REVIEWER PRAISE FOR BOOKS BY DOUGLAS GRAY

The Complete Canadian Small Business Guide (with Diana Gray)

" ... This guide is truly a gold mine ... an admirable job ... taps into the author's extensive expertise ..."

Profit Magazine

" ... I can say with absolute certainty that this guide is *the best* .. It is well organized, written in a very informative way and at the right level of detail ... The samples, checklists, glossary, and sources of other information can best be described as exemplary. Just a great piece of work ... recommended to everyone I deal with ... "

Steve Guerin, Former Project Manager, Office of Research and Innovation,
Ryerson Polytechnical University, Toronto

" ... Detailed, very informative, scrupulously objective as well as being written in a style that is refreshingly clear of jargon ... This one is a 'must buy' ... "

B.C. Business

Home Inc.: The Canadian Home-Based Business Guide (with Diana Gray)

" ... Should be required reading for all potential home-basers ... authoritative, current and comprehensive ..."

Edmonton Journal

" ... An absolute necessity for your bookshelf ... crammed with useful information ... will pay for itself in short order ..."

Victoria Times-Colonist

Making Money in Real Estate: Mortgages Made Easy; Home Buying Made Easy; Condo Buying Made Easy

" ... Gray delivers the goods. It is all-Canadian, and not a retread book full of tips that are worthless north of the U.S. border. It's chock full of practical streetsmart strategies and advice, pitfalls to avoid, samples, what-to-look-out-for checklists and information sources ... the information that Gray passes along is invaluable, thorough and eminently usable ... the book has an easy style to it that is almost conversational ..."

Business in Vancouver

The Canadian Snowbird Guide

" ... an invaluable guide to worry-free living in the U.S. ... by one of Canada's bestselling authors of business and personal finance books ..."

Globe & Mail

" ... I hate to sound like a cheerleader for Gray and his *Canadian Snowbird Guide*, but RAH! RAH! RAH! regardless ... the book is a complete how-to written in his characteristically thorough style ... Gray delivers the goods right where the Snowbirds live. If you or someone close to you winters in the U.S., you should have this book ..."

Business in Vancouver

" … Gray has written a reference book, thoughtful and complete, and prepared with the authoritative research skills and knowledge of a fastidious solicitor. To this end, the *Snowbird Guide* is as practical as a sunhat on a Tampa afternoon, and that alone warrants it a place on every southbound RV's bookshelf …"

Quill & Quire

Risk-Free Retirement: The Complete Canadian Planning Guide

(with Graham Cunningham, Tom Delaney, Les Solomon, and Dr. Des Dwyer)
" … This book is a classic … will be invaluable for years to come … It is arguably the most comprehensive guide to retirement planning in Canada today … "

Vancouver Sun

BESTSELLING BOOKS AND SOFTWARE PROGRAMS BY DOUGLAS GRAY

Small Business Titles

- *Start and Run a Profitable Consulting Business*, 5th edition
- *Start and Run a Profitable Business Using Your Computer*
- *Have You Got What It Takes?: The Entrepreneur's Complete Self-Assessment Guide*, 3rd edition
- *Marketing Your Product* (with Donald Cyr), 3rd edition
- *The Complete Canadian Small Business Guide* (with Diana Gray), 2nd edition
- *Home Inc.: The Canadian Home-Based Business Guide* (with Diana Gray), 2nd edition

Real Estate Titles

- *Making Money in Real Estate: The Canadian Residential Investment Guide*
- *Mortgages Made Easy: The Canadian Guide to Home Financing*
- *Canadian Home Buying Made Easy: The Streetsmart Guide for First-Time Home Buyers*
- *Condo Buying Made Easy: The Canadian Guide to Apartment and Townhouse Condos, Co-ops and Timeshares*, 2nd edition
- *Mortgage Payment Tables Made Easy*
- *Making Money in Real Estate* (Software jointly developed by Douglas Gray, Phoenix Accrual Corporation and McGraw-Hill Ryerson Limited)

Personal Finance/Retirement Planning Titles

- *Risk-Free Retirement: The Complete Canadian Planning Guide* (with Tom Delaney, Graham Cunningham, Les Solomon and Dr. Des Dwyer)
- *The Canadian Snowbird Guide: Everything You Need to Know about Living Part-time in the U.S.A. and Mexico*, 2nd edition

SO YOU WANT WANT TO BUY A FRANCHISE

Read this before you sign on the dotted line.

Proven steps to successful franchising in Canada

DOUGLAS GRAY

NORMAN FRIEND

McGraw-Hill
Ryerson

Toronto Montréal New York Auckland Bogotá Caracas
Lisbon London Madrid Mexico Milan New Delhi San Juan
Singapore Sydney Tokyo

McGraw-Hill
Ryerson Limited

A Subsidiary of The **McGraw·Hill** Companies

ISBN: 0-07-560419-1
1234567890 GTC 7654321098

Canadian Cataloguing in Publication Data

Gray, Douglas A.

So you want to buy a franchise: proven steps to successful franchising in Canada

(SOHO solutions for Canadians)
Previously published under title: The complete Canadian franchise guide.
ISBN 0-07-560419-1

1. Franchises (Retail trade) – Canada. I. Friend, Norman P. II. Title.
III. Title: Complete Canadian franchise guide. IV. Series.

HF5429.235.C3G73 1998   658.8'708'0971   C98-931077-9

Publisher: **Joan Homewood**
Production Coordinator: **Jennifer Burnell**
Editor: **Rachel Mansfield**
Electronic Page Composition: **Bookman**
Interior Design: **Diana Little**
Cover Design: **Sharon Matthews**

Printed and bound in Canada.

To Diana, my wife, partner, friend and fellow
entrepreneur. Thank you for your constant understanding,
encouragement and enthusiasm.

DAG

To my mother, and my dear brother Rex.
I wish that you were still here to share my joy.

To my children, Joanne and Jonathan.
Thank you for your love and understanding, especially
when I needed it the most.

To Tünde. Thanks for not giving up
and for loving me unconditionally. My life is so much richer
with you in it.

NPF

Acknowledgements

We are indebted to many individuals who have given generously of their time in the preparation of this book.

We would like to express our appreciation to Gord Metcalfe of National Franchise Data Systems for providing statistics on franchising in Canada.

We would like to thank Adia Personnel Services of Menlo Park, California, for their permission to use their questionnaire for prospective franchisees, "Are You Franchisee Material?". Thanks also to Professor Russell Knight of the University of Western Ontario for permission to include the results of his studies on personal franchise characteristics required for success.

Last, but not least, we would like to thank the editorial staff of McGraw-Hill Ryerson for their support and insightful and constructive suggestions throughout.

Preface

Every year, thousands of Canadians from all walks of life respond to the call of entrepreneurialism. Young people fresh out of college or university, mature executives who have been set adrift by their corporations, parents who are raising children at home, low-skilled workers, and new immigrants are part of this growing force of independent businesspeople. Many are attracted to franchising as a method of doing business because of what they perceive to be a greater chance of success than going it alone as an independent operator.

Franchising is not a guarantee of success or a promise of great wealth, although a good franchise is in most cases a safer bet than an independent business. The lure of fast profits for minimum effort or low-entry capital requirements attract many people who are totally unsuited to being franchisees. In addition, there are those who, in evaluating a franchise business opportunity, disregard any warning signals, brush aside any negative advice, and fail to carry out proper due diligence.

This book has been written to guide the reader, step-by-step, through all aspects of selecting the type of franchise business most suitable to his or her background and available capital. The information provides a good basic knowledge of the various types and levels of franchising and the opportunities that are available in one of the most exciting business concepts of our time.

Whatever your decision, we wish you the best in all your small business endeavours.

Douglas Gray
Norman Friend
Vancouver, B.C.
May 1998

Table of Contents

Chapter 4: Understanding the Franchise Agreement / 111
No two franchise agreements are alike. Find out what is negotiable and get clear information on the elements of an agreement.

Chapter 5: Financing the Franchise / 151
How much will you need – now and in the long-run? This chapter will show you where
to look for credit and how to arrange it.

Chapter 6: Which Legal Structure is Best for You? / 185
Might a sole proprietorship suit you – or could a partner be helpful – or would a limited
company be more effective?

Chapter 7: Business Planning / 191
Set your goals and don't skip the business plan. This chapter provides samples to budget for the start-up, forecast the first three months and project cash-flow.

Chapter 8: Buying an Existing Franchise / 214
Two for the price of one – buying an operating business from the vendor *and* buying a
franchise from the franchisor. This chapter tells you where to find them and how to check
them out.

Chapter 9: The Ten Golden Rules / 253
Write them down and read them every day.

Appendix: Franchise Regulatory Authorities / 255

The Top 500 Franchises in Canada (by number of units) / 257

CHAPTER 1

Introduction to Franchising

*Enthusiasm finds the opportunities, and energy makes
the most of them.*

Henry S. Haskins

WHAT IS FRANCHISING?

The word "franchising" is one of the most misunderstood and
misused business words in the English language. In basic terms, it is
a form of distribution or marketing. It is a method of doing business
by which the *franchisee* is granted the right to offer, sell or distribute
goods or services under a marketing plan or system prescribed in
substantial part by a *franchisor*. It is a strategy for successfully pene-
trating, developing, dominating and achieving a disproportionately
large market share.

The terms "franchise," "franchisor" and "franchisee" are used
extensively throughout this book; therefore, it is important that you
have a clear understanding of their meanings.

The **franchisor** is the company that owns and controls the franchise system and grants the licence to operate the franchise according to a certain method, and with the products and/or services that
have been developed by the franchisor.

The **franchisee** is the company or person who pays the franchisor
for the franchise and the right to use the system.

The **franchise** is the right to use the trademarks and systems, and
to promote and market the products and/or services.

THE GROWTH OF FRANCHISING

Although franchising has been used as a method of business
expansion since the turn of the century, it was not until the 1950s that
it received widespread acceptance. In Canada and the U.S. the last

two decades have seen an unprecedented expansion in both the number of franchise outlets and the range of products or services being franchised. In a study prepared for the International Franchise Association, futurist and author of *Megatrends*, John Naisbitt, predicted that "Franchising is the way of the future. Almost any service imaginable will be franchised, and many independent businesses will be absorbed by franchising. Franchising is the most successful marketing concept ever created."

With more than 3,000 franchised companies in 60 different industries, and with more than 250 new companies entering the world of franchising annually, the total number of franchised companies will have doubled by the end of the decade in North America.

The total number of business-format franchises increased by approximately 5% in 1992 to almost 430,000, while at the same time sales from this type of franchised business increased by about 6% to $246 billion. While *Fortune 500* companies eliminated approximately 3.9 million jobs throughout the 1980s and early '90s, franchises added approximately 300,000 new jobs to the economy between 1989 and 1991 alone.

Franchising in Canada

A new Canadian franchise opens every hour and forty-five minutes. According to information from an annual survey conducted by the Ontario-based company National Franchise Database Systems Inc., and published in "Canadian Franchise Facts—1996," around 1,100 Canadian franchise organizations operate a total of 74,129 outlets, which represents 65,741 franchised outlets and 8,388 outlets operated directly by the franchisor. The Canadian franchise industry directly employs 1,043,652 or 14.08 persons on average per outlet.

The survey estimates that Canadian franchising grew by:

5.48% 1994 over 1993
6.89% 1995 over 1994
7.61% 1996 over 1995

The largest franchise categories by number of units are:

1. Food Service   17,829   24.1%
2. Retail   9,926   13.4%

3. Miscellaneous Products   9,671   13.0%

4. All Others   36,703   49.5%

The survey divided the 1,100 Canadian franchise companies into 44 Standard Industrial Classifications (SIC). The top three employment categories account for 65.5% of all franchise employment.

RANK	CATEGORY	# OF EMPLOYEES	% OF FRANCHISING
1.	Food Service (6 categories)	470,048	45.0%
2.	Miscellaneous Products & Services (1 category)	135,842	13.0%
3.	Retail (7 categories)	89,265	8.5%
4.	All Others (30 categories)	348,497	34.5%

The typical Canadian franchisor:

Has: 12 corporate units and 63 franchised units for a total of 75 units

Requires: an average equity investment of $62,000

Has: an average franchise fee of $224,060, employs 952 persons

Has: been in business over 17 years

Has: an annual growth of 4.4 units per year.

The market sectors where the greatest growth is anticipated are:

- business aids and services
- construction
- maintenance and cleaning services
- retailing (non-food)
- automotive products and services
- home improvement
- home inspection services.

Franchising in the U.S.

More than 550,000 franchised businesses operate in the United States, generating more than $800 billion in sales. A new franchise business opens somewhere in the U.S. every eight minutes each business day.

Some franchise systems operate within small geographical areas within the U.S. and will probably never achieve national coverage, but since the 1960s, U.S. franchisors have been invading the

Canadian marketplace. Approximately 500 of the larger franchisors have introduced their franchise systems to Canada. Almost every industry has now been revolutionalized by franchising, but probably the most-recognized franchises are those that belong to the early U.S. franchisors who brought fast-food, real estate sales, automotive products and services, and hotels into Canada as franchise systems.

International Franchising

The removal of trade barriers within the European Community during the next few years should open up a tremendous window of opportunity for franchising. As the member nations of the European Community—France, Germany, Italy, Belgium, Luxemburg, the Netherlands, Denmark, Ireland, Greece, Spain, Portugal and the United Kingdom—standardize regulations and open their borders, franchising will have access to one of the largest and most affluent markets in the world. Combined with the opening of Eastern Europe, the potential for established North American franchisors who are interested in international expansion can be appreciated.

"It [Europe] is a market that remains largely undeveloped. European franchising is now where the United States was 10 or 15 years ago," says Michael Sellers, president of the U.S. affiliate of Franchise Development Services Ltd., a Norwich, England-based firm that helps franchise companies to become established in Europe.

Some of the greatest-volume franchised outlets in the world are located outside of North America. The largest McDonald's restaurant is in Moscow, and is actually a joint venture with McDonald's Canada. Business has surpassed all expectations.

Kentucky Fried Chicken's biggest outlet is in Beijing and it serves more than 10,000 meals a day. Franchisors such as KFC, Pizza Hut and Holiday Inns are established in China, the Soviet Union and the former Eastern Bloc countries.

One notable difference between the 1,000 franchise systems operating in Europe and those operating in North America is that approximately 75% of the franchise systems in Europe are service businesses, whereas in North America it is the exact opposite, with the majority of franchises being retail-based. This is mainly due to the short supply, and consequently the high costs, of retail premises.

France has the highest number of franchises in Europe (although its definition of franchising is broader than in most other countries), followed closely by the United Kingdom. In Japan, franchising now accounts for about 10% of all retail sales and this percentage is growing steadily.

FRANCHISE LEGISLATION

Canada

Until 1997, Canada had been relatively free of franchise legislation, with Alberta being the only province in Canada to have legislation directed specifically at franchising. However, the increasing number of law suits between franchisor and franchisee has prompted other provinces to re-assess the need to introduce some form of franchise legislation. Ontario is scheduled to introduce franchise legislation in 1998, and other provinces should be close behind. There is also the possibility that some form of national franchise legislation is imminent.

The Alberta legislation passed a new Franchises Act, Bill 33 (the "Bill"). Franchisors are no longer required to register with a government agency in Alberta. The Bill applies to the sale of a franchise in two situations: if the franchised business is to be operated either partly or wholly in Alberta; or if the purchaser of the franchise is an Alberta resident or has a permanent residence in Alberta.

Under the new Bill, a franchisor must provide a prospective franchisee with a copy of the franchisor's disclosure document at least 14 days before the prospective franchisee signs any agreement relating to the franchise, or any payments are made relating to the franchise, whichever is earlier. The disclosure document must contain copies of the following:

- all proposed franchise agreements
- financial statements of the franchisor
- reports and other documents in accordance with the regulations.

A certificate must be signed by at least two officers or directors of the franchisor, which states that the disclosure document contains no untrue statement of a material fact and does not omit to state a material fact. Experienced franchisors, with a high net worth, may be granted a Ministerial Exemption from the requirement to provide financial statements. There are also a number of situations which constitute exemptions from the requirement for a franchisor to deliver a disclosure document.

The franchisor is not required to provide a full disclosure document if an agreement contains only terms and conditions relating to one or more of the following:

- a fully refundable deposit*
- a confidentiality and non-disclosure agreement
- the designation of a territory or location of the proposed franchise location.

If a franchisee suffers a loss because of a misrepresentation contained in a disclosure document, the franchisee has the right to collect for damages against the franchisor and every person who signed the disclosure document. If the franchisor fails to provide the disclosure document within the time requirements, the prospective franchisee may rescind the agreement by giving notice of cancellation no later than 60 days after receiving the disclosure documents, or no later than two years after the granting of the franchise. A franchisor must, within 30 days of receiving a notice of cancellation, compensate the franchisee for any net losses the franchisee has incurred in acquiring, setting up, or operating the franchised business.

The legislation was a co-operative effort between the Alberta government and a committee comprised of representatives of the Canadian Franchise Association, the Franchisee Association of Alberta, and the former Alberta Franchisors Institute. It should result in a more streamlined and efficient process. Section 7 of the Bill, which requires a duty of fair dealing by all parties, will ensure that franchisors review their current practices in sensitive areas such as default, renewal, assignments, rebates and product purchasing, and termination. Please refer to Appendix for the address and phone number of the Alberta Municipal Affairs, Housing and Consumer Affairs Division. To receive a copy of the new Alberta's Franchises

---

* a fully refundable deposit is (a) a deposit that does not exceed 15% of the initial franchise fee, (b) refundable without any deductions, and (c) given under an agreement that in no way binds the prospective franchisee to enter into any franchise agreement.

Act and Regulation, please contact the Queen's Printer Bookstore at (403) 427-4952 (Edmonton) or (403) 297-6251 (Calgary).

Franchising in provinces other than Alberta is generally governed by common law. Franchisors who operate in Quebec must comply with the French-language translation requirements and conduct their business in English and French.

United States

Franchising is more highly regulated in the United States. Every franchisor who wishes to offer or sell a franchise is required by the Federal Trade Commission (FTC) to prepare an extensive disclosure document for each potential purchaser. This disclosure format is called the "Uniform Franchising Offering Circular" (UFOC).

In addition, several states have enacted laws regulating the offer and sale of franchises which are more stringent than the FTC regulations.

FRANCHISING'S SUCCESS RATE

Franchising has certainly experienced a high success rate, and a remarkable staying power through recessionary times; many franchisors quote a 90% success rate for franchised businesses. This figure is misleading and does not appear to have any basis in fact. What is not in question is that franchised businesses do have a higher success rate than independent businesses.

It is generally accepted that 40% of all non-franchised businesses don't make it to the end of their first year of operation, and 80% fail within their first five years. Even the 20% that survive are not safe, as 90% of them will fail within their next five years. So, even if they manage to struggle through the first five years, the odds are against them surviving the next five.

The University of Toronto's Faculty of Management carried out what is probably one of the most thorough studies on the performances of franchised businesses in Canada to date. Having access to provincial sales tax returns data from the Ontario Ministry of Revenue, they compared the performance of companies in several industry sectors. The businesses had been categorized as franchised or non-franchised, but the corporate names were not divulged.

The sample covered 18,000 companies in seven categories, such as convenience stores, donut shops, unlicensed restaurants, car leasing companies, etc. After analyzing the data for 1987, '88 and '89, they discovered that *in six of the seven categories the franchised companies' performances ranged between 34% and 314% better than owner-managed businesses in terms of gross sales.* This factor is extraordinarily important and demonstrates a key trend. The greater success rate was explained in terms of gross sales as a function of brand-name recognition, superior marketing, superior training, superior location and superior buying power.

While these figures do not provide an insight into the relative profitability, or the success or failure rates of the businesses, they do validate one of the single greatest benefits of franchising. The right franchisee who belongs to a good franchise system, with all other things being equal, will substantially outperform an operator of a non-franchised business.

TYPES OF FRANCHISES

The term "franchise" is used to describe several different types of agreements, although its current definition places the emphasis on the continuing relationship between the franchisor and the franchisee. Most franchises fall under the classification of *product or service*, or *business-format*. Although franchises will generally lean more heavily towards one or the other, they typically combine characteristics from both categories.

Product or Service Franchise

Early franchises were generally "Trade Name" franchises. The franchisor allowed the franchisee to distribute goods utilizing the franchisor's trademark. This type of licensing arrangement includes such businesses as car and truck dealers, soft drink bottlers, home entertainment stores and service stations.

Generally, the franchisee was required to conform to certain standards relating to the quality of the product or service, but apart from that he or she was free to carry on business without any control or guidance from the franchisor.

Business-Format Franchise

Business-format franchising is the most common form of franchising and involves not only the licensing of a product or service, but provides the method for running the business.

Real estate companies, diet centres and travel agencies are examples of business-format franchises. Fast-food franchises often combine product and business-format franchising, as do most of today's franchises.

WHAT ARE THE ALTERNATIVES TO FRANCHISING?

There are other business arrangements offering opportunities that may be more appropriate for you, such as:

- licensing
- distributorship
- dealership.

Licensing

The terms "licensing" and "franchising" are often confused, and are, in fact, sometimes used interchangeably. The term "licensing" is sometimes used in the health care industry or in the legal and accounting professions because it sounds more acceptable or appropriate than "franchising."

Technically, the term "licensing" refers to a licence to use patents, know-how and/or trademarks in a non-business-format arrangement. The licensor grants a licence to the licensee but does not prescribe the manner in which the licensee conducts his or her business.

Distributorship

In a distributorship arrangement, the manufacturer supplies the distributor with products at a wholesale price. The distributor then resells the products to dealers, or retails them directly to the public.

A distributorship differs from a franchise in that royalties are not normally paid to the manufacturer as a percentage of gross sales. The manufacturer does not prescribe the method for operating the business, but may provide training to improve selling techniques and product knowledge, and may also give advertising assistance in the form of co-operative advertising allowances. This assistance is provided with the intent of increasing sales of its products.

Dealership

A dealership is similar to a distributorship, except that the dealer normally sells directly to the public. The dealer is not usually restricted to carrying one product line, as is often the case in franchising or distribution.

Distribution and dealership agreements are traditionally shorter than franchise agreements. They are typically for a year, compared to franchise agreements which are normally a minimum of five years. All are renewed by mutual agreement.

WHAT ALTERNATIVES ARE THERE WITHIN FRANCHISING?

There are also several different methods of doing business within franchising, and these are limited only by the creativity of the people involved in the franchising:

- single-unit franchising
- turnkey franchising
- franchisee involvement (semi-turnkey)
- conversion franchising
- home-based franchising
- piggyback franchising
- multiple-unit franchising
- multi-level franchising
- master franchising
- sub-franchising
- area development agreement.

The following descriptors are generally recognized as the traditional alternatives within franchising, but the precise wording of a particular agreement should be examined to determine the actual franchise form and relationship.

Single-Unit Franchising

A single-unit franchise is the most common form of franchising and the method most recognized by the general public. Franchisees invest their own capital, management skills and effort, and accept the risks and enjoy the benefits of being in business for themselves, but not by themselves.

The franchisor grants the franchisee a licence to operate the franchised business at a specified location. Additionally, the franchisee may receive the exclusive rights to a defined trading area or territory, and may also receive the first option rights to acquire any proposed franchised locations within an adjacent geographical area.

Turnkey Franchising

In a turnkey franchise, the franchisor is responsible for locating, acquiring (by purchase or lease), developing and stocking the franchised business which is handed over to the franchisee ready to commence operations.

In addition to the initial franchise fee, the franchisor will receive from the franchisee the costs related to site selection, development and inventory. The franchisor often adds a mark-up to the base costs as a development fee.

Franchisee Involvement (Semi-Turnkey)

The usual arrangement in a semi-turnkey situation is for the franchisor or franchisee to locate a site or premises, always subject to the franchisor's approval. The responsibility for the development of the location is shared between the franchisor and the franchisee depending upon their agreement. The franchisor might provide the building and the inventory, with the franchisee responsible for the installation of leasehold improvements and equipment. The franchisor will assist in the opening of the unit and the training of the franchisee's staff.

Conversion Franchising

Conversion franchising is simply a different form of business-format franchising, and is not an alternative within franchising. This type of franchising is most commonly applied in industries where many independent businesses are firmly established in the marketplace. Prime examples would be Uniglobe, Century 21 and Re/Max.

In this form of franchising, the franchisor seeks out an existing, independent operator and offers that operator an opportunity to use its trade name and become part of a national network. The franchisee benefits from increased consumer recognition, training programs for management and staff, increased purchasing power, ongoing assistance and corporate referrals.

The franchisor is able to expand more rapidly by avoiding the construction, development and start-up phase costs associated with a turnkey franchise. Real estate and travel agencies are franchises that are most associated with conversion franchising.

Home-Based Franchising

Home-based franchises started to become popular in the 1980s and continue to gain popularity. This is due in part to the improvements and increased access to fax machines, personal computers, modems and personal copiers. Across Canada, some two million households operate a home-based business involving a part-time or full-time owner, an employee "telecommuting" from home, or an employee bringing work home. Other factors that fuel the growth of home-based franchises are:

- the lower investment and financial risk level
- the increase and numbers of women going into business
- corporate reorganization
- lifestyle benefits
- tax advantages
- the suitability of service types of businesses.

If you are considering a home-based business, refer to the best-selling book, *Home Inc.: The Canadian Home-Based Business Guide* by Douglas and Diana Gray (Toronto: McGraw-Hill Ryerson, 2nd edition, 1994).

Piggyback Franchising

"Piggyback" or "combination franchising," as it is sometimes known, is in essence a business within a business—a combination of two franchises operating under the same roof. Usually, a smaller niche-market business piggybacks onto a mass merchandiser, or on a store which retails more general merchandise. It is a good example of cross-promotion or fusion marketing between two businesses which share a common customer base. Some examples of piggyback franchising are:

- fried chicken counter within a convenience story (Church's Chicken in 7-11 stores)
- fast-food inside a home and clothing store (McDonald's in Walmart)
- submarine sandwich kiosk inside a gas station (Subway in Shell).

The franchise that piggybacks onto a larger established business in a good location with high customer traffic can reduce its risk, have faster start-up cash flow, and benefit from the credibility of the piggybacked business. The piggybacked business reduces its occupancy and labour costs.

Both businesses benefit from the synergy that is created when two complementary, yet distinct, businesses combine. As in any cross-promotion situation, both businesses are able to broaden their customer base.

Multiple-Unit Franchising

Multiple-unit franchising is the granting to a multi-unit franchisee the non-exclusive right to open a predetermined number of outlets within a certain area (usually a city or a province). In most instances, the multi-unit franchisee pays the up-front franchise fee (usually at a discounted rate) for each franchised outlet to be opened.

The grant is usually contingent on the franchisee opening a minimum number of units within a certain time-frame. If that level of performance is not achieved, the multi-unit franchise agreement is not normally terminated. Instead, the multi-unit franchisee is permitted to retain the units currently operating, but may lose the right to establish further units.

However, in this type of agreement it is usual to have cross-default provisions, which could result in the termination of all the agreements between the franchisor and the franchisee, if the franchisee is in default under any of the agreements.

Multi-Level Franchising

Although there are many variations of multi-level franchising, the three primary methods are:

1. master (or regional) franchising
2. sub-franchising
3. area development franchising.

These options allow the franchisor to grow more rapidly and at less cost than traditional single-unit franchising. This is often referred to as the "ultrastructure" of franchising.

In each instance, the franchisee still receives all of the benefits normally associated with franchising. There are some primary differences; for example, what is the nature of the ongoing relationship between the franchisee and the franchisor? Who provides the franchisee with ongoing support and assistance? To whom does the franchisee pay the required fees? Figure 1.1 provides a "Franchise Models" diagram that illustrates some of the relationships in the franchise ultrastructure.

Forty % of franchisors use some form of area development agreement, and 20% offer master or sub-franchise agreements. The following is a brief description of each of these methods.

Master Franchising

Master franchising is used when a franchisor wants to expand into a large geographic area, such as a province. The franchisor may not have the capital or organizational capacity to handle the expansion, so he or she seeks out a master franchisee. The master franchisee has the responsibility of signing up new franchisees within the area and providing them with the initial training. The ongoing support is usually provided by the franchisor. The master franchisee pays a front-end fee for the area and receives a percentage of the royalty payments paid by each of the franchisees. The franchise agreement is usually directly between the unit franchisee and the franchisor, but is sometimes a three-way relationship between the franchisor, the master franchisee and the unit franchisee.

Sub-Franchising

In addition to the recruitment of new franchisees, the sub-franchisor is also responsible for developing the area, providing the initial training, site selection, etc. The principle difference between master franchising and sub-franchising is that in a sub-franchise relationship the franchisee deals directly with the sub-franchisor and has only a limited direct involvement with the franchisor. The franchisee pays the royalty and advertising fees directly to the sub-

Figure 1.1   Franchise Models

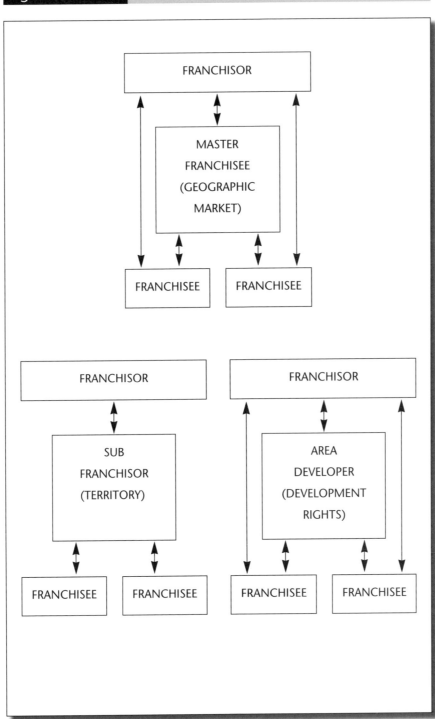

franchisor, who in turn pays a portion to the franchisee. In essence, the sub-franchisor assumes the position of the franchisor within the area. The franchise agreement is usually entered into directly between the unit franchisee and the sub-franchisor.

Area Development Agreement

In an area development agreement, the franchisor grants exclusive development rights for a particular geographic area to an area developer. The area developer can either open its own corporate units or find unit franchisees. The area developer pays the franchisor a front-end fee and is required to open a certain number of units within an agreed time-frame. The area developer may retain part of the initial franchise fees for franchises sold, and part of the royalty stream. These arrangements vary considerably. The franchise agreement in this situation is usually directly between the unit franchisee and the franchisor.

WHAT ARE THE BENEFITS OF FRANCHISING TO THE FRANCHISOR?

The benefits of franchising can be both financial and administrative and can provide:

- reduced capital requirements
- management motivation
- rapid expansion
- increased profitability.

Reduced Capital Requirements

Franchising is an alternative growth strategy to establishing company-owned outlets. It allows the franchisor to grow without the large capital requirements associated with corporate expansion. Instead of borrowing or spending existing capital, the capital comes from the franchisees themselves.

Management Motivation

Any owner who is financially committed to the success of his or her business is certain to have a higher level of motivation than a manager. Many companies are finding it difficult to hire and retain managers, and the ongoing retraining is very expensive for an organization. The franchisor also acquires the local business knowledge of the franchisee in most circumstances.

Rapid Expansion

Some new concepts are easily copied by competitors; therefore, a fast penetration of the marketplace may be important to the franchisor. It is often critical to be first into the marketplace with a new product or service in order to establish a dominant position. Franchising enables even small operators to establish a national presence rapidly and without the availability of large capital resources.

Increased Profitability

A franchise system eliminates the need for a traditional corporate structure and the associated overhead. Most day-to-day management tasks are handled by the franchisees thereby reducing the requirement for a large management staff. This translates into increased profitability for the franchisor once the franchisees have reached critical mass (i.e., sufficient revenues from franchisees' ongoing royalty payments).

WHAT ARE THE BENEFITS OF FRANCHISING TO THE FRANCHISEE?

For the franchisee, the start-up benefits are obvious:

- reduced risk
- access to a proven system
- easier access to financing
- reduced cash requirements
- increased purchasing power
- assistance with site selection
- a higher advertising profile
- opportunity to build equity
- reduction in level of stress.

Reduced Risk

As discussed earlier in this chapter, franchising does not guarantee success, but it does reduce the chances of failure.

A Proven System

With a tried and tested operating system, the franchisee avoids the obstacles and gains the opportunities. A franchisee should receive a completely proven system that includes initial training, opening assistance, accounting systems, established suppliers, manuals and use of the trademarks. The all-important "learning curve" helps prevent the franchisees from repeating previous mistakes and provides information on inventory levels, store design, competition, pricing structure and operational data drawn from the entire system.

Easier Access to Financing and Reduced Cash Requirements

Financial institutions prefer to lend to franchised businesses because of their higher success rate. The consumer awareness created by national or regional name recognition can reduce the costs of grand-opening promotional activity and advertising start-up. As well, the purchasing power of the franchisor can reduce the franchisee's initial outlay for equipment and supplies.

Purchasing Power

Collective purchasing power on products, supplies, extended health and insurance benefits, equipment and advertising can easily offset any ongoing royalties paid by the franchisee.

Site Selection Assistance

Franchisors can provide expert site selection assistance based on their operating experience and demographic knowledge.

Landlords and developers prefer to deal with someone who has an established track record. This enables franchisees as part of an established franchise system to obtain locations in major malls and other developments that otherwise would not be available to them as independent operators.

Advertising Clout

Most independent businesses cannot afford the services of advertising and promotional experts. Consequently, their advertising is often poorly conceived and inconsistent. They also cannot afford to invest in the level of advertising required to maintain a commanding presence in the marketplace.

In a franchise system, the advertising cost is spread over many units enabling the franchisor to achieve economies of scale. The franchisee can now afford well-conceived promotional campaigns and can place advertising in the most effective medium.

Building Equity

Because of the national or regional name recognition, a franchised business should eventually sell faster and for a higher value than an independent business. A buyer is motivated to purchase the business for the same reasons as an original franchisee and perceives the higher value associated with a recognized name and system such as Re/Max over John Doe Realty.

Stress Reduction

Systems which enhance the ability to operate more effectively can relieve many pressures of business. Control over job-scheduling, cash flow and inventory allow the franchisee to run the business instead of the other way around.

WHAT ARE THE DISADVANTAGES TO THE FRANCHISOR?

Some of the drawbacks for the franchisor can be:

- reduced control
- profit dilution
- uncontrolled growth
- difficulties in the selection of franchisees
- potential litigation.

Reduced Control

The franchisor must give up some control when a unit is franchised. Although establishing and maintaining control are key elements in the franchise agreement, the franchisor still runs the risk that the franchisee will operate outside of the guidelines and impair the reputation of the franchise system. Recalcitrant franchisees can obviously create problems for any franchise system which is, after all, only as strong as its weakest link.

Profit Dilution

By selecting franchising as a method of expansion, the franchisor is giving away some profit opportunity today by not operating company-owned outlets, and gambling on greater profitability in the future through an expanded system.

Uncontrolled Growth

Uncontrolled growth can be a serious problem in any business, and franchising is certainly no different. It can cause severe operational problems unless regional expansion is planned carefully and support systems are established at the appropriate times.

A good franchise system should grow outwards from its base, thereby taking advantage of its area of marketing influence and the ability to provide greater field support, including the logistical advantages of product and service supply and delivery.

Franchisee Selection

Finding franchisees who have sufficient capital, or access to the capital necessary to invest in the franchise, and who have the desire and ability to work within a system is not as simple as it may appear. The task of franchise recruitment can be time-consuming and expensive for the franchisor.

Indiscriminate franchisee recruitment by some franchisors who have either disregarded proper selection criteria, or failed to establish it in the first place, has resulted in substantial franchisee attrition. This can be costly and time-consuming and severely retard the growth of the franchise system, or destroy it entirely.

Potential Litigation

Franchisors are exposed to litigation by franchisees who become dissatisfied with the system. Either party can be the cause of the problem, but regardless of fault, it can be damaging to the overall franchise system. Problems can arise as a result of the franchisee having unrealistic expectations at the time of entering into the franchise. This places a responsibility upon the franchisor to ensure that the franchisee fully understands all of the aspects of the franchise concept and documentation, and that the ultimate performance of the franchised business depends to a large degree upon the franchisee's efforts.

WHAT ARE THE DISADVANTAGES TO THE FRANCHISEE?

Disadvantages for the franchisee can arise from a mistaken view of the undertaking, and the possibility of:

- loss of independence
- the franchisor's failure to perform
- misunderstanding the franchise agreement
- misrepresentation by the franchisor
- problems in the payment of fees.

Loss of Independence

Loss of independence can be a detriment to franchising, especially in conversion franchising where the franchisee must abandon many of his or her existing methods of doing business in favour of the system. Although many franchisees invest in a franchise because they want the guidance of the franchisor, as soon as they enter the franchise system they want to make changes. Unless a person is capable of working within a system and can accept a certain amount of regimentation, he or she should think long and hard before entering into a franchise relationship. One of the strengths of franchising is consistency, and with consistency must come compliance.

Franchisor's Failure to Perform

Some franchisors don't deliver what they promise for a couple of reasons. One reason is a shortage of available capital which can be caused by (a) unrealistic franchise sales projections; (b) underestimating the expenses associated with development of the system; (c) failure to meet unrealistic franchise sales projections; or (d) high franchisee attrition. Alternatively, it could be that the franchisor is just not capable of providing support and assistance, or of operating a franchisee organization.

Misunderstanding the Franchise Agreement

Confusion over the interpretation of certain aspects of the franchise agreement can result in a problem with either the franchisor or the franchisee. Few potential franchisees will have encountered documents similar to a franchise agreement. It requires careful explanation and scrutiny, and failure to do so will inevitably result in a conflict that may end up before the courts.

Misrepresentation by the Franchisor

Misrepresentation by the franchisor can be intentional or unintentional. Projections of income and expense can be provided to the franchisee in good faith, but may turn out to be inappropriate for the location because of the franchisor's inexperience with the area's demographics. Conversely, the figures may be total fabrications simply to get the franchisee to sign on the dotted line and pay his money.

Caveat emptor (let the buyer beware) applies to franchising as it does to any consumer purchase or investment. However, consumers are often their own worst enemy, choosing to ignore cautionary advice and warning signals, and basing their investment decision on emotion without balancing it with logic.

A good franchisor does not:

- attempt to make its profits solely from the sale of franchises (which is a non-renewable resource)
- reduce the franchisee's chance of success by pocketing cash inducements from developers and landlords
- insist on prepayment by the franchisee of three, four or five years of royalties.

A good franchisor seeks to obtain its profits from renewable resources such as royalties that are based on achieving the level of gross sales that contribute to the franchisee's success.

Problems in Payment of Fees

The franchisee pays an initial franchise fee for being granted the franchise, using the system, and receiving initial training. The initial franchise fee is paid only once during the term of the agreement; however, franchisors may charge a nominal renewal fee at the commencement of each new term of the agreement. A normal term for a franchise agreement would be five or 10 years.

The initial franchise fee is used to offset the franchisor's costs of franchise recruitment, initial training, site selection, lease negotiation, and start-up assistance. Little, or nothing, is left for profit in most cases. Franchisors sometimes charge a site selection fee of $5,000 or more, in addition to the initial franchise fee, to offset the costs of site selection and lease negotiation.

In addition to the initial franchise fee, some form of ongoing royalty is paid by the franchisee to the franchisor. Ongoing royalties fund the continuing support program and are also the franchisor's residual income, which is normally its main source of profit. Royalty fees should be set at a level that provides the franchisor with a cash flow sufficient to maintain the level of service required by the franchisees, while at the same time allowing profit for the franchisees. These royalties are paid weekly or monthly and can be a flat fee for service, or based on a percentage of gross sales.

Franchisees are also usually required to contribute to a national, regional or local advertising fund, which is in addition to any requirement that the franchisee invest a minimum amount in local advertising. Advertising funds are not recognized as revenue for the franchisor as the funds are held in trust by the franchisor and not mixed with its own funds.

An explanation of fees and royalties is provided in Chapter 3, "Evaluating the Franchise."

UNDERSTANDING THE FRANCHISEE/FRANCHISOR RELATIONSHIP

The relationship between the franchisor and the franchisee is unique and combines fundamentally different characteristics than most relationships.

The franchisee does not work for the franchisor. It would be more appropriate to say that the franchisor works for the franchisee, as it is the franchisee who pays the franchisor. The franchisor is in essence an employee who performs a variety of tasks for the franchisee as counsellor, bookkeeper, advertising advisor, purchasing agent and marketing expert.

The franchisee is defined in the franchise agreement as being an independent operator, and as such must indemnify the franchisor in various ways from any acts committed by the franchisee that may affect the franchisor. And yet, the franchisee must work within a system prescribed by the franchisor and is subject to the franchisor's controls.

The franchisee is in some ways a partner, but not so in other ways. The franchisee is an entrepreneur because he or she must be prepared to risk entry into business, but not be too much of an entrepreneur. In other words, the franchisee should not be a clone of the franchisor or he or she may be too entrepreneurial and fail to work within the system prescribed by the franchisor.

In a sense, the best way to view the relationship is as a business "marriage." In entering into the relationship, the franchisee must be prepared to relinquish some freedom and adapt to new responsibilities. The franchisor assumes a responsibility to assist the development of the franchisee and be empathetic in its approach to the new "partnership."

This illustrates the importance of careful investigation and basing the decision to enter into a franchise relationship on common sense and thorough research.

For more information on small business management tips, refer to the bestselling book, *The Complete Small Business Guide*, by Douglas and Diana Gray (Toronto: McGraw-Hill Ryerson, 2nd ed, 1994). Also refer to the internet website http://www.smallbiz.ca.

RECAP

In this chapter we discussed:

- what franchising is and how it works
- the changes and growth in franchising
- the type of person who becomes a franchisee
- the success rates of franchisees
- the alternatives within franchising
- benefits and disadvantages to the franchisor and franchisee
- some of the business characteristics needed for a successful franchise partnership.

CHAPTER 2

Is Franchising For You?

Men, as well as women, are much oftener led by their hearts
than by their understanding.

Lord Chesterfield

DO YOU HAVE WHAT IT TAKES FOR SELF-EMPLOYMENT?

It is as important to evaluate the franchise and the organization behind it as it is to evaluate your own suitability for self-employment. Do you have what it takes to become an entrepreneur? Do you have the desire, ability and confidence to be in business for yourself?

Many people romanticize about going into business and believe they could run things so much better if they were the boss. But, when the time comes to cash in their equity, mortgage their home, and write a cheque for a relatively large business investment, their confidence often rapidly disappears.

This is the time to be totally honest with yourself. Some questions to ask yourself are:

- Do you have the support of your family?
- Will you enjoy operating this type of business?
- Are you good at interacting with people?
- Can you live with the worst situation?
- Can you handle the responsibility of running your own business?

CONSIDERING THE FRANCHISE OPTION

If you are considering the franchise option, you need to review your personal and business goals. How will a franchise benefit you in attaining your goals compared with starting a business from scratch? Are you motivated by the challenge of doing it yourself? Or does that responsibility cause you more than a little worry and apprehension? Perhaps you have specialized skills which you would like to turn into a business operation, but all the many general aspects of starting a business are somewhat overwhelming and intimidating. If this is the case, then the franchise option may well be suited to your personal and business needs.

Prospective franchisees who are shy and have difficulty dealing with the general public should obviously not enter a people-oriented business such as retailing. It is not always necessary to have a background in the business, but if you don't like a particular business and are going into it primarily for the financial rewards, the chances are you are not going to be in it for very long. You must have a passion for the business. Most people enjoy doing what they are good at and, conversely, are good at doing what they enjoy. If you don't like what you are doing, your commitment to the business will be lacking. Most franchisors would rather have someone with the capacity to learn rather than someone who may have to unlearn certain habits. In other words, it's hard to teach an old dog new tricks.

The main reasons that franchisees give for buying a franchise are, in their order of priority:

- desire to be their own boss
- financial growth and ultimate riches
- to be successful
- training and guidance
- to build equity (long-term investment).

Conforming to a System

In order for the franchise system to work, the franchisor requires a high degree of uniformity, which translates into conformity on the part of the franchisee. Having many of the business decisions made for you can be a plus or minus depending on your nature. If you do not like someone inspecting or scrutinizing your work, or have a tendency to be very independent, you should think again about franchising.

If your intention is to establish your business and then diversify or expand your operation, you may be restricted from doing so because your ability to expand would be based on available territories within your geographic area. In this case, perhaps franchising is not the route you should take.

REAL LIFE: Don't Buck the System

Peppy Personnel Services had been franchising for three years and had 10 franchised units. They required their franchise applicants to have a business, sales or sales management background and strong interpersonal skills. Rhonda Headstrong applied for a Peppy franchise and completed a personality profile to determine her suitability as a franchisee. Although Rhonda did not possess the franchisor's required skills, and her personality profile indicated that she might have difficulty accepting direction, Peppy approved her application as they were anxious to sell another franchise.

It wasn't long before Rhonda's maverick behaviour caused problems. Rhonda always challenged any direction from Peppy's head office and insisted on doing business "her way." Rhonda's business was seriously underperforming and negatively affecting the other franchisees in the system, who pressured Peppy to make her comply with procedures or terminate her franchise. When Rhonda's non-compliance escalated to the point where she was obviously in default of her franchise agreement, Peppy was able to terminate the franchise.

The whole situation could have been avoided if both parties had paid heed to the warning signs at the onset. Rhonda clearly did not meet the franchisor's selection criteria and her personality was not suited to working within a system prescribed by someone else.

WHAT DOES A FRANCHISOR LOOK FOR IN A FRANCHISEE?

Many franchisors concede that they are less selective during the first months and years of starting a new franchise company because they have to establish a base of stores quickly in order to finance their growth. If, during the investigation process, you get the feeling that the franchisor would sell a franchise to anyone who could afford it, be cautious!

A study of the personal characteristics required for success was carried out by Professor Russell M. Knight of the University of Western Ontario. He compared the factors that franchisees and franchisors considered important. In general, both sides were in agreement on the critical factors, as shown in Figure 2.1, "Personal Franchise Characteristics for Success."

Figure 2.1	Personal Franchisee Characteristics for Success					
	Franchisee %			Franchisor %		
	Very Important	Important	Not Important	Very Important	Important	Not Important
Previous management experience in same industry	0	20	80	2	14	84
Previous business experience	12	46	42	16	47	37
Management ability	84	15	1	66	31	3
Desire to succeed	90	10	0	93	7	0
Willingness to work hard	92	8	0	93	6	1
Creativity	26	56	18	12	44	44
Strong people skills	63	32	5	64	34	2
Financial backing	71	27	2	67	27	6
Support from family	52	28	20	46	32	22

(Study size: 148 franchisors and 105 franchisees replied to questionnaire with follow-up interviews with 25 members of each group. The study was conducted by Professor Russell Knight of the University of Western Ontario.)

Quick Check 2.1 Are You Franchisee Material?

This quiz was developed by Adia Personnel Services of Menlo Park, California.

1. You plan to launch a training program for your staff. How do you proceed?
    a. You prepare and implement the training yourself, incorporating your own experience and ideas.
    b. You hire an expert consultant who uses a program endorsed by an industry association.

2. You have a choice between three new sales-related jobs with varying salary structures. The higher the risk, the higher the compensation. Choose one.
    a. Straight salary
    b. Base salary plus commission
    c. Entirely commission

3. You own a company. How much operational detail, from administrative to advertising and payroll, are you comfortable with?
    a. I want direct control over all operations.
    b. I delegate less than half.
    c. I delegate more than half.

4. You have three job offers, all with comparable salary, benefits and other factors. Choose one:
    a. Small company, but high management responsibility and exposure.
    b. Middle-sized company with less personal exposure, but more prestigious company name.
    c. Large firm with least personal exposure, but very well-known name.

5. You're working on a project and you've reached a major stumbling block. Do you:
    a. Seek help from others immediately.
    b. Think it through and then present possible solutions to your superior.

Quick Check 2.1 Are You Franchisee Material? (cont'd)

c.   Keep working at it until you resolve it on your own.

6. You are competing for a major potential contract that presents itself right before your vacation. It will require immediate attention, which will directly conflict with your vacation plans. Do you:

a.   Cancel or postpone the vacation.

b.   Request an extension on the deadline from the prospective customer.

7. Which investment sounds more appealing to you?

a.   A 5% fixed return on your money over a period of time.

b.   From less than 20% to more than 50% return on your money over a period of time, depending on economic conditions, such as interest rates or the stock market.

8. Which job is more appealing?

a.   You work 40-hour weeks and get 5% salary increases each year.

b.   You work 60+ hour weeks and increase your salary by 15% to 20% by the end of the first year.

9. Which business arrangement is most appealing?

a.   You're the sole owner—your name is on the door.

b.   You're in partnership, but you own a majority of the stock.

c.   You're in an equal partnership.

10. When you were a child, did you seek out activities that were somewhat risky or daring?

a.   Yes

b.   No

c.   Sometimes

11. Your company has used a successful technique for 10 years. Sales have steadily increased by 10% per year. You used a sales technique elsewhere that you feel will result in 15% to 20% annual sales increases, benefiting you and the company. Your method will require some investment time and capital up-front. Do you:

Quick Check 2.1 **Are You Franchisee Material?** (cont'd)

    a. Avoid the risk and stay with the current system.

    b. Suggest your new method, showing previous results.

    c. Privately use your different sales technique and then show results later.

12. You suggest your system to your boss and he says, "Don't rock the boat." Do you:

    a. Drop your different approach.

    b. Approach your boss at a later time.

    c. Go to your boss's boss with the suggestion.

    d. Use your own system anyway.

13. Which of these achievements would mean the most to you?

    a. Becoming president of a company.

    b. Becoming the highest-paid employee of a company.

    c. Winning the highest award for achievement in your profession.

14. As a teenager did you:

    a. Have a business of your own.

    b. Work for your parents for spending money.

    c. Receive an allowance without working.

    d. Hold a part-time job.

15. What is your typical work week?

    a. 35 hours.

    b. 40 hours.

    c. 50 hours.

    d. 60 hours.

    e. 60+ hours.

16. What would you like your work week be?

    a. 35 hours.

    b. 40 hours.

    c. 50 hours.

    d. 60 hours.

    e. 60+ hours.

Quick Check 2.1 Are You Franchisee Material? (cont'd)

17. How often have you been involved in developing a new company venture, department or innovation?
    a. Frequently
    b. Seldom
    c. Never

18. Which three of the following activities do you find most appealing? (Check only three.)
    a. Sales and marketing
    b. Administrative
    c. Payroll
    d. Training
    e. Customer service
    f. Credit and collections
    g. Management

19. You are in the middle of a stressful, crisis situation. How do you think your co-workers would describe your mental state?
    a. Composed and in control.
    b. Handling the situation, but anxious.
    c. Agitated.

20. What work pace do you generally prefer?
    a. Work on one project until it is completed.
    b. Work on several projects at one time.

21. You are about to make a sales call. Which phrase best describes your frame of mind?
    a. You will most likely make the sale.
    b. You may make the sale.
    c. There's a chance you could make the sale.

SCORING

After answering all the questions, add up your points using this guide. These categories and ranges will give you an idea about whether you are more likely to find success as a corporate player, franchisee or entrepreneur. Successful franchisees tend to fall in the middle of the

Quick Check 2.1 **Are You Franchisee Material?** (cont'd)

two extremes; however, each franchise opportunity should be evaluated individually, since each requires varying skill.

1.	a=3	b=1					
2.	a=1	b=5	c=10				
3.	a=5	b=3	c=1				
4.	a=3	b=2	c=1				
5.	a=1	b=5	c=7				
6.	a=5	b=1					
7.	a=2	b=6					
8.	a=3	b=10					
9.	a=7	b=5	c=2				
10.	a=8	b=1	c=4				
11.	a=1	b=6	c=4				
12.	a=1	b=5	c=8	c=10			
13.	a=8	b=2	c=5				
14.	a=8	b=5	c=1	d=6			
15.	a=1	b=3	c=5	d=8	e=10		
16.	a=1	b=3	c=5	d=8	e=10		
17.	a=10	b=5	c=1				
18.	a=10	b=1	c=3	d=3	e=8	f=2	g=5
19.	a=5	b=2	c=1				
20.	a=3	b=6					
21.	a=7	b=3	c=1				

Category	Range
Corporate Player	33–60
Franchise Candidate	61–142
Entrepreneur	143–169

Are You Franchisee Material?

A self-assessment test for prospective franchisees was developed by Adia Personnel Services of Menlo Park, California. See Quick Check 2.1, "Are you Franchisee Material?"

CORPORATE REFUGEES

The downsizing of companies and the rash of mergers and corporate takeovers have provided franchising with a huge window of opportunity as executives and middle managers respond to the call of entrepreneuralism. These often well-qualified prospects have either been cast aside by corporate North America, or are still employed but fuelled by the need to control their own destiny, realizing that job security is diminishing rapidly.

Corporate refugees usually have three choices regarding their future: (a) find another job, (b) go into business for themselves, or (c) retire. The job market has shrunk considerably in the past few years and the chance of finding a comparable, or acceptable, job is minimal. Most corporate refugees are too active to consider retirement. Many have a substantial net worth with savings, equity in their homes, RRSPs and are financially capable of investing in a wide range of franchises. Some have also received a significant "golden handshake" in terms of a financially attractive retirement package.

Many of those who want to go into business take a look at the failure rate of independent businesses and decide that the risk is unacceptable. Their major concern about leaping into entrepreneurship is the risk of failure and the subsequent loss of security. Many of the early franchisees were in their 20s or early 30s, whereas most corporate refugees are in their 40s or 50s and consequently are far more risk-averse as they have less time to recover financially if the business should fail. Security can serve to motivate or demotivate depending on whether it is perceived as gained or lost. Security becomes a demotivation when corporate refugees have to give up some of their assets that they have taken years to amass, and pledge others as collateral, to get into business.

Increasingly, corporate refugees are turning to franchising as a way of fulfilling their desire to become an entrepreneur. The learning curve and ongoing support offered by a good franchise system provides the safety net that is missing when people go into business as an independent operator.

Some corporate refugees are not suited to operating a franchised business for several reasons:

- They are accustomed to having a support staff to carry out menial tasks and consequently may find it difficult to fulfill all the roles from janitor to bookkeeper.
- They are unaccustomed to working outside of 9 to 5.
- They do not have a bottom-line mentality. Their corporate responsibility may have only related to operating within the guidelines of a departmental budget without influencing, or realizing the implications of their budget, on net profit.
- They are not used to dealing with the stress of totally running the show, particularly if their responsibilities or decision-making was limited to a narrow sphere of influence.
- They lack the drive, commitment and focus that are necessary to achieve success on their own. The corporate structure provided them with a certain security and insulated them from the peaks and valleys associated with the hands-on operation of a small business, particularly in the early stages.

Because of their organizational and administrative skills, many corporate refugees are better-suited to some type of sub-franchising rather than the hands-on management style required by a small business.

COUPLES IN BUSINESS

Married couples, or life partners, going into business together is believed to be one of the fastest-growing areas in business, increasing by nearly 50% in five years. Some sources quote 60% of new franchises are operated by couples.

Entrepreneurial partnerships have their own set of problems. The business is often their only source of income. Most business partnerships have problems, of course, but business couples have more of them, and they are often unique. If they fight as a couple, they carry it to work, and if they fight as business partners, they carry it home. Any weakness in the personal relationship is usually magnified in the business relationship, and vice versa. If it doesn't work, there's a lot more to lose. It's not only the business—it's the relationship.

Spouses who work well together tend to have very profitable businesses, as well as better personal relationships. However, it takes time, effort and insight to reach that point.

Consulting sessions and seminars attempt to show couples how to work together while maintaining a relationship, and how to avoid conflicts.

The stakes for couples in business are definitely much higher than for most business partnerships, so it is critical to address any potential problem areas before walking the entrepreneurial path.

HOW TO ASSESS YOUR FINANCIAL INVESTMENT COMFORT LEVEL

The financing requirements for a franchise are very similar to those for an independent business. In both instances it is imperative that the business is not undercapitalized. The following questions will help in your deciding your financial investment comfort level:

- What is the maximum amount of investment you are willing to undertake, including possible assistance from someone else?
- Are you willing to sign a personal guarantee for a business loan or financial assistance?
- If you don't have enough collateral, are you willing to give up a share of ownership in the business to a partner or investor?
- What is the type and amount of collateral that you have available to back up a loan request?
- Will you have to focus your search exclusively on franchisors who offer financial assistance?
- What is the maximum investment that you can handle without assistance?

The financial factors which are most important in assessing your potential investment level can be divided into two areas:

1. **Your net worth**, which relates to your investment potential. In other words, do you have enough money on hand, or enough security or collateral, that you can go to a lender to acquire the capital needed to start the franchised business?

2. **Your own cash-flow requirements.** Are you able to survive during the initial start-up period of the business from your own resources, or from an alternative source such as your spouse's income?

How to Calculate Your Net Worth

The first step is to calculate your net worth and unencumbered capital. Sample 2.1 gives an example of a net worth statement, which is part of a franchise application report. Different people may have the same total net worth, but assets can be distributed differently among liquid assets and equity, thereby making it easier for one person to finance a business than another.

Essentially, your personal financial statement appears very much in the same format as that of a company. You have assets on the one hand and liabilities on the other. Your assets are all the things that you own. They are your cash in the bank, your life insurance surrender value, the value of your home and RRSPs—even small items such as golf clubs.

On the other hand, your liabilities fall into two categories:

- monies you owe to other people including banks, mortgage companies, credit cards, taxes and so on
- monies which you consider you owe to yourself.

So, in other words, if you take all the things that you own (your assets) and subtract all the money you owe to other people (your liabilities), you are left with your net worth. If your sole possession is your home, which is valued at $100,000, and you have a mortgage of $60,000, your net worth would be $40,000. That is the money that you would owe to yourself when you sell your home and pay off your liabilities.

From the point of view of calculating your net worth for the purposes of obtaining bank, trust company or credit union financing, it must be understood that a bank is not interested in smaller items that you own, such as golf clubs, nor does the bank necessarily want you to cash in your RRSPs. Banks look at large assets, which are those that can be sold realistically in the event of a need to pay off a loan. So, the most important of these to the lender is your home. If you were to own shares in a publicly traded company, which is recognized by the bank as a stable venture, then these shares may also form some additional security or collateral for a loan.

Your investment in a business will come from two sources:

- loans against assets
- unencumbered capital or liquid assets from which you can obtain cash in order to invest in a business.

Sample 2.1	Personal Financial Statement

ASSETS	$
CASH IN BANK*	
NOTES DUE TO ME*	
Secured by Real Estate	
Secured by other Collateral	
Unsecured (Collectible)	
OTHER ACCOUNTS OWED TO ME	
Professional Accounts Receivable	
Other Collectible Amounts	
STOCKS AND BONDS	
Marketable Stocks	
Other Stocks	
Savings Bonds	
Other	
Other	
CASH SURRENDER VALUE OF LIFE INSURANCE	
AUTOMOBILES	
REAL ESTATE*	
Homestead	
Other Residential	
Commercial	
Rural	
OTHER ASSETS (DESCRIBE)	
TOTAL ASSETS	

ANNUAL SOURCE OF INCOME	$
Salary/Wages/Fees	
Bonuses and Commissions	
Dividends of Interest	
Real Estate	
Business, Professional or Royalties	
Other (Itemize)	
TOTAL	

LIABILITIES	
NOTES PAYABLE TO BANKS*	
1. Due to	
Collateral	
2. Due to	
Collateral	
3. Due to	
Collateral	
OTHER NOTES PAYABLE - SECURED*	
1. Due to	
Collateral	
2. Due to	
Collateral	
OTHER NOTES PAYABLE - UNSECURED*	
Due to	
Due to	
TAXES OWING	
Income Taxes	
Other Taxes	
LIFE INSURANCE POLICY LOANS	
DUE ON AUTOMOBILES	
OWING ON REAL ESTATE Lien holder	
Homestead	
Other Residential	
Commercial	
Rural	
OTHER LIABILITIES (Describe, i.e. personal bills)	
TOTAL LIABILITIES	
NET WORTH (Total Assets minus the Total Liabilities)	
TOTAL LIABILITIES AND NET WORTH	

CONTINGENT LIABILITIES	$
Guarantor Obligations	
Legal Claims	
Endorser or Co-Maker Obligations	
Leases or Contracts	
Liens or Special Debt	
Provision for Federal or Other Taxes	
Other (Itemize, i.e. alimony, child support, maintenance, etc.)	
TOTAL	

*These items require detailed explanation later in this statement.

Sample 2.1	Personal Financial Statement (cont'd)

NOTES PAYABLE

To Whom	Original Amount	Present Balance	Maturity and/or Payment Schedule	Collateral (if any)

NOTES RECEIVABLE — DUE TO ME

To Whom	Original Amount	Present Balance	Maturity and/or Payment Schedule	Collateral (if any)

STOCKS AND BONDS

No. of Shares	Name if Issuer	Where Traded	Par Value	Market Per Share	Total Value	Pledged (Yes or No)	Registered in Name of

LIFE INSURANCE

Company	Policy No.	Face Amount	Cash Surrender or Loan Value	Policy Loan (if any)	Beneficiary

REAL ESTATE

Location and Description	Present Value	Monthly Income	Title in Name of	Original Amount	Present Balance	Payment Schedule

CASH

Name and Location of Bank	Phone Number	Bank Contact	Type of Account				Identification Number	Amount in Bank
			C	S	CD	O		

C=Chequing   CD=Certicate of Deposit   S=Savings   O=Other

FOR THE PURPOSE OF SECURING CREDIT AND OTHER CONSIDERATIONS, THE UNDERSIGNED FURNISHES THE FOREGOING STATEMENT AND INFORMATION, WHICH SETS FORTH THE TRUE AND ACCURATE FINANCIAL CONDITION OF THE UNDERSIGNED. YOUR SIGNATURE CONSTITUTES YOUR APPROVAL FOR US TO MAKE A ROUTINE CREDIT CHECK.

Some of your assets may be mortgaged or have other monies owing against them. An example of this would be your personal residence. The bank will normally be very interested in using your home as security in a stable housing market; however, it has to take into consideration that if there is a mortgage against the home, it can effectively reduce the realization value upon resale. The following example may assist in clarifying this situation.

REAL LIFE: Home Equity Can Help Your Financing

Lavinia Laidoff had received $110,000 from her employer Cutback Contracting Company, as a "golden handshake" when her job was eliminated as a result of the company downsizing. Lavinia decided to use the opportunity to get into business for herself so that she would be in a position to control her own destiny. She decided to invest in a "Sammy's Subs and Pizza Store," which required a capital investment of $150,000 plus $30,000 working capital. Lavinia calculated that, based on conservative projections of revenue and provided that she took a wage of no more than $2,000 a month, the business could comfortably service a debt of $40,000. Lavinia had originally purchased her house for $90,000 but it was now worth $275,000, with only $35,000 remaining on the mortgage. The Central Bank of Canada agreed to lend Lavinia the additional $40,000 capital she required, and arranged a $30,000 line of credit for the working capital, using her house as collateral.

Although a bank may be prepared to lend you sufficient monies against your home, given that there is sufficient equity, and you are able to liquify some of your other assets to raise cash for your investment, you should also pay close attention to the extent of your liabilities. By borrowing additional funds and by liquifying your assets and investing them in a business, you may be placing yourself at undue risk. You are incurring new liabilities when you may already have excessive liabilities for other reasons. To put it simply, if you already owe too much money and have limited cash reserves, further borrowings against your home to start a business can quickly get you into financial difficulties, even if the business is otherwise a good opportunity. (Please refer to Chapter 5 for information on financing a franchise.)

Debt-to-Equity Ratios

To ensure the financial strength of the franchisee, most franchisors have built-in financial safeguards. Franchise agreements often stipulate that the franchisee must maintain at all times a certain debt-to-equity ratio. Some franchisors insist on a debt-to-equity ratio of no greater than 1:1, and others 2:1, depending on the type of business. Similarly, the franchisor will normally insist that the franchisee maintains a working capital ratio (that is the ratio between current assets and current liabilities) of not less than 1:1.

Subject to the franchisor's approval, you may have partners in your business; however, most franchisors will require that the "operating partner" has either a majority interest or operating control. This requirement is explained in more detail in Chapter 4, "Understanding the Franchise Agreement."

RECAP

In this chapter we have looked at:

- the personality traits required in a successful franchisee
- the strengths a franchisor is looking for in a franchisee
- the advantages and problems for couples in franchising
- assessing the financial investment and debt-to-equity ratios

and included were samples of:

- Personal Franchisee Characteristics for Success Survey
- Are You Franchisee Material Quick Check
- Personal Financial Statement.

CHAPTER 3

Evaluating the Franchise

When written in Chinese, the word "crisis" is composed of two characters—one represents danger and the other opportunity.

John F. Kennedy

LOOK BEFORE YOU LEAP

Every year, thousands of Canadians choose franchising as a way of going into business. Newspapers are filled with "franchise" opportunities and, while most of them are legitimate business opportunities, some are not. The rapid growth of franchising has attracted some unprincipled operators who seek to take advantage of anyone who is lured by the promise of great rewards for little risk and minimal effort. The method of operation and techniques are varied, but their objectives are the same—take the money and give little or nothing in return. Potential franchisees should not get lured by "get-rich-quick schemes," but should investigate each opportunity thoroughly.

Mutual Dependence

Once you have determined that franchising is for you, the search begins for the most suitable franchise. At this point you may have narrowed the choices down to a couple of industries, or even to a few franchises.

Success in franchising is based on mutual dependence, so it naturally follows that the search for a franchise is a mutual investigation process. In evaluating a franchise opportunity, it is important to analyze both the proposer (the franchisor) and the proposal (the franchise). Unless you have some knowledge of the former, it is very difficult to evaluate the substance and credibility of the latter.

Reputable franchisors go to great lengths to select a franchisee. If a franchisor fails to investigate you as carefully as you carry out your investigation, be cautious. If a franchise is awarded to a franchisee who is unable to operate it successfully, the franchisor will suffer almost as much as the franchisee that fails. Not only does the franchise unit fail to produce the ongoing royalty stream for the franchisor, but it can also take up a tremendous amount of the franchisor's time and effort to either salvage or resell the franchise. That is a no-win situation.

The franchise concept is very important, of course, but so is a proven track record, a financially sound franchisor, a good management team, a strong advertising program, site assessment, sound lease negotiation, and a proven concept.

Buying a franchise is similar to an acrobat performing with a net. It takes away some, but not all, of the risk. A large part of the benefit of a franchise involves the elimination of the initial learning curve that is normally associated with a new business venture. The franchisee operates within the proven guidelines of the franchise system, thereby hopefully eliminating many costly mistakes.

Franchising is not a guarantee of success or the accumulation of great wealth. However, franchising is usually a safer investment than opening a similar independent business if the franchise is part of a solid franchise concept. It is essential, however, that you carry out the same thorough research and investigation, called due diligence, as if you were starting or purchasing an independent business.

Balance Your Decision-Making

To be a successful franchisee you must have a passion for the business, as well as understand it and be capable of financing it. Obviously, a prospective franchisee should not seriously consider a franchise that is beyond his or her financial means. The other elements—emotion and logic—should be equally balanced when making the final decision about purchasing a franchise. The prospective franchisee should feel good about the business and the people involved in the franchise, and excited about the opportunity, but logic has to be applied to the decision-making process in such areas as consumer acceptance, risk analysis, availability of product, demographics etc.

In general, a prospective franchisee must ask himself or herself, "Does this all make sense?" Your emotional commitment is only one of the essential elements, and if any of these elements is missing, the franchise is probably not right for you.

THE CRITICAL FACTORS OF A GOOD FRANCHISE

There are four critical factors that combine to make a good franchise system:

1. **The Organization** Does the franchise organization have the ability to develop and maintain a franchise network?
2. **The Product or Service** Does the product or service have a widespread consumer demand?
3. **The Competitive Edge** Does this franchise offer a *better way* of providing that product or service to the consumer?
4. **The Entrepreneurial Opportunity** Will the level of investment, the nature of the industry and the appeal of the franchise itself attract enough new franchisees to ensure that the system will grow and the franchisee can be resold in the future?

Each factor is discussed in detail below, together with some questions to ask a franchisor. To help a prospective franchisee to interpret the information about a particular franchise opportunity and apply it to his or her own situation, checking off the items in Quick Check 3.1, "Franchise Assessment Checklist" is a useful exercise.

The Organization

The personality of the franchisor is one of the most crucial factors in the long-term success of a franchise. Most franchisors start out operating a small independent business, which may be the basis for the franchise concept. Unfortunately, the skills required to operate a successful small business are usually totally different from those required to run and build a franchise system.

Quick Check 3.1 Things to do

Check when answered
to your satisfaction

The Franchisor

1. How long has the franchise been in business? _____

2. Is it a well-established company? _____

3. How long has it been offering franchises? _____

4. Does it have proven experience of operating a franchise chain? _____

5. If a new firm, how long has the concept been tested? _____

6. What are the results of the concept testing? _____

7. Is it the subsidiary of another company? If so, who is the parent company? Has that company ever franchised other products or services? What is its track record? _____

8. What business is the company really in? Is it more interested in selling franchises than in marketing a viable product or service? _____

9. How does the company make its money—from "up-front" fees or from continuing royalties? (Reputable franchisors are interested in the continuing success of their franchisees; money should come from successful franchises and products, not by reselling unprofitable franchises.) _____

10. How many franchised outlets are currently in operation? How many outlets are company-owned? _____

11. Have any outlets failed in the past? If so, why? What is the ratio of successful franchises to those which have failed? _____

12. Have you received the franchisor's recent audited financial statements? Is the company financially stable? Has your accountant analyzed the statements? _____

13. Who are the franchisor's directors and officers, and what is their business experience? _____

14. Are these management people employed full-time by the franchise company? _____

15. How long has the present management been with the company? _____

Quick Check 3.1 **Things to do** (cont'd)

16. What is the depth and quality of the franchisor's management team and supervisory personnel? _____

17. Does the franchisor have a reputation for dealing honestly with its franchisees? With its customers? _____

18. What is the franchisor's standing with the Chamber of Commerce? The Better Business Bureau? Dun & Bradstreet? Its bank? Your bank? Canadian Franchise Association? _____

19. Have you discussed the franchisor's plans for future development and expansion or diversification? _____

20. What effect will development and expansion have on your dealings with the franchisor? _____

21. What innovations has the franchisor introduced since first starting? _____

22. Are there immediate plans for further expansion in your area? Will that affect your sales? _____

23. Where will new franchises be located?

24. Has the company shown a pattern of solid growth? _____

25. How selective is the franchisor when choosing its franchisees? Have your qualifications and financial standing been reviewed? _____

26. If the franchise is operating, or being offered, in Alberta, have you seen the franchisor's disclosure document? If the franchisor is a member of the Canadian Franchise Association have you seen a copy of the Franchisor's Mandatory Disclosure Document? _____

27. Has the franchisor shown you any certified figures indicating exact net profits of one or more franchisee firms which you have personally checked yourself with the franchisee? _____

28. Is the franchisor connected in any way with any other franchise company handling similar merchandise or services? _____

29. If the answer to the last question is yes, what is your protection against this second franchisor organization? _____

Quick Check 3.1 Things to do (cont'd)

30. Are there any lawsuits pending against the franchisor or its key people? What is the nature of the claim? Has there been a history of dissatisfied franchisees litigating against the franchisor? _____

The Product or Service

31. How is the firm's image in the community? How is the product regarded? _____

32. Are you prepared to spend the rest of your business life with this product or service? _____

33. Will this product/service sell all year round or will you be out of business for some months each year? Are you prepared for such a slack period? _____

34. Might this product/service just be a fad? Or will demand increase? Is it a luxury? _____

35. Is it well-packaged to promote sales? _____

36. Where is the product/service now sold? _____

37. What assurance do you have that the franchisor will be able to continue getting the product for you at a fair price? _____

38. How many people in the area are potential customers? _____

39. Is the product or service protected by a trademark or copyright? Is it patented? _____

40. What makes the product or service unique, and does it satisfy a particular need in your market? _____

41. Can the product or service be easily duplicated by your competitors? _____

42. How much of this product or service is presently sold, and have sales been increasing or decreasing? _____

43. Would you buy the product or service on its own merits? _____

44. How long has it been on the market in its present form? _____

45. Is the product or service marketable in your territory? How do you know? _____

Quick Check 3.1 **Things to do** (cont'd)

46. Is the price competitive with similar products or services on the market? Do you have many competitors? _____

47. Have you reviewed the federal/provincial standards and regulations governing the product or service? _____

48. Are there product warranties or guarantees? Are they your responsibility or the franchisor's? _____

49. Are you allowed by the franchisor to carry other product lines or provide additional services? _____

The Location and Territory

50. How well-defined is the franchised sales area? Is it outlined on a map? In the contract? _____

51. Are there proposed changes in traffic patterns or redevelopment which could affect the business in the proposed location? (Check municipal offices about local by-laws.) _____

52. How expensive are taxes and insurance in the area? _____

53. Are your franchised rights exclusive for the area? What guarantee do you have? Can the company open its own outlets? _____

54. What competition is in the area? _____

55. Can you select your own location? _____

56. Do you lease or own the premises? What are the terms? _____

57. Will you receive assistance in selecting a location? Is there a fee for this? _____

58. Will the population in the territory given you increase, remain static, or decrease over the next five years? Does the franchisor have information on these matters? _____

59. Will the product or service you are considering be in greater demand, about the same, or less demand than today five years from now? _____

60. Can you, or the franchisor, change the size of your territory in the future? _____

61. Do you have a profile of the people in your area, including age, income and occupation? _____

Quick Check 3.1 Things to do (cont'd)

The Franchise Contract

62. Does the contract fully explain your rights and obligations under the franchise agreement, and those of the franchisor? _____

63. Does the contract benefit both parties—you and the franchisor? _____

64. Can you terminate the contract if, for some reason, you have to? _____

65. What is the cost or penalty if you do terminate the contract? _____

66. Will you have the privilege of selling or transferring the franchise and under what conditions or restrictions? Will you have the option of selling it yourself, or must it be handled as a resale by the franchisor? How is the resale price then set? _____

67. Does the contract give the franchisor the right of cancellation for almost any reason, or must there be good cause? Are the reasons for cancellation outlined? _____

68. If the franchisor can terminate, will you be compensated for goodwill? _____

69. Are the payments to the franchisor spelled out in detail? What do they include? _____

70. Must you purchase a minimum amount or all of the merchandise from the franchisor? _____

71. Can you use your own suppliers? _____

72. Must you purchase or lease equipment directly from the franchisor? _____

73. Are makes and/or sources of supply for equipment, furnishings and fixtures specified? _____

74. Who is responsible for repairs to fixtures and equipment? Are warranties provided? _____

75. Do you fully understand the terms of any leasing agreement you sign? _____

76. Is there an annual sales quota? Is it realistic? Can the company terminate the contract if the quota is not met? _____

Quick Check 3.1 **Things to do** (cont'd)

77. Does the contract prevent you from establishing, owning, or working in a competing business for a certain period after termination? Do you feel this restriction is fair in the circumstances? _____

78. Before you sign the sales contract, are you sure that the franchise can do something for you that you cannot do for yourself? _____

79. Does the franchisor provide continuing assistance? Is this specified in the contract? _____

80. Is training-school attendance required? _____

81. Have you examined and seen in operation the company's franchise handbook, the accounting system and all other systems and methods to which you will have to adhere? _____

82. Will the franchisor help with the financing arrangements? What will it cost you? _____

83. Are advertising and sales support adequate? What is the cost? _____

84. If a well-known personality is involved in the advertising, does he/she assist you directly? How? What happens if the celebrity quits or dies? _____

85. What controls does the franchisor specify in the following areas? _____
    - operational procedures _____
    - product/service quality _____
    - hiring staff _____
    - advertising _____
    - accounting _____
    - insurance _____
    - prices _____
    - reporting and records _____
    - other _____

86. Are you allowed to hire a manager, or must you run the franchise yourself? _____

87. Does the franchisor perform a market study for each potential franchise location? _____

Quick Check 3.1 **Things to do** (cont'd)

88. Is the chosen franchise location right for your own needs? _____

89. What standards does the franchisor specify for the property? _____

90. If a lease is involved, are you leasing from the franchisor or from an independent landlord? _____

91. Can you sublease, assign the lease, or move the franchise if necessary? _____

92. Is the franchise contract for a specified number of years, at which time a new agreement must be negotiated? Or is the franchise term indefinite, with automatic renewal privileges, subject to certain mutually agreeable restrictions? _____

93. Does the franchise agreement provide for arbitration in the event of a dispute or default? _____

94. Are your payments to the franchisor clearly specified? Are the following shown? _____
     • the franchise fee _____
     • any fixed yearly payments the franchisor receives _____
     • royalty payments based on a percentage of gross sales _____
     • the monthly percentage of gross sales required for advertising _____
     • fees for continuing services provided by the franchisor _____

95. Are these costs realistic or overly burdensome to profitability? _____

96. What happens if supplies from the franchisor are interrupted? Can you purchase goods from alternative suppliers? _____

97. Have you the right to the franchisor's latest innovations? _____

98. Does the contract cover in detail all the franchisor's verbal promises made during the interview? _____

99. If leasing the location, will the lease be for the same term as the franchise agreement? Can the lease be renewed if you renew the franchise? _____

Quick Check 3.1 **Things to do** (cont'd)

100. Are you responsible for the construction or improvement of the premises? If so, will the franchisor provide you with plans and specifications, and can these be changed? _____

101. If you default on the contract, how much time do you have to rectify the situation? _____

102. What happens to the business in the event of your prolonged illness or death? Have questions regarding succession been clearly addressed? _____

103. Before you sign the contract, are you sure that the franchise can lead to your meeting personal and financial goals? _____

104. Will the franchisor arrange financing?

105. Does the franchisor call upon you to take any steps which are, according to your lawyer, unwise or illegal in your city or province (e.g., Sunday openings)? _____

106. Are you prepared to give up some independence of action to secure the advantages offered by the franchise? _____

107. Do you really believe you have the innate ability, training and experience to work smoothly and profitably with the franchisor, your employees and your customers? _____

108. Have you had your accountant and lawyer carefully check out the agreement, particularly those areas dealing with bankruptcy, termination, renewal, transfer and sale of the franchise? What is their opinion? _____

Questions to Ask Current Franchisees

109. Was the profit projection by the franchisor accurate? _____

110. What reports to the company are necessary? Are they reasonable? _____

111. Is there a minimum quota of sales? Is it difficult to achieve? _____

Quick Check 3.1	Things to do (cont'd)

112. Are the products and equipment supplied by the franchisor satisfactory and delivered promptly?   _____

113. How reliable is delivery from the franchisor?

114. What problems have been encountered with the franchisor?   _____

115. How did the franchisor's income projections compare with the results experienced by existing franchisees?   _____

116. What was the total investment required by the franchisor?

117. Were there any hidden or unexpected costs?   _____

118. Has the franchise been as profitable as expected?   _____

119. How long was it before the operating expenses were covered by revenue?   _____

120. How long was the franchise in operation before the business became profitable?   _____

121. How long was it before the franchise was able to pay a reasonable management salary?   _____

122. Does the franchisor respond promptly and helpfully to questions asked?   _____

123. Has there ever been a serious disagreement with the franchisor? What about? Was it settled amicably?   _____

124. What kind of management and staff training was provided? Did it meet expectations? Where was it held?   _____

125. Is the marketing, promotional, and advertising assistance received from the franchisor satisfactory?   _____

126. What steps have been taken to make the franchise with this particular franchisor?   _____

127. Do franchisees advise anyone else to start a franchise with this particular franchisor?   _____

128. If the contract could be changed, what would you change?   _____

REAL LIFE: Dictators Don't Make Good Franchisors

Harry Autocrat had owned and operated three AutoExtra stores that sold and installed automotive aftermarket accessories. He decided to sell his stores as franchised units, then expand AutoExtra by franchising new locations. Harry franchised his stores as planned and added five new franchised AutoExtra locations over a period of two years.

The franchise system started to experience severe problems. Harry had not made the transition from the autocratic, hands-on management style that had been effective in running his own stores for 15 years, to a more hands-off leadership style that is necessary to run a franchise organization. Harry was accustomed to firing his employees if they did not carry out his instructions, something he couldn't do with franchisees. He was also used to making instant radical changes with his company-owned stores, whereas, the franchise system demanded a more stable, consistent leadership style.

Harry had two major problems: (1) he didn't have a system for running the business, and (2) his management style was not suited to dealing with owner-operators. The old company-owned AutoExtra had been managed by crisis. The new franchised AutoExtra required management by objectives.

The franchisees began to resent Harry's angry outbursts and constant changes of direction. Franchisees started to dis-enfranchise their stores and operate independently from the system. Soon, Harry was involved in several law suits with ex-franchisees, which marked the beginning of the end for AutoExtra.

A franchisee must look closely at the ability of the key people involved in the franchise company. Is there a strong management team that understands the particular industry and possesses the business and legal skills necessary to build the franchise organization? Some franchise organizations who have enjoyed success in franchising one industry have been unsuccessful in their attempts to franchise a different industry because they have failed to modify their system accordingly. Success in one field of franchising does not automatically guarantee success in another field. A franchisee is not solely buying a franchised business; he is buying into a network of franchised businesses. The system must continue to grow with quality franchisees to be able to provide name recognition and purchasing power, and to ensure that the franchisee can ultimately resell the business at a profit.

Numbers also create a very important part of franchising— Synergy! Synergy occurs when the whole appears greater than the sum of the parts. In other words, the consumer perceives that the independent franchised business is part of a strong national organization; a business that is small enough to care, but big enough to do the job.

Synergy can only be achieved with a sufficient concentration of franchised units within an area.

Questions to be asked:
- How long has the franchise been in business?
- Is it a well-established company? How long has it been offering franchises? Does it have proven experience in operating a franchise system?
- Is it a subsidiary of another company? If so, who is the parent company? Has that company ever franchised other products or services? What is its track record?
- Who are the franchisor's directors and officers, and what is their background?
- Are these management people employed full-time by the franchise company? How long has the present management been with the company? What is the quality of the franchisor's management team and supervisory personnel?
- What level of ownership/management are you dealing with? Is this the franchisor or a sub-franchisor? Is the franchise agreement between you and the franchisor, or the sub-franchisor? What happens if either the franchisor or sub-franchisor fails?

Bear in mind:
Many franchisees are blinded by public relations articles about the creators or the driving forces behind franchise success stories, but they could be dealing with a level of management once, twice or even three times removed from the original franchisor (such as a sub-franchisee or area franchisee as explained in Chapter 1). This dilution of management skills and delegation of franchisor respon-

sibilities through various forms of territorial franchising can critically impact on franchisee performance.

Questions to be asked:
- What business is the company really in? Is it more interested in selling franchises than in operating a solid franchise concept?
- How does the company make its money—from "up-front" fees or from continuing royalties? Does the franchisor have adequate financial backing or is it relying on the sale of franchises to develop the system?
- Have you received the franchisor's recent audited financial statements? Is the company financially stable? Has your accountant analyzed the statements?

Bear in mind:

If a franchisor is financially weak, it may be using the sale of franchises to capitalize or subsidize its business. A franchisor may provide confirmation of financial stability by providing audited or unaudited statements, banking references, or a comprehensive, professionally prepared annual company report. This level of information will vary depending on the size, time in business, or status of the company.

A good franchisor does not rely upon initial franchise fees to generate profit. After paying the costs of advertising and marketing the franchise opportunity, start-up costs and initial training, there is usually very little, if anything, left from an initial franchise fee. Reputable franchisors are interested in the continuing success of their franchisees. The franchisor's residual income, and source of profit, should be derived from successful franchises and products, and not from the initial franchise sales or from the resale of unprofitable franchises.

Questions to be asked:
- How long has the company been franchising? Has the company shown consistent solid growth? How many franchised outlets are currently in operation? How many company-owned and operated outlets are there?

Bear in mind:

Talking to existing franchisees is one of the best ways of validating the franchise. Some franchisors will limit access to franchisees until they are satisfied that a prospective franchisee is qualified to own a franchise. At this point they will provide access to their franchisees, but even then they will insist on the prospect making an appointment and not simply calling on them at a time that could be inconvenient.

It is important to ask franchisees if the franchisor does deliver what it promises, and if there was anything that they were led to believe they would get, but never received. It is beneficial to ascertain how the financial projections provided to the franchisees by the franchisor corresponded with actual performance.

Questions to be asked:
- How selective is the franchisor when choosing its franchisees? Have your qualifications and financial standing been reviewed?
- Have any outlets failed in the past? If so, why? What is the ratio of successful franchises to those that have failed?

Bear in mind:
The fact that an outlet has failed is not necessarily a negative sign. The failure could be the fault of the franchisee, or related to unsatisfactory demographics. The real acid test is to determine how the failure was dealt with by the franchisor.

Questions to be asked:
- How long has the franchise concept been tested? What are the results of the franchise testing? Does the franchisor successfully operate a prototype? What is the performance of the prototype?

Bear in mind:
A franchisor should not expect a franchisee to do something that it cannot do itself. At least one prototype should be in operation to prove the concept, iron out any problems and test new products and services prior to introducing them to the franchise system.

Questions to be asked:
- Does your province have laws regulating the sale of franchises? If the franchise is being offered in Alberta have you received the franchisor's disclosure document? Is the franchisor a member of the Canadian Franchise Association? Is so, have you received the Mandatory Disclosure Document from the franchisor?

Bear in mind:
If the franchise business is to be located partly or wholly in the province of Alberta, or if you are a resident of Alberta or maintain a

principle residence in Alberta, the franchisor must provide you with a disclosure document at least 14 days before the signing of any agreement relating to the franchise, or the payment of any consideration relating to the franchise, whichever is earlier. See the section entitled "Franchise Legislation" in Chapter 1 for more information on franchise legislation in the province of Alberta. If the franchisor is a member of the Canadian Franchise Association they are required to provide a prospective franchisee with a Mandatory Disclosure Document setting out various information about the franchise and the franchisor.

The Product or Service

Question to be asked:
Does the product or service have widespread consumer appeal?

Bear in mind:
   Selling a new concept to the general public is expensive and risky. Ideally, consumer demand for the product or service should have already been established in the surrounding market area. Although the concept may be well established in another locale, there may be no consumer demand or awareness in your market area.
   Some potential franchisees, thinking that the market is saturated, shy away from franchise opportunities that are already well represented by other companies. Ray Kroc, the founder of McDonald's, probably summed it up best when he said "Saturation is for sponges." If there is an established consumer demand for a product or service, it then becomes a matter of gaining market share rather than gaining acceptance of the concept. Also there is often a latent consumer market demand for a concept. This can increase the potential market size when a competitor enters the marketplace and by doing so, increases the exposure of the concept.

Questions to be asked:
• Are you prepared to spend the rest of your business life with this product or service?
• Will this product/service sell all year-round or will you be out of business for some months each year? Would you be prepared for such a slack period?
• Is this product/service a trend or a fad? Or will demand increase? Is it a luxury? Is it well-packaged to promote sales?

Bear in mind:

Most people do not understand the difference between a trend and a fad. A fad starts from the "top" and works down, whereas a trend starts from the "bottom" and works up. In other words, a trend—such as fitness—starts from a demand created by the consumer. Consequently, a trend is normally long-lasting, whereas a fad—such as pet rocks and cabbagepatch dolls—rarely penetrate deeply enough into the market to have longevity.

If the franchise concept is built on a single product, the franchisee must examine the consequences of any drop in demand by the consumer. If the franchise only sells yoghurt or muffins, what would happen if the demand disappeared? If the franchisor is the only source of supply, what alternatives are there if the franchisor fails and supply is terminated?

Questions to be asked:
• Where is the product/service now sold? How many people in the area are potential customers? How much of this product or service is presently sold, and have sales been increasing or decreasing?
• Is the product or service marketable in your territory? How do you know?
• Have you reviewed the federal/provincial standards and regulations governing the product or service? Will the product sell in Halifax and Vancouver? Has the franchisor carried out any demographic studies within the area to determine feasibility? Is the franchise recession-proof?
• Can the concept be taught or is it a skill unique to the franchisor?

Bear in mind:

Franchisees should analyze the performance of the product or service during any downturn in the economy. Some franchises perform well during such periods, but the sale of durables such as furniture, electrical goods and other discretionary purchases can be diminished.

Franchisees may also benefit from the franchisor's sustained advertising during slower economic times. Some market studies indicate that companies who sustain advertising during a recessionary period increase their market share by about 12%.

The Competitive Edge

Questions to be asked:
- Is this a better way of delivering the product or service to the consumer?
- Is it well-packaged to promote sales? What makes the product or service unique, and does it satisfy a particular need in your market? Can the product or service be easily duplicated by your competitor? Is the product or service protected by a trademark or copyright? Is it patented?
- Would you buy the product or service on its own merits? How long has it been on the market in its present form?
- Is the price competitive with similar products or services on the market? Will you have many competitors?
- How is the firm's image in the community? How is the product regarded?
- Will the product or service you are considering be in greater demand, about the same, or in less demand five years from now?
- Are there product warranties or guarantees? Are they your responsibility or the franchisor's? Will the franchisor allow you to carry other product lines? What assurance do you have that the franchisor will be able to continue getting the product for you at a fair price?

Bear in mind:

A franchise must provide the franchisee with something that he or she is unable to do, or obtain, for himself or herself. In other words, the franchise should offer a competitive edge. It may be in the purchasing power, advertising economies of scale, the exclusivity of the product or service, or strong consumer name recognition.

Franchisors will normally wish to exercise control over the two areas in which product is supplied to franchisees: (a) products supplied directly by the franchisor, and (b) products supplied authorized by the franchisor.

They will also want to control the products in terms of quality control and the range of products carried by the franchisee. Such controls are necessary to ensure uniformity and consistency across the entire franchise system.

Products supplied directly by the franchisor are often trademarked by the franchisor (proprietary products), and as part of its grant to the franchisee of a license to use the trademark, the franchisor will obviously wish to impose quality standards. Similarly, the franchisor will be concerned about the goods or services sold in the franchise system and will require the ability to authorize suppliers of goods or services to the franchisees.

In most situations, the franchisee will be given a list of authorized suppliers that the franchisor has approved to supply products or services to the franchise system. The franchisor may also provide a list of products and services that the franchisee is authorized to use. Minor and infrequent purchases, such as office supplies, will probably be excluded from this list.

If the franchisee sources products that are comparable in quality and appearance, and available at a lower price than existing authorized products, approval can usually be requested from the franchisor to change suppliers. The franchisor cannot unreasonably withhold approval but will wish to make sure that the lower price and the supply of products can be sustained. This is understandable as the franchisor could jeopardize a longstanding relationship with a supplier in order to take advantage of a "one-off" deal. The franchisor will normally want to be satisfied in terms of packaging, warranties, advertising support and promotional materials.

The areas of tied selling, price concessions, exclusive dealing and market restrictions are controlled under the Competition Act by the Price Discrimination Enforcement Guidelines. The guidelines give franchisors who sell products to their franchisees greater flexibility in offering functional discounts, exclusive dealing discounts and growth bonuses, in addition to the traditionally permitted volume-based discounts.

Questions to be asked:
- Is there adequate support and training?
- Is the cost of training included in the initial franchise fee?
- How many people can attend the training?
- Who is responsible for costs of travel and accommodation?

Bear in mind:
The duration and location of the training program, and the responsibility for any costs associated with travel or accommoda-

tion, should be specified. If the franchisor provides training at a location other than the franchised location, the franchisee should make allowances for the fact that he will not be receiving income during that period.

The Entrepreneurial Opportunity

Most people do not enter a business with the thought of selling it in the future; however, it is a sensible approach to develop a business with the intention of future resale. You must have a way of liquidating your asset. A franchisee should seek to obtain a salary that is adequate to maintain his desired standard of living, provide a satisfactory annual return on investment, plus build equity in the business. The only way to realize that equity is, of course, through the eventual resale of the business. A franchise should sell faster and for a higher price than an independent business by virtue of its exclusivity, name recognition and all the other franchise advantages.

On average, franchises change hands every five years. The reasons for the change of ownership are varied: people want a fresh challenge; the transfer of a spouse to a new city; an inability to run the business profitably; illness, retirement, personal problems; or simply a franchisee's desire to capitalize on his or her efforts and make a profit.

A franchisee needs to feel confident that, whatever the reason, he or she can dispose of the business within a reasonable time-frame and for a reasonable profit, assuming of course that value has been built into the business.

Various factors positively or negatively impact a business resale. The level of investment required, type of business, hours of work and the return on investment will all influence the saleability of the business. A franchisee must look at the broad appeal of the franchise opportunity to other entrepreneurs, taking into consideration all of the factors that influence the growth of the total franchise system. Unless the system grows, many of the benefits of franchising such as advertising clout and purchasing power will be lost, and the possibility of resale will also be diminished.

WHERE TO SOURCE FRANCHISE OPPORTUNITIES

Newspapers

Franchise opportunities can usually be found in the classified section of most major daily newspapers listed either under franchises, business opportunities or businesses for sale. Some franchisors run larger display ads in the business section of the paper.

The Globe and Mail has a special section advertising single-unit and territorial franchises every week. The *Financial Post* also has a special advertising section on a regular basis. Both newspapers periodically feature special reports on franchising.

Publications

Opportunities Canada, Franchise and Dealership Guide, 4283 Village Centre Court, 2nd Floor, Mississauga, Ont. L42 1Y5. Phone (905) 276-8880, Toll free 1-800-463-7469, Fax (905) 276-9907.

Opportunities Canada is published three times a year by Prestige Promotions. It contains franchise and dealership opportunities and informative articles on franchising. It is comprehensive and updated regularly. Prestige Promotions also organizes franchise and business opportunities trade shows across Canada. Contact them for upcoming events.

Franchise Annual, Info Franchise News Inc., 9 Duke Street, P.O. Box 670, St. Catharines, Ont. L2R 6W8. Phone (905) 688-2665.

The *Franchise Annual* is published annually and lists franchises available in Canada and the United States.

Canadian Business Franchise, 395 Conway Road, Victoria, B.C., V8X 3X1. Phone (205) 744-1662; Fax (250) 744-3763.

Canadian Business Franchise is a magazine which is published six times a year and has advertisements for franchise opportunities and articles on various aspects of franchising.

Franchise Opportunities Guide, the official guide of the International Franchise Association, 1350 New York Avenue, N.W., Suite 900, Washington, DC 20005. Phone (202) 628-8000.

The guide lists more than 2,500 franchises and contains educational articles about franchising. Several other magazines, including INC., *Success, Profit* and *Canadian Business,* also carry franchise advertisements.

Entrepreneur Inc., 2311 Pontius Avenue, Los Angeles, California, 90064.

Entrepreneur magazine is published monthly. Each January they publish a Franchise 500 edition in which they assess over 1,000 franchise opportunities in the U.S. and Canada and rate them according to performance and growth.

These types of ratings may provide some indication of the performance of a franchise, but they can be misleading for several reasons. First, the information is provided by the franchise organization and may not be accurate. The performance may also vary depending on the territory or country. Claims such as "#1 Franchise" or "The Fastest-Growing Franchise in the Country" should be treated with caution. It has been proven time and time again that the general public is fairly gullible and will invest their life savings in something that promises a fast buck, without carrying out proper due diligence. Rapid growth alone does not provide evidence of a good franchise opportunity. Often franchises that grow rapidly suffer horrendous attrition in their second and third years of operation. The prospective franchisee must look beyond rapid growth and apply other criteria as suggested in this book.

Franchise Shows

Various franchise shows are held throughout the year in Canada, and these are well advertised in local newspapers. You may also want to attend some shows in the U.S. to see franchisors who are not yet established in Canada. Education seminars on different aspects of franchising are sometimes held in conjunction with the show. The prospective franchisee has a good opportunity for exposure to many different franchise opportunities and, in some instances, to meet a franchisor face to face. A show should be used to gather information and narrow down your options. We would not recommend making decisions about investing in a business opportunity of this size and nature during a show. A decision made under such circumstances is more likely to be based on emotion than logic. If you wish to pursue a specific franchise opportunity, arrange to meet at a later date to discuss the matter further.

The following organizations promote franchise and business opportunity shows on a regular basis. They can be contacted to obtain a schedule of their upcoming shows:

CANADIAN FRANCHISE SHOW
Canadian Franchise Association
5045 Orbiter Drive
Building 9, Suite 401
Mississauga, Ontario
L4W 4Y4
Phone (905) 625-2896
Toll free 1-800-665-4232

The CFA conducts trade shows in Toronto, Vancouver and possibly other cities in the future. Check for a current schedule.

CANADIAN NATIONAL FRANCHISING EXPO (Toronto)
FRANCHISE AND INVESTMENT OPPORTUNITIES EXPOSI-TION (cities outside Toronto)

Prestige Promotions
4283 Village Centre Court
2nd Floor
Mississauga, Ontario
L4Z 1Y5
Phone (905) 276-8880
Toll free 1-800-463-7469
Fax (905) 276-9907

Prestige organizes franchise and business opportunity shows throughout Canada. It is the largest promoter of this type of trade show in Canada. Prestige also publishes *Opportunities Canada* magazine three times a year.

FRANCHISE AND INVESTMENT EXPO
Mart Franchise Venture LLC
Fort Lee Executive Park
One Executive Drive, 3rd Floor
Fort Lee, N.J., 07024 U.S.
Phone (201) 461-1220
Fax (201) 461-1226

This company is the world's largest franchise expo producer with shows in various countries, including Canada. They also produce the international franchise expos in the U.S.

Franchise Consultants

Some franchise consultants only represent specific franchisors, but there are those who will work with a prospective franchisee in some type of mentor relationship to source and identify the most suitable franchise. A good franchise consultant can save you a lot of time in the selection process by narrowing down your options and weeding out the less reputable franchises.

Check with professionals in the franchise industry such as lawyers, lenders and franchise associations to find out which consultants are credible and will provide sound advice.

HOW TO EVALUATE THE FRANCHISOR'S TRACK RECORD

There are several sources and methods of checking out the franchisor's track record including audited statements, suppliers, credit ratings (through companies such as Dun and Bradstreet), Better Business Bureau, other franchisees, franchise associations, consultants, any regulatory authorities and your bank.

In general, you want to determine how long the franchisor has been in business, when the franchising program commenced, how many units are franchised and how many are company-owned, how the units are spread geographically, and if any units have failed. Find out if the business was operating before franchising took place and for how long. There are exceptions to the rule, but it is usually better to have a relatively long learning curve before the process of franchising commences. There is a significant difference between a company that franchises and a franchise company. The geographical spread of units will show if the franchise is fragmented or has grown out from the middle in an orderly fashion. This provides a concentrated marketing influence and better ability for the franchisor to service the franchisees. Any evidence of uncontrolled or fragmented growth can be a warning signal.

The more established a franchise is the more information that will be available. When validating a relatively new franchise, more emphasis must be placed on the skills and background of the franchisor and its key employees than on the experience of existing franchisees. Franchisees with less than one year of experience will normally still be in a honeymoon period and will often provide glowing validation.

Reviewing the Franchisor's Statements

If you are able to obtain copies of the franchisor's financial statements, make sure they are current and audited. In addition to checking the financial stability of the company, examine the main revenue source of the franchisor. As discussed later in this chapter, a franchisor's true income should be from ongoing royalties and not from initial franchise fees. If the main source of revenue is derived from initial franchise fees, you may have a franchisor who is focused on franchise sales and not the ongoing success of the franchisees. Advertising income should not be considered revenue as it is technically held in trust for the franchisees.

The franchisor should be incorporated and have significant assets in the company. Exercise caution if you are dealing with a company that does not have assets or an operating base in Canada because, if it should be necessary in the future for the franchisee to initiate any legal action against the franchisor, it could turn out to be a cumbersome, expensive and possibly futile exercise.

Regulatory Authorities

If the franchisor is operating in Alberta, if you are a resident of Alberta, or have a permanent residence in Alberta, the franchisor is required by the Alberta Securities Commission to provide you with a copy of the franchisor's disclosure document as discussed in Chapter 1. If you are investigating a franchise in a province other than Alberta, and the franchisor is operating in Alberta, you can request a copy of the disclosure document that the franchisor is required to provide in Alberta. If the franchisor is operating in the United States you may be able to obtain a copy of the franchisor's disclosure statement if they carry on business in a state that requires full disclosure.

This information provides a good basis for assessing the merits of a franchise operation. Don't assume because a franchisor has complied with disclosure or registration requirements it implies that the regulatory authority has approved or recommends the franchise in any way. It simply means the franchisor has conformed to the regulatory requirements. It is essential that you verify the information disclosed by the franchisor by speaking with existing franchisees, your lawyer, your accountant, or a franchise consultant. The addresses and phone numbers of the regulatory authorities in Canada and the U.S. are provided in Appendix.

Franchise Associations

A franchisor's membership in a franchise association is voluntary. If it is not a member of an association, this does not mean that it is not a competent franchisor. However, it is often a good indication that when a business elects to be part of an association that represents its industry, or method of doing business, that it is a responsible organization and has an interest in staying abreast of developments and their potential impact on franchising and franchisees.

The role of an association is to keep its members informed about any changes that may affect the way they do business, and to attempt to project an image of professionalism to the general public. In an effort to promote ethical franchising through industry self-management and self-regulation, the Canadian Franchise Association, on April 1, 1997, produced its first Mandatory Disclosure Document for its franchisor members. Key areas within the document include: the length of time the franchisor has been in business; the franchisor's business experience; the level of investment required; a list of the franchisor's shareholders and directors; and the franchisor's involvement in any litigation issues. A further two key areas concerning: (1) relations with suppliers, and (2) declaration of financial statements are to be added to the document in the future.

An association office will be able to tell you if a franchisor is a member and provide some information about selecting a franchise. They can also assist by directing a prospective franchisee to someone who can provide them with professional assistance. A list of Franchise Associations is provided in Appendix.

Provinces

Each of the provinces and the territories has a specific branch of government set up to help small business and franchising. These branches can assist through loan programs, counselling and skills development for both owners and employees.

Lenders

Some of the major banks have special franchise departments that offer a complete range of franchise services to both franchisors and franchisees. They often have information on a wide range of franchises and have pre-approved lending criteria for some of the more established franchises.

The Experience of Other Franchisees

One of the most reliable methods of validation is to talk to franchisees who have been in the system for at least a couple of years. Try to talk to franchisees who have a similar unit to one you are contemplating and operate in an area with the same type of demographics. Also, try to talk to franchisees other than those on a list given to you by the franchisor, and if possible any franchisees who are, for whatever reason, no longer in the system.

It is best to ask questions that relate to the character of the franchisor and the level of support they have received, and whether the franchisor lives up to its promises. The following questions will assist in validation:

- Were the projections of income and expense provided by the franchisor reasonably accurate?
- Were there any additional costs over and above the total investment figure that they have been given?
- Did they receive the promised level of training and opening assistance and was it adequate?
- Are there any logistical problems regarding supplies or deliveries?
- How does the franchisor respond to problems?
- Who provides them with ongoing support and is it efficient?
- Was the operations manual adequate and easy to follow?
- Are the reporting requirements required by the franchisor reasonable?
- How long was it before the business reached break-even?
- Is there anything they would change if they did it again?
- How seasonal are the sales figures?

Work in a Franchise Outlet

It may be possible to work in one of the franchise outlets for a period of time to see if you are suitable for that particular business and to get a feel for the performance of the units and the franchisor. This is not always practical as the franchisor may be reluctant to expose a potential franchisee to more of its trade secrets without having his or her firm commitment to the franchise system.

Some people are more analytical in their decision-making than others and need to examine each and every aspect of the franchise business under a microscope. Some people confuse the need for more and more information with what is really a form of buyer's remorse, or fear of actually making a final decision and commitment to proceed. They are looking for reasons to say no! We suggest that you carry out proper due diligence, but undue procrastination may indicate that you do not have the necessary self-confidence to go into business on your own, either independently or as a franchisee.

UNDERSTANDING THE FRANCHISE SALES PROCESS

Attracting, screening and selecting suitably qualified franchisees is a time-absorbing and expensive task for a franchisor. Statistics show that only one person in 2,000 who sees a franchise advertisement is likely to inquire. Only one in 20 will actually fill out the franchisor's application form, and approximately one-third of those who do apply will meet the franchisor's financial, behavioural and demographic criteria.

Franchisors have different franchise recruitment philosophies and strategies which are usually a reflection of their respective positions in the marketplace. An established, successful franchise with a strong demand may have more formalized application procedures and place a much stronger emphasis on qualifying the applicant than will a new franchise organization.

Some franchisors concede that they are less selective during the early stages of starting a new franchise company because they need to establish a base of stores quickly in order to finance their growth. Franchisors should not depend on the revenue from franchise sales to finance their growth. Any slowdown in the sales of franchises will inevitably result in the collapse of the franchise system. A slowdown in franchise sales could result in the franchisor becoming even less selective, which will also ultimately destroy the franchise. If you get the feeling that the franchisor would sell a franchise to anyone who can afford it, be cautious. It is the franchisor's obligation to decide responsibly whether the applicant is, in fact, the right sort of person for a particular franchise.

The franchisor's emphasis at all times should be on "selecting" the franchisee and not on "selling" the franchise.

Franchise Sales Psychology

Although franchisors employ a wide variety of techniques designed to motivate people to apply for a franchise, the most common psychological selling technique is some form or degree of reverse-selling. In essence, reverse-selling places the motivation on the applicant to do the selling, thereby effectively reversing the roles of customer and salesperson. The customer assumes the active role and the salesperson the resistive role. To achieve this, the franchisor will place a series of hurdles in front of the franchisee throughout the investigation process that range from minor obstacles to those requiring substantial effort and commitment on the part of the franchisee. The franchisor is looking for the franchisee to demonstrate enthusiasm, commitment and perseverance—all good behavioural traits in a franchisee.

Reverse-selling also shifts the focus of the process from selling to selecting. Part of franchise sales psychology is to create urgency and fear of loss in the applicant. The "fear of loss" is often a greater buying motivator than "the desire for gain." Consumers respond to promotions that are based on the fear of loss such as "one to a family" or "first 50 customers only." The consumer must have a perceived need for the product or service, but the idea that they may miss an opportunity is a powerful motivator. The degree to which it is applied or created is often the difference between a credible and well-intentioned franchise company concerned about the quality of its franchisees and one that is totally focused on the revenues created by the sale of franchises. Beware of any franchisor who makes it too easy to buy a franchise. Conversely, the franchisor who applies unreasonably strong reverse-selling techniques may have something to hide.

Don't give in to undue pressure to sign today. Any credible franchisor would not let you proceed unless you had investigated the franchise thoroughly.

The Initial Enquiry

The first interest in a franchise opportunity is often generated by an advertisement, exposure to the franchised business (a store or restaurant visit) or a referral by an acquaintance. An interested party (called the "applicant") contacts the franchise organization and requests information about the franchise opportunity.

What happens next varies depending upon the size, proximity, sophistication, availability and franchise recruitment philosophy of the franchise organization. Some franchises will give the caller a generous amount of information over the telephone and others will simply attempt to qualify the caller. Some will forward a comprehensive franchise information package and others will simply forward the applicant a franchise application report which must be returned before any information is provided, subject to the applicant meeting the franchisor's qualification criteria. Sample 3.1 shows a sample franchise application report.

The initial enquiry to the franchisor can tell a great deal about the franchise organization. How the telephone is answered, the amount and timing of information released, the emphasis on selling versus qualifying the applicant, and the professionalism of materials all combine to create the total image of the franchisor. Some franchises will not take a call from a prospect, but will obtain the name and telephone number of the prospect and call them back later. This gives them an opportunity to see where the prospect is calling from (home or office) and also gives the franchisor some form of control as they are the party placing the call. Franchisors prefer to remain in control of the recruitment process.

Pre-Qualification

As previously mentioned, the process of finding and selecting suitably qualified franchisees is very expensive and time-consuming. Franchisors are normally able to develop an ideal franchisee profile but, unfortunately, not everyone has all of the financial and personal resources, and characteristics required to operate a franchise. Many franchisors attempt to pre-qualify the applicant at the telephone enquiry stage and explain:

- the total level of initial investment and how much will be required as equity from the applicant

Sample 3.1	Franchise Application Report

1. PERSONAL DATA

   Name_____

   Phone (____) _____   (____) _____
           work   home

   Address _____

   City_____ Province_____ Postal Code _____

   How long at this address?____ Social Insurance No. _____

   Date and Place of Birth _____

   Marital Status _____

   Spouse's Name _____

   Dependant(s) Name and Age _____

   Have you ever been convicted of a criminal offence?_____

   Explain_____

   Are you/have you ever been party to a civil litigation?_____

   Explain_____

   Have you or any company with which you were associated ever gone bankrupt? _____

2. CURRENT & PREVIOUS EXPERIENCE: (starting with most current)

   1) Company Name_____

       Date_____ to _____

       Type of Business _____

       Duties_____

       Annual Salary _____

       Supervisor _____

       Reason for leaving _____

   2) Company Name_____

       Date_____ to _____

| Sample 3.1 | **Franchise Application Report** (cont'd) |

Type of Business _____

Duties _____

Annual Salary _____

Supervisor _____

Reason for leaving _____

3) Company Name _____

Date _____ to _____

Type of Business _____

Duties _____

Annual Salary _____

Supervisor _____

Reason for leaving _____

3. OTHER BUSINESS INTERESTS

Have you ever had your own business or been self-employed? ___

_____

What do you feel will be your most important contribution(s) to your business? _____

_____

_____

4. EDUCATIONAL BACKGROUND

Highest level of education attained: _____ Degrees _____

Major Subjects _____ Minor Subjects _____

Special Training _____

Courses Taken _____

What languages do you speak? _____

5. GENERAL INFORMATION

I became interested in a franchise opportunity because _____

Sample 3.1	Franchise Application Report (cont'd)

List any hobbies, community activities, or special interests _____

If we select each other, my involvement would be:

Full-time operator_____ Wife/husband active operator _____

Part-time supervisor with other business interests_____

Absentee operator (investment only)_____

Would you be willing to relocate to a new city?_____

My franchise location preference is:

1st Choice_____ 2nd Choice _____

Have you ever worked at one of our locations? If so, when and where?_____

Are you related to any officer, director, or employee of our company, or any of our franchisees? If so, please name the person.

6. FINANCIAL PROFILE (REFER TO FINANCIAL STATEMENT SCHEDULES)

Present Income _____

Spouse's Income _____

Net Worth approximately _____

I understand that any associates who cooperate with me in financing this operation must also complete a financial profile. Forms may be sent to:

Name _____

Address _____

Will any partners or investors be active? _____

Are you a partner or investor in any other venture? _____

Sample 3.1   Franchise Application Report (cont'd)

What level of income do you wish to earn from the operation of your franchise?_____

What is the minimum personal income you will need during the first year of operation? _____

7. CREDIT REFERENCES

     Company Name   Address   Phone No.   Account No.

   1. _____

   2. _____

   3. _____

8. BANK REFERENCES

           Account No.   Bank   Phone No.   Branch

  Chequing _____

  Savings _____

9. PERSONAL REFERENCES (excluding relatives and former employees)

     Name   Address   Phone No.

   1. _____

   2. _____

   3. _____

- the basic franchise concept
- the process used for franchisee selection.

If the franchisor is satisfied that the applicant meets the pre-qual-ification criteria, it may arrange to meet with the applicant, or alter-natively forward a franchise application report to the applicant. The process will not continue until the application has been received and approved. Established franchise companies that attract a significant number of enquiries wish to ensure that they are going to invest their time with someone who has the capital available to proceed with the franchise. In other words, they may not proceed with an applicant who must sell a residence prior to proceeding, or be satis-fied with an assurance from the applicant that they can get the money, or with someone who is evasive about the amount of capital or collateral that is available. To a franchisor, a qualified applicant is someone who is ready, willing and able to proceed with the fran-chise. Selling a home and going into a new business simultaneously can be a very emotional experience, especially if the family is mov-ing to a new area. There are too many issues to cope with all at once. So, don't be surprised if the franchisor is fairly insistent about know-ing your financial picture because the franchisor does not have time to waste with tire-kickers.

The respective locations of the franchisor and the applicant play a part in the dissemination of information. For example, if a fran-chisor was located in Toronto, and had the opportunity to obtain a key mall location in Winnipeg which required a fast response in order to secure the lease, it may immediately advertise for a fran-chisee in local newspapers. Because of the urgency, the franchisor may send a representative to the area rather than wait for interested parties to travel to its office. The franchisor would probably expedite any franchise enquiries by forwarding a franchise application to the prospect together with some limited information about the fran-chise. This application may be a simple "Application for an Interview" which only requires very basic information, or a more in-depth franchise application report. The prospect may be required to return the application immediately to the franchisor, or bring it with him or her to the first meeting. The franchisor would probably attempt to obtain several qualified prospects prior to travelling to the area to interview the applicants in order to create "a fear of loss" among the applicants, and to have some alternatives.

The Franchise Kit

The quality and professionalism of the franchise kits provided by franchise companies vary from a poorly worded letter reproduced on inexpensive letterhead to an expensive presentation brochure. The lack of care and professionalism evident in a franchise kit may be a reflection of the franchisor's image and credibility, and as such should give reason to be concerned. Conversely, it doesn't necessarily follow that an expensively prepared glossy presentation folder means the franchisor is offering a solid opportunity.

A franchise information kit is typically comprised of six parts:

- a history of the company
- a summary of the benefits to the franchisee
- qualification criteria for a franchisee
- public relations propaganda and credibility-building items such as photographs, ad-reprints, articles about the company, testimonial letters etc.
- projections of income and expense, and an initial investment summary
- a franchise application report.

Franchise materials are designed to get applicants' attention, motivate them to complete the application, and sustain their motivation during the sales process. To achieve this, the package is created to appeal to both the logical and emotional sides of the applicants. A section on analyzing the financial data such as the projections of income and expense provided by a franchisor is presented later in this chapter.

The Mutual Investigation Process

The applicant should expect to exchange information with the franchisor in order to determine that he or she is suited to the opportunity being presented. During this process the prospect can also learn a great deal about the franchisor's approach to franchising.

The following outlines the typical process and addresses topics such as the premises and inventory, which may not be present in every situation. For convenience, the various steps of the franchisee recruitment process have been numbered, although some of the steps may take place simultaneously, and some parts of the process will not apply to certain franchise opportunities.

STEP #1

Purpose	Activity	Materials Provided
• Parties become acquainted with each other	• Explanation of mutual process • Ask and answer questions • Aptitude assessment	• Confidential questionnaire • Franchise information • Complete profile package • Confidentiality agreement

Step #1 will take the form of a personal meeting with a representative of the franchisor that may take place at the franchisor's office, the applicant's home, or some other mutually convenient location. A decision to travel to the franchisor's place of business will depend on distance, cost and time, and the appeal of the opportunity. At this point in the process the applicant may have received an information package from the franchisor and submitted a franchise application report.

If the franchise application report has not already been submitted, the applicant will probably be asked to complete it at this time. This is required by the franchisor for the purpose of qualifying the applicant in the areas of:

- financial capability
- personal reputation
- business experience
- suitability and aptitude relative to the type of business
- ability to work within a system.

Financial projections may not be provided until the next meeting. Franchisors want to release their information in a sequential manner in order to avoid providing information prematurely.

Confidentiality/Non-Disclosure Agreement

Most franchisors require applicants to enter into some form of confidentiality/non-disclosure agreement, thereby preventing the applicant from using the franchisor's information or disclosing the information to another party. The applicant also agrees not to use the information to compete with the franchisor, and to return all materials and documents if he or she does not proceed with the franchise. Sample 3.2 shows a typical confidentiality/non-disclosure agreement.

Personality Profile

Several franchisors use some type of psychological-personality testing designed to identify a match between the applicant's psychological profile to their ideal franchisee profile. It has been found that the "ideal psychological profile" is very similar for all franchises as the tests focus on personality or behavioural traits in the areas of dominance, extroversion, patience and conformity.

Dominance is a control trait, and franchisors are usually looking for applicants who are in the mid-to-high range of this trait. A moderately high degree of dominance is required for a person to overcome any adversity or problems, but if the dominance level is too high it can translate into the applicant being too strong-willed or too entrepreneurial to be a franchisee. Such a personality tends to be more of a maverick than a team player.

Applicants should score 50% to 75% in the extroversion trait. People with high scores in this trait are usually excellent in sales and customer service. They tend to interact well with people and are outgoing and enthusiastic. However, a very high mark in this trait can be a disadvantage as it can indicate that a person is far too outgoing, and may appear shallow and superficial with a tendency to try to talk himself out of situations instead of dealing with a problem rationally. Someone with a very high mark in this area may require close supervision to keep him on track.

An ideal score for the patience trait is in the lower end of the scale, somewhere between 25% and 50%. Although patience and steadiness are admirable qualities, people who have high scores tend to procrastinate, react slowly to situations, and fail to make changes when they are necessary. They are normally patient, calm and sincere, which are admirable qualities, but they are not usually goal-setters, decision-makers, or risk-takers which are qualities crucial to the successful operation of a franchise.

Sample 3.2	Confidentiality/Non-disclosure Agreement

THIS NON-DISCLOSURE AGREEMENT made the *** day of *******, ****,

BETWEEN   (franchisor)

                  having a place of business at

                  ****************, (Postal code)

                  (hereinafter called the "Company")

AND:

                  ****************, (Postal code)

                  (hereinafter called the "Applicant")

WHEREAS:

A. The Company is the owner of a system identified and distin-guished by unique and standardized design, uniform standards, specifications, procedures of operation and by high quality style and uniformity of services provided to the general public of a ***** (service or product) ****;

B. The Company has developed a franchise system in Canada for the exclusive provision of these services;

C. The Company wishes to maintain the development secret and confidential and to protect trade ideas, business concepts and sys-tems so developed.

D. The Applicant is desirous of having the developments disclosed to it and is willing to evaluate the developments in confidence and not to make use thereof except pursuant to mutual agreement between the Company and the Applicant.

E. The Applicant considers the disclosure to be real and valuable consideration.

NOW THEREFORE THE PARTIES AGREE AS FOLLOWS:

1. The Company will disclose the developments to the Applicant. The Applicant shall endorse receipt of any written documents comprising part of this disclosure by signing and dating a copy thereof to be retained by the Company if the Company so elects.

Sample 3.2   **Confidentiality/Non-disclosure Agreement** (cont'd)

2. The Applicant agrees not to communicate the developments to any person, firm, corporation or business without the Company's prior written consent. The Applicant specifically agrees not to use, for personal gain, any trade ideas, business concepts or systems introduced by the Company.

3. The Applicant shall not make copies of an information, documents, materials, diskettes, tapes or other information appertaining or relating to the developments without the Company's prior written consent. The Applicant shall forthwith upon demand by the Company return to the Company all specifications, documents, materials, diskettes, tapes and any copies thereof or any materials of any kind delivered to the Applicant or any materials arising out of the foregoing and shall not retain copies thereof for any purpose.

4. If the Applicant contends that any concepts or information disclosed to it by the Company are in the public domain or were in the possession of the Applicant prior to such disclosure, the Applicant shall within ten (10) days of the receipt by the Applicant of such disclosure give written notice of such contention to the Company, which written notice shall include a complete identification of the information in question and the derivation thereof, including particulars of any contract in which the Applicant or any other person has made use of such concept or information. If the Applicant has not within ten (10) days of the receipt of the disclosure as contemplated in this Agreement given such written notice to the Company, then and in that event it shall be conclusively presumed that all information disclosed by the Company to the Applicant concerning the developments originated with the Company and constituted secret and confidential information and know-how.

5. The Company makes no warranty that any information or concept contained in any disclosure made pursuant to this Agreement is or may be of value to the Applicant. The Applicant, however, shall be bound by the terms of this Agreement whether or not the

Sample 3.2	Confidentiality/Non-disclosure Agreement (cont'd)

Applicant elects to enter into future written agreement with the Company for the exploitation of the developments to the mutual advantage of the parties.

6. It is expressly understood and agreed that the agreement herein shall not be construed as to create any partnership, joint venture, agency or any other business relationship which would authorize either party hereto to act in the name of or on behalf of the other party and it is further understood and agreed that each of the parties are to remain completely independent of one from the other and that neither party has authority of any kind to create any liability or obligation on behalf of the other party.

SIGNED SEALED AND DELIVERED
in the presence of:

_____   _____

Witness   Applicant

The degree of conformity required by franchisors varies depending upon the nature of the franchisor's business. Certain businesses require a high degree of conformity due to the high degree of technology in the operation of the business. Others require more creativity and innovation from the franchisee, which translates into a lower mark being required in this trait. One of the most important elements in franchising is consistency, which requires compliance by the franchisee. So, it follows that a franchisor does not want an operator who will continually fight the system.

It is not unusual for the applicant to be asked to pay between $50 and $200 (depending on the sophistication and comprehensiveness of the test) for the franchisor to process a psychological-personality profile. The applicant is demonstrating commitment by paying for the test and by providing the information. The decision to pay for the test is a judgement call by the applicant, taking into consideration the overall benefits including his or her level of interest in the particular franchise, the market position of the franchisor, and the cost of the test. It makes a great deal of sense to take this type of test as it could prevent a lot of grief in the future should the applicant prove to be unsuitable to franchising in general, or to this particular opportunity; however, it must be remembered that any type of personality profile is only one element in the selection of a franchisee.

STEP #2

Purpose	Activity	Materials Provided
• Explanation of financial opportunity • How is the money made	• Discuss the financial opportunity • Discuss financial procedures	•Interim agreement • Examples of financial opportunity

---

At the second meeting, the franchisor will usually provide more detailed information about the franchise, including projections of income and expense. An interim agreement may be given to the applicant for their review. This may take the form of an offer to purchase agreement, as shown in Sample 3.3.

Under the Alberta Franchises Act, a franchisor must provide a prospective franchisee with a copy of the franchisor's disclosure document at least 14 days before the signing by the prospective franchisee of any agreement or the payment of any consideration. (See Chapter 1 regarding Franchise Legislation.)

Note that this is a legal document and as such should be reviewed by the applicant's lawyer prior to execution or upon submitting a deposit. The interim agreement will contain a specific time-frame in which the franchise agreement must be executed and will normally be subject to certain events taking place, such as final approval of the application by the franchisor, the applicant's lawyer reviewing the franchise and lease documentation, and the applicant obtaining financing on satisfactory terms and conditions. If the applicant considers that the time allowed for completion and removal of the conditions precedent is insufficient for him or her to carry out proper due diligence, he or she should ask for it to be extended. The interim agreement may also contain some form of non-competition clause.

Sample 3.3	Offer-To-Purchase Agreement

TO: **************************

(the "Franchisor")

FROM: **************************

(the "Applicant")

The Applicant hereby makes application to enter into a Franchise Agreement with the Franchisor upon substantially the same terms and conditions as are generally contained in the Franchisor's standard form of Franchise Agreement subject to such reasonable modifications as may be mutually agreed upon:

1. The Franchisor shall grant the Applicant the right to use the Franchisor's system, business format, methods, procedures, standards and such trademarks as are established from time to time in connection with the operation of a ************* Franchised Business at the following location *************************.

2. A fully earned nonrefundable Initial Franchise Fee in the amount of TWENTY-FIVE THOUSAND DOLLARS ($25,000.00) for the opportunity to establish a ************* Franchised Business is to be fully paid by the Applicant upon execution of the Franchise Agreement.

3. The Applicant will pay monthly to the Franchisor's Advertising Fund two percent (2%) of Gross Sales.

4. The Applicant will pay monthly to the Franchisor a Continuing Royalty of four percent (4%) of Gross Sales.

5. The Franchise Agreement shall have an initial term of five (5) years, and if the Applicant qualifies as provided in the Franchise Agreement, may be renewed for one additional renewal term of five (5) years.

6. The Franchise Agreement and the provisions of the application shall be construed in accordance with the laws of the Province of ************* and the laws of Canada applicable therein.

7. The Applicant understands that prior to executing the Franchise Agreement the Franchisor may furnish information and material which will be of a confidential nature concerning the Franchisor and the franchise system including, without limitation, the con-

Sample 3.3 **Offer-To-Purchase Agreement** (cont'd)

tents of the Franchise Agreement and the Franchisor's other standard documents. The Applicant agrees to keep all such information confidential and not to disclose same to any competitor of the Franchisor or any other person, firm or corporation or obtain any benefit therefrom, directly or indirectly, without the prior written consent of the Franchisor and concurrently with this application the Applicant has entered into the Franchisor's present form of NON-DISCLOSURE AGREEMENT.

8. The Applicant hereby accepts this application as notice in writing of and consents to the obtaining from any credit reporting agency, bank, credit grantor or any other party with which the Applicant has financial relations, such information concerning the Applicant as the Franchisor may require at any time in connection with the franchise hereby applied for.

9. The Applicant hereby authorizes the Franchisor to take whatever actions and make whatever enquiries it may consider necessary to confirm and verify the information contained in this application and the Confidential Qualification Report of the Franchisor provided by the Applicant and to contact any of the references set forth therein.

10. The Applicant shall submit to the Franchisor such other information and documents concerning the Applicant as the Franchisor may reasonably request.

11. The Applicant herewith encloses a deposit in the amount of FIVE THOUSAND DOLLARS ($5,000.00). It is understood that if the Franchise Agreement is entered into between the Franchisor and the Applicant, such amount will be credited towards payment of the Initial Franchise Fee without interest of deduction.

12. Upon receipt of notice of acceptance of this application from the Franchisor, the Applicant shall have fifteen (15) days in which to enter into the Franchise Agreement with the Franchisor, and pay the balance of the Initial Franchise Fee. In the event that the Applicant fails to enter into the Franchise Agreement and pay the balance of the Initial Franchise Fee within the above noted time period, the Applicant understands and agrees that TWO THOU-

| Sample 3.3 | Offer-To-Purchase Agreement (cont'd) |

SAND DOLLARS ($2,000.00) of the deposit referred to in paragraph 10 herein will be retained by the Franchisor for its absolute use as consideration for processing this Application.

In the event that a Franchise Agreement is not entered into between the Applicant and the Franchisor, the Applicant shall promptly return any and all material, together with any and all copies made by the Applicant of such material, received from the Franchisor.

13. If the Franchisor fails to accept this Application within fifteen (15) days of the date hereof, the Applicant understands that the entire deposit will be returned without interest or deduction.

Dated at *************** in the Province of *************** this **** day of **************, ****.

_____   _____
Witness   Applicant

Name _____

Address _____

_____

_____

********** (franchisor's name) ************* hereby acknowledges the foregoing together with the receipt of the deposit referred to above and agrees to consider the Applicant as a candidate for a **************
Franchised Business.

Dated at ********* in the Province ************* this *** day of **********, ****.

(insert franchisor's name)

_____

Name _____

Title _____

As part of the mutual investigation process, the applicant may be required to attend an interview with the franchisor's selection committee. A selection committee is usually comprised of some members of the franchisor's staff and is part of the screening process.

Deposits

An interim agreement usually calls for the applicant to make a significant cash deposit. The amount of deposit required, and whether it is refundable, non-refundable, or partially non-refundable, varies from franchise to franchise. There are no hard and fast rules regarding deposits and there are varying opinions as to whether or not any or all of the deposit should be non-refundable. Some people within franchising feel strongly that franchisors should not retain any part of the deposit. In essence, it is similar to charging the applicant a fee to review the franchise agreement. However, this has to be balanced against the value of the information that the franchisor would have to provide without the benefit of receiving any form of financial commitment by the applicant.

It is not unreasonable for a franchisor to require a deposit of at least $5,000. Part of that deposit, such as $2,000, may be non-refundable in the event of non-performance by the applicant. The total deposit is normally returned without interest or deduction if the franchisor decides not to approve the application. (Please refer to Chapter 1: Franchise Legislation.)

Most franchisors will not provide applicants with certain materials such as the franchise agreement, or allow any review of the operations manual by the applicant, until it has an executed offer to purchase agreement and is paid a deposit. Most franchisors will allow applicants to inspect the operations manual, but will not actually hand it over until the franchise agreement has been executed and the initial franchise fee paid.

There may be a requirement for the applicant to increase the deposit within a stipulated time-frame or upon certain events taking place such as the applicant's receiving financing approval, the elapsing of a period of time, or the completion of a legal review of the franchise agreement. The deposit may become totally non-refundable at that time. For instance, an offer to purchase may call for a $5,000 deposit, of which $2,000 is non-refundable should the applicant fail to proceed. It may call for the deposit to be increased within a certain time, or upon the occurrence of a certain event (such as the signing of a lease) by a further payment of $5,000, thereby raising the total deposit to $10,000. At that point the original $5,000, or the total $10,000, may become non-refundable.

Another contentious issue is the holding of the deposit. Is it to be held by the franchisee's lawyer in trust for release upon execution of the franchise agreement, or is it to be paid directly to the franchisor? This may be a matter for negotiation or the franchisor may insist that it receive the deposit or alternatively its lawyer, to be held in trust.

STEP #3

Purpose	Activity	Materials Provided
• Established commitment to business	• Deposit • Complete offer to purchase/interim agreement	•Copy of franchise agreement

---

This may be the first opportunity for the applicant to review the franchise agreement. A comprehensive review of the terms and conditions normally present in a franchise agreement is provided in Chapter 4, "Understanding the Franchise Agreement." Most credible franchisors thoroughly review the franchise agreement with the applicant prior to review by the applicant's lawyer, in order to provide the applicant with a general understanding of the intent of the various clauses and the agreement itself.

It is imperative that the franchise agreement, and any ancillary documentation such as the offer to purchase agreement or any leases for premises or equipment, be reviewed by a lawyer experienced with franchising, and any laws relating to franchising. A lawyer must be conversant with not only the contents of the agreement, but also with what might be excluded from the agreement.

Although it is often the case that there are more applicants than locations, the applicant should not allow himself to be subjected to pressure from any franchisor who blatantly warns the applicant "If you don't buy it today, you will have missed your chance." The applicant may in fact "miss his chance" and regret the fact that he did not act faster. However, the possibility of making the wrong decision has far greater implications for the applicant. At least by carrying out a full review of the franchise opportunity and obtaining professional advice, the applicant still has his investment safe.

STEP #4

Purpose	Activity	Materials Provided
• Review franchise agreement	• Discussion • Preliminary site investigation	•Set date for closing of franchise

---

If it is necessary to locate premises, this may be the point when preliminary site investigation commences. Some site investigation can be carried out simultaneously with the lawyer's review of the franchise agreement, although it may be pointless to invest too much time in site investigation until the applicant is satisfied that he or she is in fact going to proceed with the franchise.

It may be the responsibility of the franchisor or the applicant to find a suitable location for the franchise. Alternatively, it could be a mutual responsibility. The franchisor should provide a list of site selection criteria based on their previous experience and demographic requirements. If the franchisor has the responsibility for site selection and lease negotiation, the applicant may be charged a "Site Selection Fee" of $5,000 or more, in addition to the initial franchise fee.

STEP #5

Purpose	Activity	Materials Provided
• Orientation to training program	• Establish training schedule •Discuss company policies and procedures	•Operations manual

---

The franchisor should have a structured program that may require the applicant (and possibly management and staff) to spend time training at a corporate office or store. A training schedule and critical path prior to opening should be established at this time based on a planned opening date, and operational policies and procedures reviewed with the applicant.

STEP #6

Purpose	Activity	Materials Provided
• Closing date agreement and fee	• Secure premises	•Site design and layout

---

At this stage the franchise agreement and ancillary documentation are executed and the applicant pays any balance of the initial franchise fee, or other agreed fees such as lease deposits or partial inventory payments. The applicant may also be required to sign a lease, or sub-lease. Any site layouts or store designs should be available at this point. The topic of location, leases etc., is covered in Chapter 6, "Understanding Territory, Location and Leases."

STEP #7

Purpose	Activity	Materials Provided
• Prepare for the opening of the store or outlet	• Training at company store • Training at franchise location • Initiate advertising campaign for opening	•Improvements to premises •Equipment and inventory delivered

---

The franchisor should provide assistance with the preparation of the store (pre-opening) and may conduct part of the training (probably staff training) in the actual premises prior to opening. In the case of a food franchise, there may also be a "dry run" with family, friends and invited guests to iron out any problems before opening the doors to the general public.

Some businesses such as printing franchises will have equipment installed at this time, and the franchisor should be on hand to check the installation and equipment. It may be necessary to have employees on hand prior to opening to assist in the preparation and receive training. Their wages during this period have to be included in the initial start-up costs.

A promotional grand opening campaign is normally established at this point. It may be designed to create impact a short time after the business opens, so as not to put too much pressure on the system in the early stages; in other words, a few weeks later.

STEP #8

Purpose	Activity	Materials Provided
• Opening week	• Representative from corporate on hand	•Ongoing support from corporate office staff on hand, no materials *per se*

The level of training and assistance provided by the franchisor varies depending on the nature of the business and the policy of the franchisor. Some franchisors will have a representative in the franchise location for three weeks working alongside the franchisee and his staff. Others will leave the franchisee to operate the business immediately after the grand opening and pay periodic visits over the next few months to ensure that everything is operating smoothly.

ESTABLISHING FINANCIAL VIABILITY

Assessing the Franchisor's Profit-and-Loss Projections

There is no way that a franchisor can accurately project the future performance of a franchise business. All of the known elements can be factored into the equation, but the biggest variable, which will invariably skew the whole equation, is the performance of the franchisee. A franchisor can only provide a "financial picture," taking into account information and demographics from past experience. For the franchisor's protection any projections of future financial performance will carry a disclaimer similar to the following:

> *These projections are for illustration purposes only and in no way represent actual or potential sales volumes, expenses or profit that can be realized by a franchisee at any location.*
>
> *There is no warranty or guarantee that these projections reflect actual performance which depends on numerous factors including the franchisee's business and management skills.*

Franchisors may provide franchise applicants with:

- no written financial statements or projections, or
- a financial projection of income and expense with a number of different scenarios based on varying performances.

The Alberta Franchises Act requires the franchisor to provide details of any earnings claims information used by the franchisor, including material assumptions underlying its preparation and presentation, whether it is based on actual results of existing outlets and the percentage of outlets that meet or exceed each range of results. The earnings claim information must have a reasonable basis at the time it is prepared. The disclosure documents must also state the place where substantiating information is available for inspection by franchisees. If the information is given in respect of a franchisor-operated outlet, the franchisor must state that the information may differ in the respect of a franchisee outlet. Earnings claims consist of information from which a specific level or range of actual or potential sales, costs, income or profit from franchisee or franchisor outlets can be ascertained.

The franchisor has a considerable responsibility to ensure that any projections of earnings and expenses provided to a prospective franchisee have been qualitatively researched and are relevant to the particular location. Most franchise agreements contain an "Entire Agreement" clause (see Chapter 4) which requires the franchisee to acknowledge that what is contained in the franchise agreement constitutes the whole agreement. This means any financial projections provided by the franchisor, whether oral or written, which may have influenced the franchisee to buy the franchise, are not considered to be part of the agreement. The courts consider the use of entire agreement clauses to be fair and reasonable; however, they take into consideration the franchisor's relative sophistication and negotiating power when determining the enforceability of such clauses.

Most franchisors provide several scenarios based on increasing annual sales volumes, together with the respective operating costs and ratios. These scenarios are normally based on the averages of actual operating figures achieved by existing franchisees and should be relevant to the particular location. This should provide the prospective franchisee with an indication of what might be achieved in the initial years of operation, based on a reasonable set of circumstances.

Prospective franchisees occasionally insist on seeing actual operating statements of a franchised location. The main reason for this request is probably lack of trust of the franchisor; however, there is some danger in the franchisor, or the franchisee, placing too much reliance on the track record of an individual franchisee.

Franchises are people-driven and results can vary considerably based on personal effort, attitude, customer service and product quality. If the franchise for sale is an operating business, then actual financial statements should be made available. A typical Pro Forma Income Statement that may be provided by a franchisor is shown in Sample 3.4.

Some franchisors will not provide any estimates of financial performance and will encourage prospective franchisees to create their own projections after talking to franchisees already in the system. This method forces the prospective franchisee to carry out thorough due diligence and protects the franchisor from any claim that it has provided the franchisee with misleading financial information or earnings claims.

The following questions are grouped under various headings to allow the prospective franchisee to properly scrutinize and review the financial information provided by the franchisor.

Are the sales volumes and gross profits realistic?

- for franchises already in operation
- for the proposed location
- and attainable in the particular circumstances.

Are operating expenses realistic?

- What expenses would change for the particular area?
- Would expenses change due to the franchisee's particular circumstances?

- Are any expenses understated?
- Have any expenses been omitted?

What is the cash flow?

- Will the cash flow from sales be sufficient to cover cash requirements while the business is becoming established?
- Will there be a requirement for additional financing?

What will be the return on invested capital?

- What is the current rate of return on funds invested in safe investments?
- What salary could the franchisee earn if employed?

Sample 3.4	A Typical Pro Forma Income Statement (in 000's of dollars)						
Sales	250.0	300.0	350.0	400.0	450.0	500.0	550.0
Cost of Goods Sold	150.0	180.0	210.0	240.0	270.0	300.0	330.0
Margin	100.0	120.0	140.0	160.0	180.0	200.0	220.0
EXPENSES							
Wages	30.0	30.0	30.0	30.0	30.0	30.0	30.0
Benefits	1.2	1.2	1.2	1.2	1.2	1.2	1.2
Bad Debts	0.3	0.3	0.3	0.3	0.3	0.3	0.3
Interest	3.0	3.0	3.0	3.0	3.0	3.0	3.0
Royalties	10.6	12.8	14.9	17.0	19.1	21.3	23.4
Advertising	8.8	10.5	12.3	14.0	15.8	17.5	19.3
Insurance	0.8	0.8	0.8	0.8	0.8	0.8	0.8
Telephone	2.4	2.4	2.4	2.4	2.4	2.4	2.4
Rent, Taxes, etc.	30.0	30.0	30.0	30.0	30.0	30.0	30.0
Supplies	2.4	2.4	2.4	2.4	2.4	2.4	2.4
Utilities	2.4	2.4	2.4	2.4	2.4	2.4	2.4
Office (General)	2.4	2.4	2.4	2.4	2.4	2.4	2.4
Travel	1.2	1.2	1.2	1.2	1.2	1.2	1.2
Repairs/Maintenance	1.2	1.2	1.2	1.2	1.2	1.2	1.2
Accounting	1.2	1.2	1.2	1.2	1.2	1.2	1.2
Miscellaneous	1.2	1.2	1.2	1.2	1.2	1.2	1.2
TOTAL EXPENSES	99.1	103.0	106.8	110.0	114.6	118.5	122.3
INCOME	0.9	17.1	33.2	49.3	65.4	81.6	97.7

- Do the profits as adjusted for the franchisee's circumstances provide a greater return than can be obtained through other investments and salary?

Oral Representations

Franchisees should have reason for concern if the franchisor provides only oral representations regarding the possible financial performance of the franchise. A franchise should only rely on written information. If information provided orally is critical to the performance of the franchise, insist that it be provided in writing. Most franchise agreement expressly provide that no oral agreements shall be deemed to exist or to bind any of the parties.

Profitability Ratios

When investigating either a new or resale franchise, it is helpful to have an understanding of certain ratios. These ratios measure the overall ability of the firm to produce a profit. There are various ways the small business owner/operator can determine profitability. Determining the ratio of gross profit margin to net sales can be a useful exercise. The information required to do this calculation can be located on the balance sheet and income statement (see Samples 3.5 and 3.6).

$$\text{Formula:} \quad \frac{\text{Gross profit}}{\text{Net sales x 100}} = \%$$

Interpretation: The purpose of this ratio is to determine the percentage of gross profit on each sales dollar. It reveals the actual percentage of sales revenue available to cover the operating and general expenses and taxes, and provide a profit. If you compare gross profit with average desired markup, you can see the effect of discounts and theft or spoilage on a business. If the ratio is different from budgeted ratios, you will want to examine the reasons very carefully.

If the ratio is lower than the average for the industry or is decreasing, it may mean that the markup is too low or the cost of merchandise is too high. Solutions include:

- increase sales
- decrease costs
- increase the markup.

Sample 3.5	Balance Sheet

As of (Current Date/Year)

Assets	19____	19____
	(Current Year)	(Previous Year)

Current Assets

Accounts receivable (attach aged list)	$_____	$_____
Less: Allowance for bad debts (net)	_____	_____
Cash & balance in bank accounts	_____	_____
Prepaid expenses (e.g., insurance, rent, etc.)	_____	_____
Inventory at market value	_____	_____
Other current assets	_____	_____
Total Current Assets	$_____	$_____

Fixed Assets (net book value after depreciation)

Land and buildings	$_____	$_____
Furniture, equipment & fixtures	_____	_____
Other fixed assets	_____	_____
Total Fixed Assets	_____	_____

Other Assets (nonfixed, e.g. automobiles)	$_____	$_____
Total Assets	$_____	$_____

Liabilities

Current (due within 12 months)

Accounts payable	$_____	$_____
Bank loans	_____	_____
Loans—other	_____	_____
Employee deductions and sales taxes payable	_____	_____
Income taxes payable	_____	_____
Current portion of long-term debt	_____	_____
Other current liabilities		
Total Current Liabilities	$_____	$_____

Long Term (over one year)

Mortgages payable	$_____	$_____
Less: Current portion noted above		
Loans from shareholders & partners	_____	_____
Other loans of long-term nature	_____	_____
Total Long-Term Liabilities	$_____	$_____

Total Liabilities	$_____	$_____
Net Worth (Total AssetsTotal Liabilities)	$_____	$_____

Shareholders' Equity

Share capital	$_____	$_____
Retained earnings	_____	_____
Total Shareholders' Equity	$_____	$_____
Total Liabilities & Shareholders' Equity	$_____	$_____

Sample 3.6 Income Statement

(Also referred to as profit-and-loss statement,
P & L statement, or operating statement)

For Month and Year-to-Date Ended_____, 19_____

	Current Month Relative to Total Income		Year-to-Date Relative to Total Income	
	Amount	%	Amount	%
Sales	$		$	
Gross sales				
Less returns and allowances				
(discounts)	$_____		$_____	
Net Sales	$_____	100%	$_____	100%
Cost of Goods Sold				
Beginning inventory	$_____	___%	$_____	___%
Plus inventory purchases	$_____	___%	$_____	___%
Plus plant & other				
manufacturing costs	$_____	___%	$_____	___%
Less closing inventory	$_____	___%	$_____	___%
Total Cost of Goods Sold	$_____	___%	$_____	___%
Gross Income (Subtract total cost of goods sold from net sales)	$_____	___%	$_____	___%
Operating Expenses				
Advertising & promotion	$_____	___%	$_____	___%
Bad debts	$_____	___%	$_____	___%
Bank service charges	$_____	___%	$_____	___%
Depreciation (e.g., equipment)	$_____	___%	$_____	___%
Employees' wages	$_____	___%	$_____	___%
Insurance	$_____	___%	$_____	___%
Owner's salary	$_____	___%	$_____	___%
Repairs & maintenance	$_____	___%	$_____	___%
Supplies	$_____	___%	$_____	___%
Taxes and licences	$_____	___%	$_____	___%
Telephone and utilities	$_____	___%	$_____	___%
Miscellaneous expenses	$_____	___%	$_____	___%
Other (itemize)	$_____	___%	$_____	___%
Total Operating Expenses	$_____	___%	$_____	___%
Net Operating Income (Subtract Gross Expenses from Gross Profit)	$_____	___%	$_____	___%
Less: Income Taxes	$_____	___%	$_____	___%
Net Profit (Loss) after Taxes	$_____	___%	$_____	___%

WHAT RATE OF RETURN ON INVESTMENT SHOULD BE EXPECTED?

There is probably no easy answer to this question. Everyone has a different expectation level. Certainly, many franchise opportunities provide excellent returns on investment, but it would be ridiculous to assume that all franchises yield fantastic profits. The reality is that they don't; in fact, many produce profits far less than suggested by the franchisor, and many operate at a loss.

Simply put, your working investment should offer you a return that is two to three times greater than a non-working investment for the same amount.

The return should be on your total investment of:

- the value of your time
- capital expenditure
- cost of capital (interest on loans).

Return on Investment

$$\text{Formula:} \quad \frac{\text{Net profit (after taxes)}}{\text{Total assets (tangible net worth)}} \times 100 = \%$$

Interpretation: This ratio determines the effective use of all financial resources. While it can serve as an indicator of management performance, you should use it in conjunction with other ratios to confirm that assessment. A high return, normally associated with effective management, could indicate an undercapitalized firm. A low return, usually an indicator of inefficient management performance, could reflect a highly capitalized, conservatively operated business. If net profit is lower than the industry average, it could mean that you have made unwise investments or have a poor product. It could also mean that you should analyze the assets for possible disposal and conversion to cash.

WHAT IS THE TOTAL INVESTMENT COST?

Obviously, the total initial investment varies considerably among different types of franchised businesses. For instance, the cost of setting up a McDonald's fast-food restaurant is considerably higher than the cost of setting up a service franchise such as a travel agency or a home-based franchise. However, the nature of the costs (categories of expenditure) are similar among the different types of franchises. The differences between the costs of the components will obviously vary. A checklist of up-front franchisee costs is provided in Quick Check 3.1.

The typical costs involved in setting up a franchise business are as follows:

- the initial franchise fee
- leasehold improvements
- equipment
- inventory
- deposits and legal fees
- opening advertising and promotion
- working capital.

The Initial Franchise Fee

Initial franchise fees vary from quite small amounts (perhaps only a few thousand dollars) to relatively large amounts which may exceed $100,000 for the master franchise rights to a city, province or perhaps even a country. Typically, single-unit franchise fees are in the range of $25,000 to $35,000. The initial franchise fee will be relative to the magnitude of the business opportunity and the market dominance of the franchisor. New franchisors entering the market often set the initial franchise fee lower than comparable rates and gradually increase it as they gain franchisees.

Lenders will not normally finance the initial franchise fee because it is considered an intangible asset.

Leasehold Improvements

Leasehold improvements are the major expenditure when setting up a franchise. These costs can often be reduced or eliminated by "tenant incentives" that many landlords provide to new tenants. There is obviously a great deal of variance in these costs depending on the type and size of business.

Equipment

Equipment is another variable cost. Although considerable savings can often be made purchasing used equipment, lenders normally prefer to finance brand-new equipment. Franchisors, because

Quick Check 3.2 | Checklist of Up-Front Franchise Costs

Initial Franchise (License) Fee $_____

Land—include legal, zoning and associated costs   _____

Architectural Fees—permits, utility deposits   _____

Building—include site work, basic construction and
    landscaping   _____

Leasehold Improvements—alterations to leased premises   _____

Rental Costs—security deposit or last month's rent   _____

Sign Package—interior and exterior signage and
    installation   _____

Furniture, Fixtures and Equipment—include taxes, freight
    and installation charges   _____

Trucks and Automobiles—alterations, taxes, licenses, signage   _____

Site Selection Costs—consulting fees, travel expenses   _____

Legal Costs—review of contract   _____

Initial Accounting Fees—projections, bank presentation
    material   _____

Franchisor Investigation Costs   _____

Telephone Installation & Yellow Pages   _____

Opening Inventory   _____

Insurance—annual premium   _____

Training Costs—tuition fees, travel and accommodation
    (owner and key staff)   _____

Pre-Opening Costs—staff salaries, hydro, heat, supplies,
    wastage   _____

On-Site Start-Up Aid—special staff promotion package   _____

Cash Drawer Fund & Petty Cash   _____

Initial Bookkeeping Supplies, Business Cards & Stationery   _____

Grand Opening—Advertising and Promotion   _____

Financing Costs   _____

Working Capital (if credit business)   _____

Living Expenses (while establishing business)   _____

Total Investment Cost $_____

of their purchasing power, are usually able to acquire equipment at competitive prices and will pass along all or most of this saving to the franchisee. The franchisee should make certain that all manufacturer's warranties can be transferred from the first-time purchaser (the franchisor) to the franchisee.

Equipment can also be leased which reduces the initial investment cost. Some franchisors offer in-house leasing programs. The terms and conditions of franchisor leasing programs should be carefully examined and compared to other independent leasing programs.

Inventory

The cost of inventory will also vary considerably, as will the terms of payment. In most situations the inventory must be paid for some time prior to the opening of the franchise. Since revisions to the Bankruptcy and Insolvency Act, lenders have been reluctant to lend against inventory as suppliers have a 30-day window in which to recover unpaid inventory from the franchisee.

Deposits and Legal Fees

Deposits and legal fees are items that are often omitted from the initial investment estimates. These deposits include lease of the premises, equipment leases, telephone and hydro. Legal fees must be budgeted for review of the franchise documentation, leases and other agreements, and incorporation costs.

Opening Advertising and Promotion

Opening advertising and promotion is another "soft cost" which is sometimes omitted when calculating the cost of setting up the franchise. This is a very important budget item if you wish to build your cash flow quickly. If people don't know you are there, they are unlikely to patronize your business. Businesses that operate in high-traffic locations usually pay higher rent and a portion of that rent can, in fact, be attributed to an advertising cost. After all, the reason that you are paying that type of rent is to be in front of people, which is really what advertising is all about.

As a condition of the franchise, the franchisee may be required to spend a specified amount on grand opening advertising and promotion, or alternatively pay the agreed amount to the franchisor who will make the necessary arrangements on behalf of the franchisee. If the latter is the case, the franchisor should provide evidence to the franchisee as to the expenditure(s).

Working Capital

Working capital is a very important component of the start-up costs of a franchise business. Monies must be available to cover any cash shortfalls while you are getting your business going. You will need money to pay your staff, yourself and your rent, finance receivables and replenish your inventory. This need not necessarily be cash on hand, but could be provided by way of a "line of credit".

WHAT ARE THE ONGOING FEES?

Ongoing Royalties

The majority of franchise systems charge the franchise some type of ongoing royalty or service fee. The exception would be product franchises that derive their income from wholesaling products to franchisees, in which case the relationship should be examined to determine if it truly is a franchise.

In most instances, the royalty is based on a percentage of the franchisee's gross sales (excluding any sales taxes paid to various levels of government). Royalties as a percentage of gross sales vary from 1% to 10%, or even higher, with a median range of 3% to 6%. Retail operations average between 5% and 6%; however, units with high sales volumes often pay 1% or 2% less.

Service franchises tend to have royalties in the 8% to 10% range, or even higher. This is offset by the potential for the franchisee to achieve higher profits on lower sales volumes (e.g., the operator of a service franchise could earn profits of $85,000 on sales of $120,000, yet the franchisor has to provide the same level of service to the franchisee as a franchisor receiving 3% or 4% on unit sales of $2 million).

A few franchisors charge a flat fee (often in areas of business where it may be difficult for the franchisor to monitor the franchisee's sales). Although at first glance this arrangement may appear attractive to a prospective franchisee, it can actually be counterproductive as there is no financial incentive in this type of arrangement for the franchisor to help increase the franchisee's sales. Flat fees are usually indexed to allow an increase corresponding to any annual increases in the Consumer Price Index.

When assessing the amount of the royalty levied by the franchisor, the franchisee should focus on what he receives rather than on what he pays. It is natural to view the royalty as an expense, but the franchisee must consider the tangible and intangible value received such as ongoing assistance, name recognition, purchasing power, research and development, training programs, etc. Cost is a function of value, and the royalty paid should reflect the value received.

The royalty rate should be established at a point where it is affordable to the franchisee yet high enough for the franchisor to be able to provide the support necessary for the franchise system to be successful. A common mistake when evaluating different franchises is to make a direct comparison of royalties between franchise companies operating in the same industry. Often this is like comparing apples and bananas rather than apples and apples. The total value offered by the franchise must be considered including length of time established, performance of the franchisees, purchasing power and name recognition. Neophyte franchisors are sometimes tempted to set their royalties unrealistically low. If the royalties are set too low and the cost of servicing the franchisees exceeds the franchisor's revenues, it could ultimately lead to a deterioration in the level of service and support and the eventual collapse of the franchise system if the franchisees will not agree to an increase.

An alternative arrangement is used by a relatively few franchisors who usually supply all, or most, of the franchisee's products. They may collect a significant percentage of the franchisee's gross profit as a royalty and in return accept responsibility for the payment of major expenditures such as rent, advertising and product purchases. In addition, they may do all invoicing and collection, as well as providing the franchisee's accounting. This leaves the franchisee free to focus on the store's performance, although it begs the question at what point does he or she cease to be a franchisee and merely become an employee with an investment in the company.

Advertising Fund Contributions

In addition to the payment of the ongoing royalty, most franchises require the franchisees to contribute to a national or regional advertising fund. These funds are pooled to finance the advertising and promotion of the franchise and to create name recognition for the equal benefit of all franchisees. The franchisee will still need to carry out sufficient local advertising to generate business for his or her individual unit.

The advertising fund contribution is normally paid at the same time as the ongoing royalty. This contribution may be a set fee or a percentage of gross sales and will vary from franchise to franchise.

Contributions to an advertising fund are not considered as income to the franchisor and should be segregated from the franchisor's other funds and administered as a trust account. Any company-owned stores operated by the franchisor should contribute to the fund at the same rate as its franchisees. A regular accounting of the fund should be given to the franchisees by the franchisor, and an audited statement provided within 90 days of the fiscal year-end. The franchise agreement usually gives the franchisor the right to retain a percentage of the fund as an administration fee. Any such percentage should be reasonable and established at the start.

Co-operative Advertising

The franchisee may be required to enter into regional campaigns in co-operation with other franchisees who are operating in the same region. The decision to enter into any co-operative campaign should be subject to a vote of 75% of the franchisees. In the event that the campaign is approved, all franchisees must participate.

Local Advertising

National and regional advertising funds are for the purpose of building name recognition for the benefit of all franchisees; therefore, most franchisors will require a franchisee to spend minimum regular amounts on promoting their individual location. This is achieved by the franchisee agreeing to spend a certain percentage of sales on local advertising. Most franchises require in the range of 1% to 3% of sales to be committed to local advertising.

Discount Coupons

You may be required to accept and honour discount coupons issued by the franchisor or other franchisees. Accepting numerous coupons can significantly reduce profit margins while increasing the franchisor's royalty stream. The acceptance of coupons should be limited or the franchisees should be given the option as to whether or not they wish to participate in such programs.

WHAT PROFIT CENTRES ARE AVAILABLE TO THE FRANCHISOR?

A franchisor's true profit source is the ongoing royalty stream. However, there are other profit centres available to franchisors which are outlined below. There is nothing wrong with a franchisor being reasonably compensated for their risk, bargaining power, or efforts on behalf of the franchisee. The adage in these situations is, "Tell the cow you are going to milk it—and don't milk it dry." In other words, the franchisor should act fairly by passing along some savings to the franchisee (that in part is why they are in the franchise) and always disclose any profit taken.

Other sources of profit available to franchisors are:

- initial franchise fees
- advertising fund
- lease of premises
- construction of premises
- sale or lease of equipment
- sale of inventory and supplies
- internal accounting and bookkeeping services
- renewal fees.

Initial Franchise Fees

Initial franchise fees are not recognized as a profit source for the franchisor but are designed to cover the cost of advertising, screening, selecting and training franchisees. Nevertheless, as a franchise grows, a small part of the fee may become profit.

Advertising Fund

The advertising fund is not, *per se*, a profit centre for the franchisor, although the franchisor is usually allowed to levy an administration charge for handling the fund.

Lease of Premises

If it has the financial strength, one of the best methods for a franchisor to achieve greater control over the franchise system and to build an investment portfolio is to acquire real estate and lease it to the franchisees.

Franchisors who do not possess the desire or capital to own the property may choose to lease the premises directly from the landlord and sublet it to the franchisee. The franchisor's negotiating strength and covenant may allow the franchisor to secure a lease at below market rates, in which case it may use the opportunity to mark up the lease, partly as compensation for any risk involved, and partly for profit.

Landlords often provide substantial incentives to tenants for improvements and fixturing. These should be passed on to the franchisee by the franchisor.

Construction of the Premises

If the franchisor is responsible for the construction or improvement of the premises on behalf of the franchisee, it may charge a management fee; or, if a fixed price is quoted, a profit may be built into the construction agreement.

If the franchisee is responsible for the construction or improvements in accordance with the franchisor's plans and specifications, the franchisor may charge a reasonable fee for preparing the plans and specifications, or a *per diem* charge for inspection and supervision.

Franchisor-profits from the construction or improvement of premises are often a source of conflict between the franchisor and franchisee. Any profit realized by the franchisor should be reasonable and must be fully disclosed in writing to the franchisee.

Sale or Lease of Equipment

Franchisors often have the opportunity to purchase new or used equipment in volume which they can in turn sell or lease to the franchisees. Again, there may be room for a franchisor to realize a profit, but the franchisee should end up paying less than he would pay for the equipment if he negotiated independently.

Sale of Inventory and Supplies

The franchisor may be in a position to make a profit by acting as a distributor or buying agent for inventory supplied to franchisees. Other sources of profit, which can be very significant for a franchisor, are rebates, discounts and advertising allowances from suppliers of goods to the franchisees.

These are areas with great potential for conflict even if the franchisor makes full disclosure; the franchisees may resent the franchisor making a profit on their purchases.

Internal Accounting and Bookkeeping Services

The provision of internal bookkeeping or accounting is a valuable service to franchisees, and most franchisors charge a minimal fee which is generally lower than if provided by an outside contractor.

Renewal Fees

Most franchise agreements provide for the payment of a fee (a renewal fee) to renew the franchise agreement at the expiration of the set term. If the franchise agreement provides for a renewal fee it may specify: (1) a percentage of the initial franchise fee; (2) a set dollar figure; or (3) a reasonable amount required to cover the franchisor's legal and administrative costs associated with renewing the franchise agreement.

The renewal fee should not be a profit centre for the franchisor, but should be enough to compensate for any time or costs associated with renewing the agreement.

RECAP

In this chapter we have evaluated:

- the critical factors of a good franchise and the questions you should ask
- the sources for information on available franchises

- converting your business to a franchise
- a franchisor's track record
- franchise associations
- the franchise sales process from the initial inquiry through successive meetings
- the documentation required when making an offer
- the vital financial information you need regarding the franchise
- the future prospects for the franchise
- sources of revenue for the franchisor
- financial, legal and day-to-day practical items, such as advertising, to be included in an agreement
and included were samples of:
- Franchise Assessment Quick Check
- Franchise Application Report
- Confidentiality Agreement
- Offer-to-Purchase Agreement
- Pro Forma Income Statement
- Balance Sheet
- Income Statement
- Up-front Costs Quick Check

Understanding the Franchise Agreement

Once a cat sits on a hot stove, he'll never sit on a hot stove again…nor will he sit on a cold one.

Mark Twain

A good franchise agreement not only incorporates all of the elements of a sound business contract, but also expresses in legal terms business decisions vital to the proper operation of the franchise. In other words, it is a legal contract that reflects the franchise program.

The agreement will usually appear to be biased towards the franchisor which is necessary in order for the franchisor to maintain control over the franchise system. A franchisor is risking its name and reputation on your performance, and it is only fair and reasonable that it has the right to place certain obligations upon your purchase of the franchise.

A franchise agreement is both vertical and horizontal in nature. It is vertical in nature because the flow of functions commences with the franchisor and descends through the franchisee to the customer. It is horizontal in nature because it deals with the relationship created between the franchisee and every other franchisee in the system, and must provide the franchisor with controls that are designed to achieve and maintain the integrity and uniformity of the system. In other words, the system is only as strong as its weakest link. The emphasis should be on the flow of functions and responsibilities, etc., rather than on the products and services.

Despite common beliefs, there is no such thing as a standard franchise agreement, and no two franchise agreements are alike. This is understandable because franchises cover many types of businesses in many different industries and have different characteristics. Approximately 70% of franchise agreements may be similar as they deal with "business" issues such as trademarks, terms of the agreement and restrictive covenants. The other 30% deals with "issues" such as supply of products, control of premises, training and support.

WHAT IS CONSIDERED NEGOTIABLE?

There are differing opinions regarding just how negotiable a franchise agrement can be. Franchise agreements can generally be considered non-negotiable except for items such as location, exclusive territory and opening date. Some clauses may require clarification, and franchisors are usually happy to provide it in writing wherever necessary. A franchisor may negotiate a point that is specific to a particular franchisee, but will be unwilling to make any changes that will violate the franchise system. There may be more flexibility, or opportunity for negotiation, with a new franchisor whose agreement is still evolving and has not yet stood the test of time or the scrutiny of a number of franchise lawyers, reviewing it on behalf of clients who are prospective franchisees.

To prevent the need to constantly make amendments or revisions to the franchise agreement, items that are subject to change, such as approved suppliers, products or services, will not normally be contained in the franchise agreement. They are often in the form of schedules to the agreement or in the operations manual. As the operations manual is enforced through the franchise agreement, the franchisor simply has to send the franchisee a bulletin or replacement page if changes are required.

LEGAL REVIEW

The franchise agreement and all ancillary documents should be reviewed by a lawyer who has franchise experience. Credible franchisors would not let you execute the agreement unless they were assured that you had received legal counsel.

Any information, or representations made by the franchisor, that are critical to the franchise relationship should be written into or incorporated as part of the agreement before the signing.

TYPICAL CLAUSES INCLUDED IN A FRANCHISE AGREEMENT

The following is a list of clauses that are typically contained in franchise agreements. Some sections may be presented in a different sequence in a franchise agreement or combined with other sections.

Introduction

A typical franchise agreement will define both parties, one as the "Franchisor" and the other as the "Franchisee." On occasion the franchisor may be referred to as "Licensor" or "Company" and the franchise as "Licensee."

Recitals

The recital establishes the purpose and some of the basic assumptions underlying the proposed relationship between the franchisor and franchisee. These may include:

- a description of the type of business and the franchisor's system
- the intent of the franchisor to grant franchises to suitably qualified applicants
- an acknowledgement by the franchisee as to the importance of the franchisor's high and uniform standards of quality and service
- that the franchisor is the owner of the franchise tradenames and trademarks
- that the franchisee wishes to be granted a franchise and to operate it in accordance with the high and uniform standards of quality and service
- an acknowledgement by the franchisee that he or she has had the opportunity to review the agreement prior to signing it
- acknowledgement by the franchisee that he or she is aware of the business risks involved in entering into the agreement.

Definition and Interpretation

It is common to provide specific definitions of terms that are used throughout the franchise agreement. Examples of some typical terms that may be defined are gross sales, lease, advertising fund, manual, premises, system, territory and trademarks.

This section may also explain certain words or phrases such as "the singular shall include the plural," "the masculine shall include the feminine or neuter, and vice-versa." It may also state that the section headings are for convenience and are not part of the agreement.

Grant of Franchise

GRANT

This section will describe the rights granted to the franchisee and should include the right or license to operate the franchised business in accordance with the franchisor's system at the premises in the territory, and the non-exclusive right and license to use the franchisor's trademarks. The grant will be for an initial term which should be specified. If specific premises have not been determined at the time of execution of the agreement, reference should be made to the location under consideration and the exact address filled in at a later date.

TERM

The initial term of franchise agreement is usually five or 10 years with a five-year renewal option, or in some cases it may be tied to the term of the lease of the premises to facilitate any bank financing. The initial term should be long enough to allow the franchisee to operate the franchise profitably, taking into consideration the initial investment.

The conditions for renewal may be included here, or later in the agreement.

EXCLUSIVITY

If the franchisor does not award exclusivity, the agreement may state that it is exclusive in respect of the franchised location only and shall not extend to any place or territory beyond the franchise location. If no reference is made to exclusivity, then the grant should be considered non-exclusive. Any restrictions imposed, either on territory or customers, should be reviewed as to their legality and compliance with applicable provincial and federal competition laws, and in particular the Competitions Act.

In awarding exclusive territory, the franchisor is promising that it shall not, so long as the agreement is in effect and the franchisee is not in default under the terms of this agreement, directly or indirectly operate or grant to any other person the right to operate a franchise within the exclusive territory, and in addition may specify that no other unit will be situated within a certain distance from your location. The franchisee cannot be prevented from selling to customers outside the territorial boundaries. In other words, the territory constrains the franchisor, not the franchisee.

If the franchisor grants an exclusive territory, it should be clearly defined in the agreement. If the exclusive territory cannot be easily defined in writing by incorporating some reference to fixed boundaries such as municipal limits, census tracts or a radius extending from the franchise location, an addendum should be incorporated into the agreement and the limits of the territory clearly outlined on a map to avoid confusion.

There may be exceptions to the exclusivity such as in the case where the population in the territory increases by a specified number or percentage, which would give the franchisor the option to establish, or franchise, an additional store in the territory. In this case the franchisee should negotiate a right of first refusal to acquire the additional franchisee prior to the franchisor exercising its option. It may also be possible to negotiate a right of first refusal for expansion into any adjacent unoccupied territories prior to the franchise being awarded to anyone else.

Some franchise agreements contain a provision whereby the franchisee is assigned an "area of prime responsibility" within which he or she must focus sales and marketing efforts. Failure by the franchisee to meet certain performance levels, or quotas, could result in the franchisor placing a second franchise in the territory; conversely, if the franchisee exceeds any quota, the size of the territory may be increased. Very few franchise agreements carry these provisions; however, if they are included the franchisee should consider the performance levels and the consequences carefully.

REAL LIFE: Franchisors Must Be Careful Too

Superlush Lawn Care had franchises throughout Ontario and decided to expand into Western Canada. The first applicant for a Superlush franchise in B.C. was Gordon Bigpicture. Superlush wanted to award a Superlush franchise for the area of Bigbucks, B.C., an affluent area that fitted their demographic profile, but Gordon was insistent that he be granted a large exclusive territory that included two other municipalities.

His rationale was that if he developed the Bigbucks area successfully it would make the surrounding areas more profitable, and he should be allowed to capitalize on the value of the goodwill he had created. Gordon assured Superlush that he would add more trucks as his business grew, and as a result Superlush would benefit from the increased royalties. Superlush agreed to grant Gordon a larger-than-usual territory as they thought it would assist them in getting established in Western Canada.

Gordon worked hard in the Bigbucks area for two years and built his Superlush franchise into a very profitable business with four trucks. Meanwhile, Superlush was referring calls to Gordon from potential customers in the surrounding municipalities; however, he had changed his mind about expanding his business and was not interested in servicing customers outside of his Bigbucks area, but was also unwilling to surrender any of the surrounding territory.

Superlush was now shut out of two municipalities and unable to respond to consumer demand, which opened the door to their competition. The situation could have been prevented if a clause had been included in the franchise agreement whereby Gordon would have had to relinquish his rights to the additional territories if he had not established the business in those territories within a reasonable specified time-frame.

Location

SITE SELECTION

The agreement should stipulate who is responsible for the site selection and for lease or purchase negotiations. In most situations the franchisor will assist the franchisee in obtaining suitable premises, but it may be the sole responsibility of the franchisee, or a third party such as a professional agent. If the franchisor provides assistance, ask that the nature and level of assistance be specified.

In any event, the franchisor will insist on site approval, and if premises have not been approved at the time of signing, there will be a specified period of time (usually 90 days) in which the parties must agree in writing upon an acceptable location. If such premises are not located within the time-frame, the agreement may be terminated by either party, or alternatively, there could be a further extension. In such an event the franchisor will normally refund the initial franchise fee to the franchisee, less any reasonable expenses that the franchisor may have incurred in connection with the franchise agreement and for other services rendered.

If necessary, the franchisee should negotiate a longer time-frame, and extension if required, for site selection, taking into consideration problems such as zoning approvals or variances. Most franchise agreements state that approval of the location by the franchisor "shall not be unreasonably withheld." The word "reasonable" is quite common in franchise agreements, but its meaning can vary considerably depending on which side of the fence you are sitting. To avoid having to depend on the franchisor's interpretation of "reasonable," in the event of the failure to agree on the suitability of a location, insist on incorporating into the agreement a list of the franchisor's exact location selection criteria.

In addition to the initial franchise fee, the franchise agreement may provide that the franchisor can charge a site selection/lease negotiation fee. If so, the fee should be stipulated.

The franchisee is relying upon the franchisor's experience in selecting a location where the business will prosper. The franchisor should possess the overall knowledge of demographics, traffic flow and other factors that bear on the selection of a site; however, a local real estate expert will probably be more informed about local market conditions. If you are using a local realtor, keep in mind that unless he or she is being retained solely by you, or the franchisor, the realtor is in essence working for the owner of the real estate company and not necessarily in your best interests.

ALTERNATIVE LEASE ARRANGEMENT

The franchisor may wish to enter into the lease and then sub-lease the premises to the franchisee pursuant to an agreed form of sub-lease. Alternatively, the franchisor could have the franchisee enter into the lease directly with the landlord. If the latter is the case, the franchisor will normally require that, subject to the landlord's approval, the lease contains a conditional assignment to the franchisor. In the event the franchise agreement is terminated for whatever reason, the franchisor has the right, but not the obligation, to assume the franchisee's status under the lease and replace the franchisee as lessee.

The franchisor may also require that the lease contains other provisions protecting the franchisor's best interests, including the right to enter the premises and make any modifications necessary to protect the franchisor's trademarks; notification of any default by the franchisee under the lease; a covenant prohibiting any assignment or sub-lease by the franchisee without the franchisor's prior written consent; and a provision authorizing the landlord to disclose to the franchisor any information furnished by the franchisee to the landlord.

The disclosure of information by the franchisee may enable the franchisor to verify certain information such as the franchisee's gross revenues.

OPENING OF PREMISES

The franchisee will normally be required to open the premises for business within a certain time-frame after the location has been selected and agreed upon. This is understandable from the franchisor's point of view as it does not want the premises sitting idle. However, from the franchisee's point of view any such deadline must be realistic and enable the franchisee to carry out any improvements, install equipment, and train staff.

CHANGE OF FRANCHISE LOCATION

The franchisee will be restricted to operating the business from the premises and will not be able to relocate without the franchisor's prior written consent. This should not be a problem unless the premises are destroyed or the lease, or sub-lease, expires through no fault of the franchisee.

The other situation that could arise is if, in the opinion of the franchisor, there was a change in the character of the location of the premises that was sufficiently detrimental to its business potential, the franchisor could insist on its relocation.

PLANS AND SPECIFICATIONS

The franchisor may provide customized, or standard, plans and specifications, or insist on approval of the layout and design of the premises. The location must be furnished and equipped in accordance with such specifications and no changes can be made without the prior written approval of the franchisor.

The franchisor may charge a fee for preparing, revising or inspecting any plans or specifications. If so, any fees should be specified in the agreement.

FIXTURES, FURNISHINGS, EQUIPMENT AND SIGNS

The franchisee will be required to only use fixtures, furnishings, equipment and signs that meet the specifications of the franchisor, and may be required to purchase all, or some, of these items from the franchisor, or from suppliers designated by the franchisor.

The agreement should include a covenant that the prices charged for these items be competitive with those generally charged by suppliers of similar equipment.

Trademarks

OWNERSHIP OF MARKS

The agreement should state in the Recitals, or in this section, if the franchisor is the exclusive owner of the trademark/s, or that an application for registration of the trademark/s has been filed with the Registrar of Trademarks (Canada). If the franchisor is in the process of applying for the trademark/s and is unsuccessful in the application, the franchisee may be required to change all signage, materials, etc. that carry the trademark. If the franchisor is a U.S. company, the franchisor should seek legal confirmation that the trademark(s) is registered in Canada. If it is not registered in Canada, someone else could do so, and the franchisor and franchisees may be forced to change names.

The franchisee will be required to acknowledge and agree that the franchisor is the owner of all title, right and interest in and to all of the marks and will not represent that it has any interest in the marks other than the rights to use them in accordance with the franchise agreement. All goodwill arising from the franchisee's use of the trademarks enures to the benefit of the franchisor. The franchisee agrees that during or after the term of the agreement he will not dispute or contest, directly or indirectly, the validity or enforceability of the trademarks.

REGISTERED USER APPLICATION

In June 1993, the federal government passed legislation deleting the provisions of the Trade-Marks Act which required franchisees (as licensees of the trademark) to be registered as registered users of the trademark. Some franchise agreements may still have provisions for the franchisee to execute a registered user agreement, although it is no longer required.

The new legislature requires that a licensee of the trademark (the franchisee) obtain its license to use the trademark directly from, or with the authority of, the trademark owner (the licensor). The owner must exercise direct or indirect control of the character or quality of the goods or services that the licensee uses in connection with the trademark. Subject to conforming to these requirements, the licensee of the trademark is deemed to have the same effect as use by the owner.

Consequently, it is important to ensure that the franchisor is the actual owner of the trademark(s) and is capable of assigning their non-exclusive use to the franchisee.

USE AND DISPLAY OF MARKS

The franchisees will be required to agree that the use of the franchisor's trademarks applies only to their use in connection with the franchised business and they will not use the trademarks, without the franchisor's prior written consent, as part of their corporate, partnership or legal name, or for any other purpose.

Franchisees shall use the trademarks on all signs, forms, stationery, and other materials only in the manner prescribed by the franchisor.

INFRINGEMENT OF MARKS

Any unauthorized use of the trademarks is considered to be an infringement of the franchisor's rights. The franchisee must notify the franchisor immediately of any infringement or challenge to the franchisee's use of the marks, and the franchisor shall have the sole discretion to take any action it deems appropriate.

CHANGE OF MARKS

If it becomes necessary at any time—usually in the sole discretion of the franchisor—to modify or discontinue the use of any of the marks, the franchisee agrees to do so at his or her own cost unless the change is needed as a result of a successful challenge as explained in the above paragraph.

DISPLAY OF NOTICE

The franchisee may be required to affix in a prominent place at the franchised premises a notice indicating that the trademarks are owned by the franchisor and that the franchisee is an independent franchised operator using the trademarks under license by the franchisor.

Training and Assistance

Almost every franchise agreement will deal with training and assistance. This section should describe in detail the initial and ongoing training and support provided by the franchisor.

INITIAL TRAINING

This clause should specify the location and the duration of the training; who can attend the training; who is responsible for costs of accommodation, travel and living expenses during training; and whether there is a charge for additional persons attending training. Initial training will probably be provided to the franchisee and a manager. If the costs associated with the initial training are not included in the initial franchise fee, the franchisee must allow for these costs in his or her budget for up-front expenses. There may be a provision that no compensation is payable to the franchisee during training even for work performed in a franchised or company-owned unit.

COMPLETION OF TRAINING

The franchisor will generally require that the franchisee (and the manager if relevant) complete the training program satisfactorily prior to the opening of the franchised business. In the event that the franchisee fails to complete the training program to the satisfaction of the franchisor, the franchisor may reserve the right to terminate the franchise agreement and refund all, or a portion of, the fees.

START-UP ASSISTANCE

The franchisor should covenant to provide assistance at the actual location for a specific number of days prior to, during and after the opening of the franchised business. There should be a provision indicating that the franchisee is not responsible for any of the franchisor's costs of travel, accommodation or living expenses, or remuneration for any of the franchisor's staff during this period of start-up assistance.

If the franchisee requires assistance beyond the specified number of days, it will normally be at the franchisee's expense.

REFRESHER COURSES

Ongoing education such as refresher courses and seminars are part of the benefit of belonging to a franchise system. It should be specified if attendance at these programs is optional or mandatory. If it is determined that the programs are mandatory, the franchisee should require that the duration, location and the maximum number of programs in each year be specified.

Franchisor's Obligations

This section is in essence a description of the franchise program. It should be examined carefully to ensure that the franchisor is in fact obligated to provide you with the things you require to make the franchise business successful.

ONGOING ASSISTANCE

This clause should specify the type and level of operating assistance that will be given to the franchisee on an ongoing basis. The description of the various obligations are usually general in nature and some may be optional. If the franchisee considers that any of the obligations are not sufficiently specific, he or she should ask for more detail, and if necessary any further clarification could be provided as an addendum to the agreement. Items that are normally covered in this section may include:

- periodic visits to the franchise location by the representatives or employees of the franchisor for consultation, assistance and guidance of the franchisee in all aspects of the operation and management of the franchised business
- assistance in the selection and control of inventory
- bookkeeping and accounting services
- hiring and training of employees
- provision of the operations manual and all revisions made from

time to time
- formulation and implementation of advertising and promotional programs
- additional training materials developed by the franchisor
- additional training programs and refresher courses
- financial advice and consultation.

ADDITIONAL ASSISTANCE

Some franchise agreements contain a clause that gives the franchisor the right to charge the franchisee for actual time expended and actual expenses incurred if the franchisee requests in writing additional assistance to solve problems which are beyond the scope of the franchisor's normal obligations.

CONSISTENCY OF STANDARDS

The franchisor promises to use its best efforts to maintain uniformly high standards among franchisees within the system.

PRODUCT DEVELOPMENT

The franchisor agrees to use its continuing efforts towards the research and development of new products or services.

INTERNALIZED ACCOUNTING SERVICES

Some franchisors make available to their franchisees an internalized accounting or bookkeeping program. Any costs associated with such a program should be specified in the agreement and should be less expensive than if the franchisee contracted those same services to a third party. It should also be stipulated whether the program is mandatory or optional.

Franchisee's Obligations

QUALIFIED MANAGEMENT

Most franchise agreements provide that the franchisee actively participate on a full-time basis in the management and operation of the franchised business. If the franchisee is not present, he or she must ensure that the business is at all times under the direct supervision of a manager, or a trained and competent employee who is acceptable to the franchisor. This clause may also require that the franchisor approve the hiring of any person to act as manager, and may further require that this person undertake all or part of the franchisor's training program. The franchisee may be required to keep the franchisor informed as to the identity of the employee acting as manager. Any charges for such training should be specified.

COMPLIANCE WITH LAWS

The franchisee will be required to operate the franchise business in compliance with any applicable laws.

TAXES AND RENTS

The franchisee will be required to pay all municipal, local, provincial or federal sales taxes, business use or property taxes, and rate levies and fees relating to the operation of the franchised business.

ADHERENCE TO WARRANTY OR GUARANTEE PROGRAMS

This section may cover several issues involving warranties and guarantees depending on the nature of the business and should be examined to ensure there is a clear understanding of the scope of any warranty or guaranty claims that the franchisee may incur. There may be a requirement for the franchisee to honour any of the franchisor's warranties. Any warranties should be specified in the operations manual. The franchisor may prevent the franchisee from making any other warranties or guarantees to its customers other than those specified in the manual.

There may be a clause requiring the franchisor to reimburse any franchisee who replaces or performs corrective work with respect to a product sold, or service performed, if it was necessitated by an improper or defective installation carried out by the franchisee.

LICENSES AND PERMITS

The franchisee is required to secure and maintain all licenses and permits that may be required for the operation of the business, and to operate the business in compliance with such licenses and permits.

INSURANCE

The franchise will be required to purchase and maintain insurance policies as are reasonably required by the franchisor, and to provide the franchisor with a certificate of coverage and prior notice of termination, change or expiry of each policy.

WORKING CAPITAL REQUIREMENTS

The franchisee will be required at all times to maintain a specified working capital ratio (i.e., the ratio between current assets and current liabilities). The normal working capital ratio is not less than 1:1. There may also be a requirement to maintain a specified debt-to-equity ratio. This ratio may vary, but a typical ratio is not greater than 2:1.

CREDIT CARD ARRANGEMENTS

Depending on the type of business, the franchisee may be required to make arrangements with specified credit card companies for the convenience of his or her customers.

INSPECTION BY THE FRANCHISOR

The franchisee authorizes the franchisor or any of its representatives to enter the premises at any reasonable time to inspect the premises, fixtures, equipment and inventory and the general operations of the franchised business.

OPERATING PROCEDURES

The franchisee agrees to operate the business in strict compliance with the franchisor's standard procedures, policies, systems, rules and regulations as set out in the operations manual.

USE OF PREMISES

The premises may only be used for the purposes of operating the franchised business. This is necessary to achieve consistency amongst the outlets.

HOURS OF OPERATION

The franchisor may specify that the business is open during normal business hours on all normal business days and in accordance with the provisions of the lease which may require the business to be open during specific times over and above normal business hours. The franchisor will have to approve any deviation from the specified hours.

DEVOTE FULL TIME AND BEST EFFORTS

The franchisee agrees to devote his or her full time and best efforts to conducting the business.

STAFFING REQUIREMENTS

Sufficient staff must be employed to properly operate the franchise in accordance with the terms of the franchise agreement.

EMPLOYEE COMPLIANCE

The franchisee will ensure that each of his or her employees is familiar with the policies and procedures of the franchisor.

UNIFORMS

The franchisee and its employees may be required to wear uniforms which conform to the franchisor's design and specifications. The agreement may also provide that the uniforms be purchased from the franchisor or a designated supplier. While this is necessary to maintain consistency amongst the franchises, as is the case with supplies purchased from the franchisor or designated suppliers, the costs charged to the franchisee must be competitive.

CUSTOMER RELATIONS

The franchisee will be required to ensure that prompt, courteous and efficient service is provided to customers.

USE OF PHOTOGRAPHS

The franchisee may be required to agree that for the purposes of advertising and public relations related to the franchise concept, the franchisor may make, reproduce and publish photographs of the franchised business.

CONDITION AND APPEARANCE OF PREMISES

This clause is to ensure that the franchisee maintains the premises, equipment, machinery, furnishings, etc. in a clean and attractive manner in accordance with the requirements of the operations manual.

PERIODIC MAINTENANCE AND REPAIR

In addition to the "Condition and Appearance of Premises" clause, there may be an additional clause requiring the franchisee to carry out periodic maintenance and repair of the premises, machinery and equipment to ensure that the business runs efficiently.

Advertising and Promotion

This section covers the various responsibilities of the franchisor and franchisee concerning the advertising and promotion of the system. This is one of the most important sections in the agreement because the administration and use of advertising funds is often one of the most contentious issues in a franchise system.

One of the main complaints from franchisees is that they are not receiving advertising benefits in proportion to their contribution to the advertising fund. To prevent this occurrence, most franchisors insert a clause in the agreement to the effect that "the franchisee understands and acknowledges that the advertising and promotion fund to be administered by the franchisor is intended to maximize general public recognition and acceptance of all franchised outlets for the benefit of all franchisees of the system and the franchisor, and that the franchisor undertakes no obligation to ensure that any particular franchisee (including the franchisee) benefits directly or *pro rata* from the placement or conduct of such advertising or promotion."

ADVERTISING FUND

Most franchisors require franchisees to contribute to an advertising fund. The purpose of the fund should be specified in the agreement, but generally it is used to cover the costs of producing and financing advertising and promotional materials, and for the advertising and promotion of the name recognition of the franchise. The fund may be used for regional and/or national advertising campaigns depending on the franchisor's geographical coverage.

ACCOUNTING OF FUND

Another contentious area is the franchisor's accounting of the advertising and promotion fund. The advertising fund is administered by the franchisor on behalf of the franchisees, creating a fiduciary responsibility on the behalf of the franchisor. Consequently, the agreement should provide that advertising funds are maintained in a separate trust account and not mixed with the franchisor's general operating accounts.

APPROVAL OF ADVERTISING COPY, MATERIALS, PACKAGING AND PROMOTIONAL MATERIALS

The franchisee will have to obtain the franchisor's approval of advertising copy prior to placing any advertisements, and for any packaging or promotional materials, particularly where the franchisor's trademarks are used.

LOCAL ADVERTISING

In addition to any contributions the franchisee is required to make to the advertising fund, the franchisee will probably be required to spend a minimum amount on local advertising. In most cases this will be a minimum percentage of gross revenues, but in a few situations it may be a flat fee.

CO-OP ADVERTISING

The franchisee may be required to participate in regional co-operative advertising campaigns or promotions designed to enhance the value of all the franchises within the region. If so, there should be a requirement that a vote of 75% of the franchisees operating within the region is required to approve such a campaign. If the campaign is approved, each franchisee must agree to participate and share costs proportionately. This democratic process prevents dissenting franchisees from getting a free ride on the backs of the participating franchisees.

GRAND OPENING ADVERTISING REQUIREMENTS

There may be a provision for the franchisee to spend a certain amount on the advertising and promotion of the grand opening of the store. The franchisee may be required to pay the franchisor who has the responsibility of advertising and arranging the promotion. In the latter case, the franchisor should be required to provide the franchisee with an accounting of the expenditures together with invoices.

TELEPHONE DIRECTORY LISTINGS

The franchisee may be required to participate in Yellow Page advertising with other franchisees located within the same region. Alternatively, he or she may be responsible for placing an advertisement at his or her own cost in all Yellow Page directories servicing the area. The franchisor may provide the ad layouts for such advertising, but in any event the franchisee will be required to obtain the franchisor's approval of the advertisement prior to placement.

ADMINISTRATIVE COSTS

There is normally a provision for the franchisor to charge a fee for the administration of the advertising fund. It may defined as a percentage of the annual revenue in the fund in which case the percentage should be defined, or it may be necessary to fix a ceiling in terms of a maximum dollar figure that can be charged against the fund.

DELEGATION OF ADVERTISING RESPONSIBILITIES

The franchisor will normally have the right to delegate its responsibilities and duties in connection with the advertising fund to an arm's-length third party such as an advertising agency.

COUPONS AND DISCOUNTS

The franchisee may be required to accept all promotional coupons and special discount offers of the franchisor. Although this can be a valuable marketing technique, it can seriously reduce the franchisee's gross margins. The agreement should contain an option whereby the franchisee can choose not to participate under certain terms and conditions.

Purchase and Sale of Products and Services

A well-structured supplier program is essential to the success of a franchise. To ensure consistency throughout the system and the maintenance of uniform quality standards to the general public, the franchisor will require a certain amount of control over the products and services that the franchisee sells. To achieve this, the agreement will contain provisions that require the franchisee to sell only the goods and services that meet the franchisor's standards and specifications. This can vary from a requirement that the raw products used by the franchisee must meet the franchisor's specifications, that the franchisee only purchase from suppliers designated by the franchisor, and that the franchisee buy all his products directly from the franchisor.

The franchisee may be in a precarious position if the success of the franchise is founded upon the consumer's brand loyalty to a product that is manufactured by, or only available from, the franchisor. If the franchisor experiences financial difficulties resulting in its collapse, the source of supply could dry up resulting in severe consequences to the franchisee.

A list of authorized products and services is usually published in the franchisor's operations manual, and may be revised from time to time.

ALTERNATE SUPPLIERS

A franchisee cannot be forced to purchase supplies and products directly from a franchisor (unless they are trademarked products) or its designated supplier. Most franchise agreements are drafted to provide the franchisee a "window" whereby the franchisee may purchase such products and supplies from any other source or supplier provided that such products are of equivalent quality at prices lower than those charged by the franchisor or its designated supplier. The franchisee may purchase such lower-priced products or supplies from such alternate suppliers for as long as such lower prices prevail, provided that any such alternate supplier is first approved in writing by the franchisor (approval shall not be unreasonably withheld). The franchisor shall require the franchisee to submit samples of any product or supplies to be purchased from such alternate supplier to the franchisor for approval.

REBATES AND DISCOUNTS

There is normally a provision for the franchisor to retain any volume rebates and discounts from suppliers who provide products or supplies to the franchisees. There is nothing fundamentally wrong with this practice as long as it is disclosed to the franchisees and does not impede the competitive purchasing power of the franchisee.

SUGGESTED PRICES

Provisions of the Competitive Act prevent the franchisor from setting minimum prices, and the franchisee cannot suffer in any way from any action of the franchisor for selling at prices below those set by the franchisor; however, the franchisor may set maximum prices and these are binding upon franchisees.

SUBSTANDARD SUPPLIES

There may be a provision whereby the franchisee is required (usually with a notice period) to remove from sale or use any items that have not been approved by the franchisor or do not conform to the franchisor's specifications. The franchisor may also have the right of entry to the premises to remove any substandard supplies.

PAYMENTS FOR SUPPLIES

The franchisor will normally require that the franchisee covenant to pay all suppliers (including the franchisor) promptly when an account is due. This is to prevent the tardy payment practices of one franchisee from harming the reputation of the franchisor and adversely affecting the relationship between the franchisor (and other franchisees) and the suppliers.

Operations Manual

The operations manual is enforced through the agreement, and the contents of the manual may be revised from time to time by the franchisor to reflect changes in the operating procedures or approved suppliers. The operations manual is the "bible" of the franchise system, and most agreements will have clauses to ensure that the franchisee adheres to its policies and procedures and to protect its confidentiality.

CONFORMING TO THE MANUAL

The franchisees will be required to conform to all the specifications, policies, standards, procedures and methods that are contained in the operations manual. The provisions of the operations manual, including any revisions, are deemed to constitute provisions of the franchise agreement as if fully set out in the agreement. Consequently, there should be an assurance to the franchisee that no such revisions shall substantially alter the franchisee's rights under the franchise agreement.

CONFIDENTIALITY

The franchisee will be required to acknowledge that all of the information contained in the manual is confidential and constitutes trade secrets of the franchisor. The franchisee must maintain the absolute confidentiality of this information, both during and after the term of the agreement, and to disclose to his employees only the information that is necessary for the operation of the franchisee's business.

PROPERTY OF FRANCHISOR

This provision specifies that the operations manual is the property of the franchisor at all times, and is loaned to the franchisee for its use only during the term of the agreement.

Payments by the Franchisee

INITIAL FRANCHISE FEE

The franchisee is normally required to pay an initial franchise fee upon execution of the agreement. Any deposits previously paid should be credited against the fee. It may specify that the initial franchise fee is paid in consideration for the right and license granted in the franchise agreement, or for the opportunity to establish the franchised business.

The initial franchisee fee is normally non-refundable (in whole or part) and is deemed to be fully earned upon the execution of the franchise agreement. It may be possible for a franchisee to negotiate for the fee to be held in trust by either the franchisee's or the franchisor's lawyer until the location is agreed upon or the franchise business is open. There may be a provision that the initial franchise fee can be refunded (in whole or in part) if the franchisee does not complete the initial training to the satisfaction of the franchisor.

CONTINUING ROYALTIES

The continuing fees are the royalties payable by the franchisee to the franchisor for the ongoing rights and privileges that are contained in the franchise agreement and the amount and method of calculating the fees should be specified.

Most royalty fees are based on a percentage of the franchisee's gross sales and some are calculated on a flat-fee basis. In some instances, percentage royalties may be calculated on an increasing or reducing scale as sales increase, and some agreements call for a minimum amount of royalties to be paid monthly. Some agreements (mainly those based on a flat-fee royalty) allow for an annual increase based on the Consumer Price Index or some other method of inflation.

PAYMENTS

Royalties are paid either monthly or weekly. Monthly royalties are paid on or before the 10th day of the month following the month in which the sales are made.

ADVERTISING CONTRIBUTION

The advertising contribution is often calculated and submitted in the same manner as the ongoing fee. Again, the fee could be a percentage of gross sales or a flat fee, but whichever, it should be specified in the agreement.

DEFINITION OF GROSS SALES

A definition of gross sales may be provided in this section or in "Definitions" earlier in the agreement. Gross sales are usually defined as the total revenues derived by the franchisee in and from the franchised location during the period (whether evidenced by cash, cheque, credit card or otherwise in any manner) from the sale of goods or the provision of services arising out of the operation of the franchised business, minus sales taxes which are separately stated and payable to the federal, provincial or local tax authority.

ROYALTIES DURING AN EVENT OF FORCE MAJEURE

This clause specifies a method of calculating the royalties that would be paid by the franchisee upon the receipt of the proceeds of any business interruption insurance paid to it due to the franchised location being closed down because of circumstances beyond the control of the franchisee, such as fire or a hurricane. Usually, the average sales figures for a specified period of time prior to the closure of the franchise business is used as the basis for calculation of the royalties payable to the franchisor.

Franchisee's Business Records and Reporting

BOOKKEEPING, ACCOUNTING AND RECORDS

The franchisee will be required to maintain a standard bookkeeping, accounting and record-keeping system as approved by the franchisor. Such a system may be provided as part of the franchise system. Some franchisors provide valuable feedback to franchisees by using management information systems which require standardized reporting by franchisees in order to compare various ratios.

PRESERVATION OF RECORDS

The franchisor may require that the franchisee keep all business records for a period of time.

MONTHLY AND ANNUAL REPORTING

The franchisee may be required to provide the franchisor with monthly reports (normally due at the same time as the royalties) regarding gross sales, inventory levels, gross profit margin, aged accounts receivable and payable, and expenses for the current month and year-to-date.

AUDIT RIGHTS

The agreement will normally contain a provision giving the franchisor the right to audit the franchisee without prior notice to inspect the business records, accounting records, invoices, statements, reports, etc. The franchisee will be required to co-operate fully with the representatives of the franchisor and any accountants hired by the franchisor.

Renewal

Subject to certain terms and conditions, the franchise agreement usually provides the franchisee with an option to renew the franchise agreement for one additional period, which is often equal to the current term of the agreement. The franchisor may renew the existing agreement for a further term or require the franchisee to enter into the franchisor's then current standard form of franchisee agreement, which may contain different terms and conditions than those contained in the expiring agreement. Most franchisees are concerned that the franchisor may increase the ongoing royalty rate at the time of renewal. Although possible, it is not probable, as the franchisor will want to retain a good franchisee and increasing the royalties is not, in most circumstances, a good business decision.

Each franchise agreement should be examined carefully to determine the renewal rights of the franchisee. Agreements ordinarily contain the right to renew for only one additional term, although in most cases each new, or renewed, agreement will contain provision for one further renewal term. However, a franchisor may only offer an initial term of 10 years and one renewal term of five years with no further opportunity to renew the franchise. At the end of this renewal period the franchise grant may revert to the franchisor. In this case, the agreement should contain a buy-back agreement stipulating the terms and condition under which the franchisor will repurchase the business from the franchisee, including an acceptable method of valuing the business. If the franchisee decides to sell the business to a third party prior to the end of the initial term and its renewal period, obviously the value of the franchise will diminish relative to the length of the term remaining on the franchise agreement.

NOTICE OF RENEWAL

Most franchise agreements call for the franchisee to provide the franchisor with written notice of its election to renew the agreement within a set period of time prior to the expiration of the current agreement. Sixty to ninety days' notice is a reasonable notice period.

ABILITY TO REMAIN IN PREMISES

A common condition for renewal is the franchisee's ability to remain in the franchised location; therefore, it is critical for the franchisee to ensure that he or she is in a position to renew the lease. If the lease renewal is the responsibility of the franchisor, the franchisee should attempt to get confirmation from the franchisor that a renewal has been, or is in the process of being, negotiated. If the franchisor is unable to, or has failed to, renegotiate the lease, this could place the franchisee in the position of being forced to relocate, which may require a substantial capital expenditure that the franchisee is unable to afford.

UPGRADING REQUIREMENTS

Some franchisee agreements provide that, as a condition of renewal, the franchisee shall have completed to the franchisor's satisfaction, all such maintenance, refurnishing, renovating and remodelling of the premises, equipment and furnishings as the franchisor shall reasonably require. The franchisee should seek some assurance that any improvements will be reasonable, limited to a dollar figure, or can be carried out over a period of time.

MUST BE IN COMPLIANCE WITH FRANCHISE AGREEMENT

Another condition of renewal is that the franchisee is in compliance with all of the terms and conditions of the existing agreements, therefore franchisees should ensure that any defaults under the agreement are remedied prior to renewal.

RENEWAL FEE

A renewal fee is charged by most franchisors and may be a large percentage of the initial franchise fee, a fixed sum such as $2,500, or no fee at all. Some agreements simply give the franchisor the right to recover its reasonable expenses associated with renewing the agreement.

Restrictive Covenants

The agreement will contain covenants or conditions restricting the franchisee from competing with the franchisor or any of its affiliates or any of its franchisees during, and for a period of time (usually two years) after, the termination or expiration of the franchise agreement.

NON-COMPETITION DURING THE TERM OF THE AGREEMENT

The first covenant relates to non-competition during the term of the agreement (in-term) and requires the franchisee to agree that he or she will not, during the term of the agreement, in any manner whatsoever, directly or indirectly, carry on or be engaged in or be concerned with or interested in any business competitive with or similar to the franchised business.

NON-COMPETITION FOLLOWING TERMINATION OR EXPIRATION OF THE AGREEMENT

The second covenant relates to non-competition following the termination or expiration of the franchise agreement (post-term) and restricts the franchisee from using his or her knowledge and experience gained during the term of the agreement from competing within a specified geographic area, and for a specified term with the franchisor or any of the franchisees.

Courts are reluctant to enforce restrictive covenants, and even if they do find them to be justified they will insist that any restriction be reasonable.

Some agreements contain a clause which requires the franchisee to agree that such restrictions are reasonable and that all defences to the strict enforcement of such restrictions by the franchisor are waived. In agreeing to this clause, the franchisee is waiving his rights to defences in matters which are generally considered to be within the equitable discretion of a court of law. Franchisees should be reluctant to part with any such rights.

NO SOLICITATION OF EMPLOYEES

Most agreements also include a clause preventing the franchisee from soliciting employees of the franchisor, or any of the franchisees in the system, without the prior written consent of the franchisor. This is reasonable as it prevents other franchisees from poaching experienced or valued employees.

Termination of the Franchise Agreement

Although this section is necessary to give the franchisor control of the system, and for the ultimate protection of the franchisees within the system, it is usually the section that a prospective franchisee finds most offensive. However, in the event that a recalcitrant or defaulting franchisee is damaging the goodwill of the franchise system, the franchisor must have the power to terminate the particular franchise agreement.

The franchisor will claim the right under a variety of circumstances to terminate the agreement in the event of default by the franchisee. Generally, events of default are divided into two categories:

1. Critical events that allow the franchisor to terminate the agreement without notice, or opportunity to remedy the problem.
2. Events of default where the franchisee is first given notice and an opportunity to remedy the default prior to the franchisor being entitled to terminate the agreement.

The following are events of default which might be considered critical, or material defaults allowing for immediate termination of the agreement:

- failure to complete all required training

- failure to open the location for business as provided in the agreement, or failing to actively and continuously operate the franchised business for a specific number of days without the franchisor's approval
- if the franchisee declares bankruptcy or becomes insolvent, or a receiver or other custodian of the franchised business is appointed
- if the franchisee assigns, or attempts to assign, transfer or sell the whole or any part of his or her rights under the agreement without the prior written consent of the franchisor
- if the franchisee wilfully or fraudulently misrepresents any fact, condition or report to be made under the franchise agreement
- if the franchisee understates gross sales by a specified percentage
- if the franchisee engages in misleading advertising or operates the franchised business in a dishonest, illegal or unethical manner, or has its business license suspended
- if the franchisee has received during any consecutive 12-month period three notices relating to one or more defaults under the agreement, irrespective of whether the default(s) was remedied by the franchisee
- if the franchisee attempts to unilaterally repudiate the agreement or the observance or performance of any terms, conditions, covenants, provisions and obligations contained in the agreement.

Events of default which require the franchisor to give notice of default with an opportunity for the franchisor to cure such default within a specified period might normally include:

- failure to comply with any obligation of the lease
- failure to pay any sums due to the franchisor, or any supplier of equipment or supplies to the franchised business (including any sub-lease)
- unauthorized use of trademarks.

Some events of default listed here as having an opportunity to remedy may be regarded as critical or material defaults with no opportunity to remedy in some franchise agreements.

Obligations Upon Termination

In the event that the agreement is terminated, the franchisee will be required to agree to a number of items including:

- discontinue the use, directly or indirectly, of the trademarks, and any confidential methods, procedures and specifications associated within the system
- immediately return to the franchisor all copies of the operations manual
- notify the telephone company and listing agencies of the termination of the franchisee's right to use all telephone numbers and all classified directory listings of the franchised business, and authorize the transfer of the telephone number and listings to the franchisor
- pay all amounts owing to the franchisor, or any affiliate of the franchisor
- immediately cease to operate the franchised business and not operate or do business under any name or in any manner that might tend to give the general public the impression that it is, directly or indirectly, associated with or related to the franchisor or part of the franchise system
- surrender all signs or sign faces under the terms of any sign leases
- if franchisee is not a tenant of the franchisor under the lease, remove all signage from the premises and repaint the premises in a different colour scheme and decor
- discontinue using any signs, equipment, fixtures, furnishings, inventories, advertising or promotional materials, invoices, supplies, forms, or other products or materials which display the franchisor's trademark, or any distinctive feature associated with the system, and
- cancel any permitted business or divisional name registrations incorporating the trademarks.

FRANCHISOR'S RIGHT TO SIGNAGE AND ITEMS IDENTIFIED BY TRADEMARK

If the franchisor holds the head lease, or a conditional assignment of the lease, the franchisee will not be able to remain in possession of the premises. In any event, the franchisor normally has the right to re-enter the premises and remove certain items that carry the franchisor's trademark. If so, the agreement should provide for the payment by the franchisor of some amount to the franchisee, such as a percentage of original cost to the franchisee, for such materials.

If the franchisee has the right, and wishes to remain in business at the location, the surrender of the telephone number and listings normally prove onerous to the franchisee. Wherever possible, any requirement to modify the appearance of the premises following termination should be specific and not left to the discretion of the franchisor.

FRANCHISOR'S OPTION TO PURCHASE

Most franchise agreements provide the right, but not the obligation, to the franchisor, upon the termination (or expiration) of the agreement to purchase from the franchisee any or all of the equipment, inventory, supplies, furnishings, leasehold improvements and fixtures owned by the franchisees or used in connection with the franchised business. The option period should be set at a reasonable time, such as 15 days. The calculation of the purchase price should be specified in the agreement and is usually based on one of the following methods:

- original cost to the franchisee, less a re-stocking fee
- depreciated book value of the items as reflected in the franchisee's current financial statements
- fair market value as determined by agreement of the franchisor and the franchisee, or failing such agreement, by an independent arbitrator selected by a mechanism outlined in the agreement
- replacement cost, or
- any combination of the foregoing based on a greater or lesser option.

The agreement may provide that the franchisor is entitled to deduct from any monies payable to the franchise any monies owed by the franchisee to the franchisor or any of its affiliates.

LIQUIDATED DAMAGES

The agreement may also contain a provision whereby the franchisee understands and agrees that if he or she does not discontinue using the trademarks, trade secrets and operating procedures, etc., the franchisor will have the right to claim and recover damages from the franchisee. The franchisee will also be required to agree that for each day that the franchisee continues to operate the business he or she will pay to the franchisee a specified sum per day as liquidated damages.

Assignment

ASSIGNMENT BY THE FRANCHISEE

A franchisee is normally given the right to assign, sell or transfer his or her rights under the franchise agreement with the prior approval of the franchisor. This section will include the franchisee's rights in this regard.

A relatively small number of franchisors, principally to prevent franchisees from flipping the franchised business for a quick profit, have provisions in their agreements whereby for an initial period they receive a specified percentage of the profit realized by the franchisee upon resale of the franchised business. For example, they may receive 25% of the profit if a sale was achieved in the first year, 20% in the second, and reducing by a further 5% each year to year five. After the fifth year, the franchisor may just require a flat assignment fee.

FRANCHISOR'S RIGHT OF APPROVAL

As the franchise was originally granted to the franchisee based on his or her personal qualifications, a requirement for any assignment will be the approval by the franchisor of the personal qualifications of the proposed franchisee (such approval is not to be unreasonably withheld by the franchisor). The agreement will contain several conditions to the franchisor's approval of an assignment of the franchise and may include the following:

- that all outstanding accounts and obligations have been settled with the franchisor
- the franchisee is not in default in the performance or observance of any of the franchisee's obligations under the franchise agreement or any other agreement with the franchisor
- the franchisee has executed a complete release of all claims against the franchisor

- the proposed assignee in writing shall have assumed and agreed to be bound by all of the covenants of the franchisee, or at the option of the franchisor, shall have executed a new franchise agreement in the form then being used by the franchisor
- the assignee shall have completed the franchisor's training program
- the franchisee has returned to the franchisor the operations manual
- an assignment or transfer fee has been paid to the franchisor as prescribed by the franchise agreement
- the franchisee shall submit all proposed advertisements for the sale of the franchised business to the franchisor for its prior written approval, and
- the franchisor may within a specified period, at its option require the franchisee to sell its interest in the franchise agreement to the franchisor.

FRANCHISOR'S RIGHT OF FIRST REFUSAL

Franchise agreements often provide a right of first refusal or option to the franchisor to acquire the franchised business from the franchisee upon the same terms and conditions as proposed by a third party acting at arm's length. The agreement should specify the franchisor's option period which should be no longer than 30 days and preferably shorter. If the option is exercised, the franchisor should then have a reasonable time period such as 30 days in which to complete the sale. If the franchisor decides not to proceed with the purchase of the business, the franchisee is free to proceed with the sale to the third party subject to the normal terms and conditions of assignment as specified in the franchise agreement conditions stated above. However, the agreement may provide that if the proposed assignment or transfer should materially change, the franchisor shall again be given the right of first refusal.

ASSIGNMENT FEE

Most franchisors require the payment of an assignment fee to offset their costs of approving and training the new franchisee, together with any associated legal costs. This fee may be a set dollar amount, a percentage of the initial franchise fee, or the agreement may provide for the franchisor to recover any reasonable costs associated with the assignment. The word "reasonable" has a tendency to appear frequently in franchise documents as it is a convenient word to describe these kind of situations. However, it has a different meaning to different people in different circumstances. What is reasonable to the franchisor may not necessarily appear reasonable to the franchisee; consequently, it is preferable to fix a specific number or percentage, thereby avoiding any hidden surprises or conflicts.

NO ENCUMBRANCE OF FRANCHISE

The franchisee may be required to agree that he or she will not grant, issue or allow any lien charge or encumbrance whatsoever on the lease or over the franchisee's machinery, equipment, fixtures, furnishings, leasehold improvements and supplies, and not to pledge or otherwise give any third party a security interest in the franchise agreement without the consent of the franchisor. The franchisor will agree to not unreasonably withhold its consent to the franchisee granting a security interest to a Canadian chartered bank for monies advanced in connection with the franchised business.

ASSIGNMENT BY THE FRANCHISOR

In case a franchisor wishes to sell the entire franchise system, or just the master or sub-franchise rights, it usually reserves the right to assign the franchise agreement to any person that the franchisor in its sole discretion deems appropriate. The agreement should provide that any such assignee shall agree in writing to assume all of the obligations undertaken by the franchisor in the franchise agreement.

ASSIGNMENT TO A CONTROLLED CORPORATION

Many franchisees wish to operate the franchisee business through a company that they have formed. As the franchise agreement is personal to the franchisee and relies to a large part on the franchisee's characteristics and skills, the rights to operate the franchise must be transferred to the franchisee's corporation. Most franchisors will allow, coincident with or any time after the execution of the franchise agreement, the franchisee to assign the rights granted under the franchise agreement to a corporation in which the franchisee is the major shareholder. This is normally achieved by the franchisee executing a form called "Assignment to a Controlled Corporation Agreement." In connection with such an assignment, the franchisee may be required to:

- include in its articles of incorporation a provision that its business will be confined exclusively to the operation of the franchised business
- restrict the issue of shares of the corporation so that the franchisee shall continuously own greater than 50% of the issued and outstanding voting shares of the corporation
- execute such assignments and guarantees of the obligations of the corporation as the franchisor may require
- execute other documents in respect of the assignment that the franchisor may require such as a lease, or sub-lease agreement
- pay the franchisor's legal expenses and any other fees and charges incurred by the franchisor in connection with the assignment
- have the corporation and its directors and shareholders acknowledge the franchise agreement and agree in writing to be bound by it.

The restriction on the issues of shares and the requirement for the franchisee to own greater than 50% of the shares is to prevent a change of ownership without the approval of the franchisor. Some agreements may provide that the franchisee must own more than 75% of the shares. The requirement that the corporation must be confined exclusively to the operation of the franchised business prevents franchisees from investing their profits, or excess cash flow, into other ventures that could negatively impact the franchised business in the event of failure.

Death or Incapacity of the Franchisee

This section also deals with assignment of the franchise in the event of the death or permanent incapacity of the franchisee. Some agreements will deal with these situations in fairly general terms and others will be more specific. A reasonable time-frame of at least 90 days should be allowed for the heirs or representatives of the franchisee to organize themselves and make arrangements as to the operation or the disposition of the franchised business in the event of the death or incapacity of the franchisee.

SURVIVORS CAN APPLY TO CONTINUE

Subject to the franchisor being satisfied that arrangements have been made for the ongoing active management of the franchised business, the franchisee should be allowed to transfer his or her rights under the franchise agreement to his or her heirs or personal representatives upon the franchisee's death or permanent incapacity. The agreement may include a specific description of the persons to whom the franchise agreement may be transferred, such as the franchisee's spouse or children of a legal age. If the rights under the franchise agreement have been assigned to a controlled corporation and the controlling shareholder dies (i.e., the franchisee), the corporation may be allowed to retain the rights if throughout the term of the agreement the heirs or personal representatives are the beneficial and registered owner of greater than 50% of the shares, and if satisfactory arrangements have been made for the management of the business.

SURVIVORS CAN SELL

In a situation where the franchisee's heirs or representatives are unable to devote their full attention to the management of the franchised business, the right to sell or transfer the business will normally be in accordance with the general terms and conditions relating to assignment.

FRANCHISOR'S RIGHT OF FIRST REFUSAL

Many agreements contain a right of first refusal or some type of option to purchase for the franchisor to acquire the franchisee's business in the event that a *bono fide* offer is received from a third party. The rights granted to the franchisor would be similar to those granted under the general section on assignment.

FRANCHISOR'S RIGHT TO MANAGE

The franchisor may also reserve the right to operate the franchised business if the heirs or personal representatives of the franchisee cannot devote their full time and attention, or lack the ability to operate the franchised business during the 90-day period.

Independent Contractor

This section defines the legal relationship between the franchisee and the franchisor. The franchisee will be required to acknowledge that he or she is, and will always remain, an independent contractor and will not represent himself or herself to be an employee, agent or partner of the franchisor. Neither can the franchisee carry out any acts which could establish any such relationship and the franchisor will not be bound by any such acts.

The franchisee must idemnify the franchisor from any such claims, suits, actions or demands of any kind directly or indirectly arising from the operation of the franchisee's business and agree to pay any costs associated with the defence of any such actions.

Arbitration

Not all franchise agreements provide for arbitration procedures in the event of a dispute. There are differences of opinion as to whether arbitration is a useful alternative method of dispute resolution. Although it is generally regarded as a less costly and faster method of dispute resolution, the inclusion of an arbitration clause may weaken the legal remedies available to a franchisor, particularly in situations where the franchisee withholds royalty payments. It is also subject to the competence of the arbitrators with a limited right of appeal. Even in the absence of an arbitration clause, a dispute can still be referred to arbitration subject to the agreement of both parties.

If arbitration is provided for, the agreement may provide for certain exceptions. It may also specify a procedure for the selection and numbers of arbitrators, and to provide for arbitration to be subject to any applicable laws including reference to the Arbitrations Act of the province whose laws govern the franchise agreement.

Overdue Amounts

Most agreements will include provisions dealing with any overdue amounts that may be owed by the franchisee to the franchisor. It will normally state that overdue amounts bear interest at a specified rate of interest usually calculated as a certain percentage above the prime rate as charged by one of the major chartered banks. The acceptance of any interest payments will normally be deemed not to constitute a waiver by the franchisor or its rights with respect to the default that has resulted in the overdue amount, and shall be without prejudice to the franchisor's right to terminate the franchise agreement because of default.

General Contract Provisions

There will be a number of general contract provisions that may include the following:

Waiver of Obligations

The franchisee will be required to acknowledge that the franchisor may unilaterally waive any obligation or restriction upon the franchisee under the agreement. Also, no acceptance by the franchisor of any payment by the franchisee, and no failure, refusal or neglect of the franchisor to exercise any right under the agreement, or to insist on the franchisee's full compliance with the agreement, will constitute a waiver of any provision of the agreement.

In other words, if the franchisor elects to look the other way, or neglects to enforce any provision in the event that the franchisee commits a default, it does not mean that it is relinquishing its rights or disclaiming any provision of the agreement. This clause may also state that any nonenforcement against other franchisees by the franchisor will not constitute a waiver against the franchisee.

The franchisee should have mutual rights in this regard by having the benefit of the non-waiver provision in the event of default or non-compliance by the franchisor.

Notice

This clause will specify the method by which all written notices must be given and the addresses of both franchisor and franchisee to which the notices must be forwarded.

Entire Agreement

This clause ties together the franchise agreement and any other agreements referenced in the franchise agreement as the entire agreement and no other agreements, oral or written, are considered to exist or bind the parties in any way. This agreement also supersedes any and all prior agreements or understandings. If the franchisee considers that something is fundamental to the agreement, this should be included and incorporated into the agreement prior to the execution of the agreement.

Amendments in Writing

The agreement cannot be modified or changed except in writing and signed by both the franchisor and franchisee.

Severability

If any part of the agreement is found to be invalid, illegal or unenforceable for any reason, the particular section of agreement will be severed from the agreement and the remainder of the agreement will not be affected in any way.

Applicable Law

This clause specifies which province's laws apply in the event that any legal proceedings prove to be necessary. It is normally to the benefit of either party to be able to process or defend any claims in their home province; however, the location will normally be at the choice of the franchisor.

Acknowledgements

The franchisee will be required to acknowledge that he or she has carried out an independent investigation of the franchised business and recognizes that the business venture contemplated involves business risks, and that the success of the venture largely depends on the ability of the franchisee. The franchisee must also acknowledge that he or she received, read and understood the franchisee agreement and has had adequate opportunity to obtain professional advice and review the agreement with independent legal counsel.

The franchisor will disclaim making, and the franchisee will acknowledge that he or she has not received, any representation, warranty or guarantee, express or implied, as to the potential profits or success of the franchised business. This acknowledgement is very important for the franchisor as it is intended to nullify the effect of any pro formas or inducements made to the franchisee prior to the execution of the franchise agreement.

Right of Set-Off

The franchisor reserves the right, at its option, to deduct any amounts unpaid by the franchisee to the franchisor from any monies or credit held by the franchisor.

Franchisee May Not Withhold Payments

The franchisee must agree to not withhold payment of any royalty, or any amounts due to the franchisor, on the grounds of the alleged non-performance by the franchisor of any of its obligations contained in the franchise agreement.

This means that in the event the franchisee considers that the franchisor is not living up to its obligations, he or she must seek satisfaction through the courts or by some alternative dispute resolution and not arbitrarily cease paying royalties or other payments.

Rights Cumulative

The rights of the franchisor are cumulative and no exercise or enforcement by the franchisor of any right or remedy under the franchise agreement shall preclude the exercise or enforcement by the franchisor or any other right or remedy.

Counterparts

This clause allows for the franchise agreement to be executed in counterparts or portions of the whole agreement and provides that each counterpart that is executed shall be deemed to be part of the original.

Successors and Assigns (Enurement)

This clause states that the franchise agreement enures to the benefit of and is binding upon the franchisor, the franchisee and his or her respective heirs, legal representatives, successors and permitted assigns.

Joint and Several

If the franchise is comprised of two or more persons, their liability under the agreement will be combined and whole.

Powers of Attorney

Although there may be reference throughout the agreement to the franchisee granting its power of attorney to the franchisor in certain situations, it may also be included in general clauses. The franchisee will also be required to ratify and confirm all actions taken by the franchisor while using those powers of attorney. A power of attorney is an instrument authorizing another to act as one's agent or attorney and as such should not be given up lightly.

Survival of Contents

Certain provisions, covenants and conditions, such as confidentiality and non-competition, require continued performance after the termination or expiration of the franchise agreement and as such remain enforceable after termination or expiration.

Fair Dealing

The Alberta Franchises Act requires a clause in the franchise agreement which imposes an obligation on the parties to act reasonably and in good faith concerning the performance and enforcement of the agreement.

RECAP

In this fourth chapter we have discussed the intricacies of the most important document involved in the whole venture, The Agreement, with clauses covering:

- negotiable terms
- exclusivity of territory
- site selection
- opening and furnishing the premises
- the use and display of trademarks
- training and start-up assistance
- the franchisor's and franchisee's obligations
- advertising and promotion
- the purchase of products and services from suppliers
- the operating manual
- payments to the franchisor and records and reporting
- restricting covenants
- renewal, termination or assignment of the agreement
- arbitration in the case of disputes.

CHAPTER 5

Financing the Franchise

*They all observe one rule, which woe betides the banker who fails
to heed it, which is you must never lend any money to anybody
unless they don't need it.*

Ogden Nash

ASSESSING YOUR FINANCIAL NEEDS

Understanding the Stages of a Business

When starting a business, you have to consider the financial needs from start-up to ongoing daily needs, to expansion, to getting through difficult economic periods.

Managing your business effectively means understanding and anticipating the different stages and planning for them—especially in terms of financing. One of the keys to the long-term success of your business is adequate capitalization—having the financial strength to carry you through any tough times.

Start-up Needs

Whether you are opening a new franchise and starting from scratch or buying an existing operating franchise, this stage will involve the largest expenditure. Franchisors normally insist that franchisees have a substantial amount of their own equity invested in the business as unencumbered capital. This way the franchisee has more of a personal stake in the business and will be more committed to the success of the franchise than if all, or a large part, of the capital was borrowed.

Funds may be required for purchasing equipment, leasehold improvements, inventory and supplies, legal fees and security deposits (see Chapter 3). When preparing your start-up financing needs, you must also provide for contingency and reserve funds. The contingency fund is set up to cover unexpected expenses. This may represent from 10% to 25% of planned expenses. A reserve fund is established to carry the new business through the initial period of operation when there may be reduced revenue. You may be fortunate enough to have an immediate customer base and will require only a modest reserve fund of a minimum of three months' expenses to cover overhead costs and salaries. In most cases, sufficient funds for a period of six months to a year should be set aside to carry the business until it can sustain itself. It is often a condition of the franchise agreement that the franchise maintains a minimum working capital.

Ongoing Daily Needs

After the start-up needs have been assessed, your secondary financing needs will be for your day-to-day operations, otherwise referred to as working capital. Working capital is defined as the difference between the current assets and current liabilities of a business. It is the amount by which your current assets such as accounts receivable, cash and inventory exceed your current liabilities such as a short-term bank loan or trade credit payables. Working capital should be sufficient to provide for payment of your current liabilities and for the financing of your day-to-day operations including inventory and payroll.

Expansion

Funds may be required for sustained growth or expansion. Funds for growth capital may be required for the hiring of new employees, acquisition of additional inventory, or new equipment. Your business at this point should have a clear financial track record so that projections can be based on reality and history. Because of this higher degree of certainty, and therefore reduced risk to a lender, your likelihood of accessing funding is enhanced. Your request for funding is based on a greater probability of cash flow than you would expect from a start-up operation.

Lean Economic Periods or Special Needs

In some cases, specific financial needs can be anticipated; in other cases, they cannot. For example, if competition opens up across the street, interest rates go up, or key employees quit, you may require financing to get you through a difficult period.

If your financing needs during lean times are strictly for sound business reasons, then the bank may seriously look at the underlying cause for your financial shortfalls. If you need financing because your service or product is not being accepted in the marketplace, or because of management difficulties, the lender may come to the conclusion that the business may not be able to sustain itself and cure the problems that are causing the financial difficulties. Your only recourse at that point is to inject further money into your business through personal loans or by finding other private investors who are prepared to take the risk.

Planning Your Financial Needs

Many small business owners do not anticipate their financial needs until they are faced with an urgent problem, or they are overly optimistic when preparing their projections. It is important to be conservative and realistic.

As part of your financial plan, you will have to complete various financial documents such as a capital expenditure budget, projected income statement, balance sheet and cash flow. The franchisor should provide you with assistance in this area; however, it is a good idea to have a sound grasp of financial planning and forecasting.

The following guidelines should help you to prepare meaningful and reliable forecasts. Your financial forecasts should:

- reflect the most current and accurate information available
- include an explanation of your assumptions
- be realistic and reasonable
- provide documentation to support your forecasts (published industry ratios, etc.)
- provide an opportunity for input from management and professional advisors to increase the quality and accuracy of the forecast.

Your accountant may be able to provide computerized financial forecasts based on various factors and scenarios; such forecasts will help you monitor your cash flow and inventory levels. The franchisor may also supply this information.

Quick Check 5.1 Sources of Financing Checklist

	Possible Source	Need Further Info	Further Info Obtained
Conventional Sources of Financing			
1. Banks			
(a) Short-term loans:			
• demand loans	____	____	____
• secured commercial loans	____	____	____
• unsecured commercial loans	____	____	____
• operating loans	____	____	____
• lines of credit	____	____	____
• accounts receivable loans	____	____	____
• warehouse receipt loans	____	____	____
• bridge financing	____	____	____
(b) Medium- and long-term loans:			
• term loans	____	____	____
• fixed charge debentures	____	____	____
• floating charge debentures	____	____	____
• conventional mortgages	____	____	____
• collateral mortgages	____	____	____
• business improvement loan	____	____	____
• chattel mortgages	____	____	____
• leasing	____	____	____
(c) Other financing services:			
• charge card for business expenses	____	____	____
• charge card for personal use	____	____	____
• factoring services	____	____	____
• leasing services	____	____	____
• letters of credit	____	____	____
• letters of guarantee	____	____	____
2. Business Development Bank of Canada (BDC)			
• term loans	____	____	____
• loan guarantees	____	____	____
• bridge financing	____	____	____
• equity financing	____	____	____

Quick Check 5.1 Sources of Financing Checklist (cont'd)

	Possible Source	Need Further Info	Further Info Obtained
• leasing	_____	_____	_____
• financial broker program (packaging loans to external lenders)	_____	_____	_____
• joint ventures	_____	_____	_____
• equity participation	_____	_____	_____
3. Trust Companies			
• long-term loan	_____	_____	_____
• mortgage financing	_____	_____	_____
4. Credit Unions			
• term loans	_____	_____	_____
• working capital loans	_____	_____	_____
• mortgage financing	_____	_____	_____
• equity participation	_____	_____	_____
5. Insurance Companies			
• mortgage loans	_____	_____	_____
• loans based on insurance policy (cash surrender value)	_____	_____	_____
6. Investment Dealers			
• equity purchase	_____	_____	_____
• private placement	_____	_____	_____
• public issue of stock	_____	_____	_____
7. Commercial Finance Companies			
• equipment leasing	_____	_____	_____
• real estate loans	_____	_____	_____
• factoring	_____	_____	_____
• machinery and equipment loans	_____	_____	_____
• inventory financing	_____	_____	_____
• accounts or notes receivable financing	_____	_____	_____

8. Government Funding/Incentive/ Purchasing Services

(a) Federal government:

Quick Check 5.1	Sources of Financing Checklist (cont'd)

	Possible Source	Need Further Info	Further Info Obtained
• Industry Canada	_____	_____	_____
• Human Resource Development Canada	_____	_____	_____
• Public Works and Government Services Canada	_____	_____	_____
• Small Business Loans Act	_____	_____	_____
• Small business bond program	_____	_____	_____
• Business development centre (Community futures program)	_____	_____	_____
• Other_____			
_____			
_____			

(b) Provincial government:

	Possible Source	Need Further Info	Further Info Obtained
• Small business ministries	_____	_____	_____
• Provincial development corporations (Crown corporations)	_____	_____	_____
• Provincial purchasing commissions	_____	_____	_____
• Other_____			
_____			
_____			

(c) Municipal/Regional governments:

	Possible Source	Need Further Info	Further Info Obtained
• Economic development commissions	_____	_____	_____
• Municipal government	_____	_____	_____
• Small business incubator start-up program	_____	_____	_____
• Other_____			
_____			
_____			

Creative Sources of Financing or Saving Money

1. Modifying Personal Life-style

	Possible Source	Need Further Info	Further Info Obtained
• reducing personal long-distance telephone calls	_____	_____	_____

Quick Check 5.1 Sources of Financing Checklist (cont'd)

	Possible Source	Need Further Info	Further Info Obtained
• minimizing entertainment expenses	_____	_____	_____
• minimizing transportation costs (e.g., car pool, using more fuel-efficient car)	_____	_____	_____
• cutting down on tobacco and alcohol	_____	_____	_____
• reducing number of restaurant meals by packing your own lunch	_____	_____	_____
• combining personal and business travel	_____	_____	_____
• taking on a part-time job	_____	_____	_____
2. Using Personal Assets			
• using credit cards	_____	_____	_____
• using personal line of credit	_____	_____	_____
• reducing premiums by reassessing insurance policy	_____	_____	_____
• using funds in personal bank accounts	_____	_____	_____
• renting out part of your home or garage	_____	_____	_____
• selling stocks and bonds			
• cashing in pension plans (e.g., RRSP)	_____	_____	_____
• selling unnecessary personal possessions (e.g., second car)	_____	_____	_____
• selling personal assets to the business	_____	_____	_____
• remortgaging your home	_____	_____	_____
3. Using Private Investors Known to You			
• previous employers	_____	_____	_____
• previous co-workers	_____	_____	_____
• friends	_____	_____	_____
• neighbours	_____	_____	_____
• doctor	_____	_____	_____

Quick Check 5.1 Sources of Financing Checklist (cont'd)

	Possible Source	Need Further Info	Further Info Obtained
• lawyer	_____	_____	_____
• accountant	_____	_____	_____
• dentist	_____	_____	_____
• stockbroker	_____	_____	_____

4. Using Other Private Investors

	Possible Source	Need Further Info	Further Info Obtained
• through word-of-mouth contacts (various network groups)	_____	_____	_____
• answering ads in newspapers and magazines that read "investment capital available"	_____	_____	_____
• placing ads for a private investor in newspapers and magazines	_____	_____	_____

5. Family Assistance

	Possible Source	Need Further Info	Further Info Obtained
• loans from relatives	_____	_____	_____
• loans from immediate family members	_____	_____	_____
• equity financing from relatives	_____	_____	_____
• equity financing from immediate family	_____	_____	_____
• employing family members	_____	_____	_____
• sharing an office used by family members	_____	_____	_____
• using a family investment company	_____	_____	_____

6. Using Customers' Funds

	Possible Source	Need Further Info	Further Info Obtained
• having a cash-only policy	_____	_____	_____
• invoicing on an interim basis	_____	_____	_____
• asking for advance payments or deposits	_____	_____	_____
• providing discounts for prompt payments	_____	_____	_____
• charging purchases on customers' credit card accounts	_____	_____	_____
• getting signed purchase orders or			

Quick Check 5.1 Sources of Financing Checklist (cont'd)

	Possible Source	Need Further Info	Further Info Obtained
contracts (collateral for bank)	_____	_____	_____
• third-party billing long-distance phone calls to a customer's account	_____	_____	_____
7. Employees as Investors			
• asking staff to co-sign on loan guarantees	_____	_____	_____
• asking staff to invest in the business	_____	_____	_____
• direct loans from staff	_____	_____	_____
• paying partial salary in the form of stock	_____	_____	_____
8. Using Suppliers' Funds			
• supplier loans	_____	_____	_____
• establishing credit accounts with suppliers	_____	_____	_____
• buying goods on consignment	_____	_____	_____
• floor planning	_____	_____	_____
• equipment loans from manufacturer	_____	_____	_____
• rack jobbers	_____	_____	_____
• instalment financing	_____	_____	_____
• conditional sales agreement	_____	_____	_____
• leasing equipment	_____	_____	_____
• co-op advertising	_____	_____	_____
9. Selling Ownership			
• incorporating and selling shares	_____	_____	_____
• taking on partners or shareholders	_____	_____	_____
10. Renting			
• sharing or subletting rental space, staff, and equipment costs with another business	_____	_____	_____
• renting a packaged office (office space, telephone answering, mailing			

Quick Check 5.1 Sources of Financing Checklist (cont'd)

	Possible Source	Need Further Info	Further Info Obtained
address, secretarial services, equipment, etc.)	_____	_____	_____
• renting office space, furniture and equipment	_____	_____	_____
11. Leasing			
• selling your assets and leasing them back through a commercial leasing company	_____	_____	_____
• leasing assets rather than purchasing	_____	_____	_____
12. Factoring Companies			
• factoring without recourse	_____	_____	_____
• factoring with recourse	_____	_____	_____
• company sets up its own factor	_____	_____	_____
• block discounting	_____	_____	_____
13. Volume Discounts			
• buying groups	_____	_____	_____
• agency discounts	_____	_____	_____
• co-op advertising	_____	_____	_____
• group rates on insurance	_____	_____	_____
14. Financial Matchmaking Services (lists of interested private investors)			
• federal government—entrepreneur immigrants under immigration legislation	_____	_____	_____
• provincial government small business departments	_____	_____	_____
• regional/municipal economic development commissions	_____	_____	_____
• Business Development Bank of Canada	_____	_____	_____
• chartered banks	_____	_____	_____
• COIN investors' network (Canadian Chamber of Commerce)	_____	_____	_____

Quick Check 5.1 Sources of Financing Checklist (cont'd)

	Possible Source	Need Further Info	Further Info Obtained
15. Other Creative Financing Techniques			
• advance royalty deals	____	____	____
• licensing your product or service	____	____	____
• franchisor financing	____	____	____
• franchising your business	____	____	____
• joint ventures	____	____	____
• limited partnerships	____	____	____
• business brokers	____	____	____
• mortgage brokers	____	____	____
• mortgage discounters	____	____	____
• mutual fund companies	____	____	____
• overseas lenders and investors	____	____	____
• pension fund companies	____	____	____
• small business stock savings plans (provincially regulated)	____	____	____
• small business venture capital corporations (provincially regulated)	____	____	____
• venture capital companies	____	____	____
• local venture capital clubs	____	____	____
• financial consultants	____	____	____
• business consultants	____	____	____
• obtaining services in exchange for equity	____	____	____
• contra bartering (exchanging service/product for service/ product)	____	____	____
• RRSP (defer tax)	____	____	____
• assigning exclusive rights to copyright or patent, etc.	____	____	____
• proposal under Bankruptcy and Insolvency Act	____	____	____

DECIDING BETWEEN DEBT AND EQUITY FINANCING

Essentially, there are two types of financing: debt or equity. The use of either method, or both, to finance the business is of critical importance to its success. The nature of the financing will strongly determine the company's very chances of survival, as well as its rate of growth.

The distinction between debt and equity is that a person who contributes money to a company by way of equity becomes an owner of the company, whereas a person who contributes money by way of debt becomes a creditor of the company. Your professional advisors should guide you in making the ultimate decision on the best combination of debt and equity.

With debt financing, you are borrowing money and will have to pay interest for the privilege. If you take on too much debt, it could become cumbersome and you could find yourself at the mercy of the lender if things don't go according to plan and you are unable to service the debt. One of the advantages of debt financing as opposed to equity financing is that you retain ownership and control. (See Quick Check 5.1 for various sources of finance.)

Methods of Equity Financing

Equity is the money that is put into the business in exchange for shares. A balanced debt-to-equity ratio is an integral part of a successful business operation, and most franchise agreements stipulate a permitted ratio. The greater amount of debt, of course, the greater amount of risk. Circumstances that may require equity financing for your business include:

- when you have borrowed to your lending limit, or have used all available assets as collateral for other credit
- buying out a retired or deceased partner's share of the business
- when a company is expanding and its working capital needs have exceeded retained earnings
- a major equipment purchase, plant expansion, or introduction of a new product line
- research and development
- turnaround purposes when purchasing an insolvent company.

The primary source of equity financing is usually through the owners of the company. The equity may come from personal savings, the sale of real estate, or other assets or investments.

If some of the equity financing comes from other people, you must expect to give up something in return. This usually means a share of ownership in the company which in turn means a reduction in your control. Note that most franchise agreements require that the franchisee must at all times own the majority of shares in the business.

Family and Friends

A common source of equity financing is OPM (Other People's Money). In many cases, this means family and friends. You should give careful consideration to involving family and friends in your business. Consider how you would be obligated to them and their financial capability to provide funds.

If you decide to approach family and friends, deal with the situation in a businesslike manner and present them with a formal proposal just as you would a lender or another investor. Structure a formal agreement with agreed terms of repayment and interest. If they proceed, treat their investment as a business arrangement and not as a gift.

REAL LIFE: Beware of Borrowing from the Family

Billy Borrows was 28, married with one child, and hated his job. When he visited the booth of Snappy Signs at a local franchise show he was determined to raise $90,000 and get into business as a Snappy Signs franchisee. Billy approached his in-laws, Edgar and Amy Welloff, who arranged for the funds Billy required by placing a second mortgage on their home.

Around eight months later, Edgar Welloff lost his job and needed his money back urgently, but Billy was not in a position to return the funds. As Edgar Welloff had time on his hands he started to spend more time at Billy's Snappy Signs business, which led to disagreements between the two who had completely different approaches to doing business. Eventually, Billy had no alternative but to tell Edgar to stay away from the business.

After two years in business Billy had a strong enough track record that he was able to secure a loan from a financial institution and repay Edgar and Amy, but it took a long time to rebuild the relationship with his in-laws.

Investors

Aside from family and friends, you may find an investor from these sources: employees, private individuals, clients of professional advisors, suppliers, customers and other parties.

Partnership

You may consider entering into the franchise with a partner in order to share the work and the risk. As discussed in Chapter 7, "Which Legal Structure is Best For You?", the casualty rate of partnerships is very high. If you choose the partnership route, it is imperative to set the rules before you start the game and draw up a partnership agreement.

Franchisor Financing

Some franchisors may offer their own in-house financing. If so, the terms and conditions of the financing should be examined carefully and compared with other sources of financing. A failure to make loan repayments to a franchisor usually results in default, and therefore possible termination of the franchise, under the cross-default provisions of the franchise agreement. Also, if the franchisor provides unrealistic financial projections, resulting in the franchisee's inability to service the debt, it leaves the franchisee in a very precarious position.

Many franchisors have established relationships with financial institutions and are able to provide the prospective franchisee with a comprehensive financial package.

Methods of Debt Financing a Business

Raising money for your business by means of borrowing money is called "debt financing." There are numerous forms such financing can take, as debt financing generally has evolved into a very flexible vehicle. Each financial source generally provides only a limited number of methods of debt financing. Therefore, you will need to learn the sources of the various modes of debt financing should you choose to utilize debt in one or more of its forms. Some of the most commonly used forms of debt financing are briefly described below.

Demand Loan

The simplest form of loan is generally referred to as a "demand loan." The reason it is so named is that the loan is immediately repayable by the borrower "on demand" from the lender. This type of loan is available from Canadian chartered banks for many different purposes, generally has no fixed repayment schedule and is frequently unsecured. It is generally intended for a shorter term than many other forms of debt and usually has a floating interest rate tied into the prime rate. Well-established businesses which are considered extremely creditworthy by Canadian chartered banks may be charged interest as low as the current bank prime rate. This is the lowest interest rate banks charge their most creditworthy customers, while others may pay as much as 5% to 6% above prime in interest to the bank. Higher interest rates may be charged by other lenders, and they usually reflect a perceived higher-risk business enterprise.

Shareholder Loan

A company may borrow money directly from its shareholders just as a proprietorship may borrow money from its owner(s). After all, who better to believe in the prospects of the business? A bank will often not lend money to a start-up business, but it may loan money to a shareholder against his or her personal assets as security. He or she can then inject money into the company either in the form of equity through purchasing shares or in the form of debt through making a shareholder loan to the company. There are a number of advantages to the shareholder in contributing money through a loan rather than equity. For example:

- it is easier for the shareholder to withdraw his or her money from the company when it is needed for another purpose than if it were contributed in the form of shares
- the company can deduct as an expense for tax purposes the interest it pays to the shareholder on the loan, whereas dividend payments to shareholders are not tax deductible
- if the shareholder-lender loans the money to the company as the company's initial source of funds and then registers a security

document against the company in order to secure the loan, the shareholder-lender may be able to create a preferred position for his or her loan, as against the claims of unsecured creditors of the company, in the event of the failure of the business.

Interim Financing (Bridge Financing)

"Bridge financing" is so named because it functions as a "bridge" during an interim period between the start-up of a project and the moment that the project receives some form of long-term financing. Interim financing can be applied to many different situations and projects. For example, interim financing may be arranged for a growing company during the period between the capital injection by the founders and the point at which the company goes public and receives equity funding through an initial public offering. In real estate projects, it is often the debt financing (i.e., a loan) that is added onto the owner's equity in order to finance the completion of construction. It is ultimately repaid by the owner after obtaining long-term financing from a mortgage company. (This long-term financing is sometimes referred to as "take-out" financing because it pays back or "takes out" the bridge financing and often pays back or takes out some or all of the owner's original equity contribution.) Depending on the type of project, bridge financing may be available through chartered banks, venture capital companies, the Business Development Bank of Canada (BDC), private investors and other sources. (See Sample 5.1 for typical Loan Proposal Letter.)

Line of Credit (Operating Bank Loan)

Canadian chartered banks will make available to a wide variety of businesses, which they consider to be creditworthy, a line of credit up to a set maximum amount. As long as all of the conditions of borrowing are satisfied, the borrower is free to borrow money up to that agreed maximum. This form of loan is generally to provide working capital to a business and the outstanding balance will rise and fall with the cyclical needs of the business. For example, retail stores frequently utilize most of their available line of credit in purchasing inventory for the peak Christmas season. The loan is repaid as stock is sold and converted into cash.

Sample 5.1   Loan Proposal Prepared By Lender

From: XYZ Bank

To: ABC Limited

Term Sheet
(for discussion purposes only)
Confidential

Borrower: ABC Limited

Lender: XYZ Bank

Amount: $70,000 Demand Operating Facility
              $3,000 Corporate VISA

Availment: Operating Facility may be availed of by way of over-
              draft.

Purpose: To assist with general corporate financing and specifi-
              cally to finance day-to-day operations and purchase of
              inventory.

Repayment: Demand facility to fluctuate.

Interest
  Rates: Demand overdraft facility—Bank Prime + 1% payable
              monthly

Fees, etc.:   Operating overdraft will be subject to an administra-
              tion fee of $25 per month; service charge will be at the
              standard rate plus $10 per month; night deposit ser-
              vice will be at the standard rate of $1.10 per deposit
              bag.

Security: • Specific Security Agreement (for accounts receiv-
                able) registered in province

              • Assignment of inventory under Section 426 of the
                Bank Act, with fire insurance over inventory, loss
                payable to the Bank first. Proof of coverage to be
                provided.

              • Personal guarantees and postponement of claim (of
                shareholder's loan) by the two principals.

Sample 5.1	Loan Proposal Prepared By Lender (cont'd)

Covenants:

1. Total debt-to-equity shall not exceed 1:1. Equity shall be defined as the sum of paid-up capital, retained earnings, shareholders' loans and deferred management salaries less advances made to shareholders or associated companies.

2. Operating overdrafts will not exceed 50% of total assigned inventories and eligible assigned accounts receivable.

3. There are to be no dividend payments, unusual withdrawals, redemption of shares or shareholder loan paybacks without the prior written consent of the Bank.

4. Capital expenditures in any one year shall not exceed $10,000 noncumulative without the prior written consent of the Bank, such consent not to be unreasonably withheld.

5. Monthly inventory declarations and receivable listings will be provided during those periods where an operating facility is in effect.

6. Annual financial statements prepared consistent with generally acceptable accounting principles by an accredited accounting firm shall be provided within 120 days of the borrower's fiscal year-end.

7. Monthly profit-and-loss statement prepared internally by the borrower shall be provided to the lender.

8. The Bank may request any other financial information it considers necessary for the ongoing administration of the credit facility.

9. The Bank agrees to pay interest on credit balances in excess of $10,000 in your current account #0000 at the rate of the Bank's Prime Lending Rate less 3%

| Sample 5.1 | **Loan Proposal Prepared By Lender** (cont'd) |

> per annum to be calculated on the average daily credit balance and payable monthly.
>
> Events of
>   Default: The usual events of default shall apply.
>
> Review of   The credit is subject to periodic review relative to the Credit: financial information to be provided, as well as an annual review by no later than May 30, _____, in light of annual statements.
>
> This Term Sheet is for discussion purposes only. It is not an offer and represents no commitment, express or implied, on the Bank's part. During our further analysis, information could come to our attention which would detract from the merits of the application and we reserve the right to discontinue the application at any time.
>
> R.B. Jones
> Manager, XYZ Bank

You should be aware of the policy that is sometimes applied by the banks through what is known as a "clean-up provision." The bank may require you to "clean-up" the loan by reducing the outstanding balance to NIL at least once a year, and maintain a NIL balance for a certain period of time, for example, one month.

Floor Planning

This is a method of borrowing frequently used by retailers of large-ticket merchandise, such as automobiles, recreational vehicles, boats and appliances. The lender is frequently a finance company associated with the manufacturer of the goods, such as Chrysler with automobiles or Bombardier with recreational vehicles, or alternatively, another large financial institution. With this method of debt financing the lender frequently maintains legal ownership of the merchandise while it is "floored" (i.e., financed while the merchandise is physically on the dealer's showroom or warehouse "floor.") This method enables the merchant to acquire a significant inventory of merchandise without the requirement of providing purchase funds in advance of selling the merchandise.

Inventory Financing

This form of financing is a close cousin of floor planning but differs significantly in that title to the goods transfers to the merchant because he or she has paid for the goods. The goods are then used as collateral for a loan. The financing is usually secured by the lender, normally a chartered bank or commercial finance company, by entering into formal security documentation and arrangements, such as utilizing a registered debenture or other security documentation, or by taking Bank Act security on the company's inventory. Recent changes to the Bankruptcy and Insolvency Act have made banks reluctant to finance inventory. As each situation is different, you should discuss what is available with your lender.

Accounts Receivable Financing

In this type of financing, the borrower's accounts receivable from his or her own customers become the collateral to support a loan from a financial institution. In Canada, financial institutions will sometimes loan as much as 75% of the value of the outstanding accounts receivable which are not more than 60 days old. As security, the lender will usually take an "assignment of book debts" (i.e., accounts receivable) so that in the event of default by the borrower, the lender can take steps to realize payment of obtaining from the customers of the borrower the accounts receivable owed to the borrower. This type of debt financing is fairly easy to obtain and is available from chartered banks, factoring companies and commercial finance companies. It is sometimes combined with inventory financing to help a business get through a period where its capital needs are high, such as is often the case in cyclical industries.

Conditional Sales Agreement

A businessperson who needs to acquire a capital asset, such as equipment of one kind or another, and who requires financial assistance in the purchase, may often obtain debt financing from the manufacturer of the equipment in the form of a conditional sales agreement. The essence of a conditional sales agreement is that while the purchaser is able to obtain immediate possession of the purchase, ownership of the goods remains with the seller until such time as the purchase is paid. The sale is "conditional" upon the purchaser finally paying in full for the merchandise of which he or she has had possession. As a rule of thumb, many manufacturers require that 25% to 33% of the full purchase price be paid as a downpayment, therefore leaving 67% to 75% of the price available to be financed.

Letter of Credit

This is an interesting device frequently used by a domestic purchaser (in any country) to obtain credit from a foreign supplier. An "L/C," as a letter of credit is called, is a form of guarantee issued by a bank on behalf of a client (such as a domestic purchaser) to a third party (such as an overseas supplier). The L/C represents a guarantee by the bank to the supplier that when the purchaser receives the goods ordered, the supplier will be paid. For the enterprising Canadian entrepreneur, if he or she does not have the financial resources to back a letter of credit, then a third-party investor could be approached to put up the L/C in return for some remuneration. The investor may be able to obtain the L/C very easily on the strength of his or her own credit with the bank, so will only have to pay a modest fee to the bank as a service charge. It can be a very important piece of financing for the entrepreneur purchaser, who will work out an appropriate compensation to the investor for obtaining the L/C.

Leasing

Leasing an asset, whether it is a car, a computer, or real estate such as an office or warehouse, is a way of obtaining the use of an asset to help generate income without the need to invest capital in the property being utilized. By signing a lease agreement you create a legal obligation to pay the leasing company a set monthly rate for a fixed term, while at the same time acquiring an asset to use in your business. Leasing is an especially interesting way to help finance the start or growth of a business when there is a high capital cost required to purchase some necessary equipment or property, yet the company has inadequate capital to make the purchase. The attractiveness of leasing, particularly equipment leasing, also depends on current income tax laws, as well as on a number of other considerations, so it is wise to obtain professional advice before committing yourself to a leasing agreement.

Government Assistance

There are a number of federal and provincial financial assistance programs designed especially to assist emerging companies across Canada. These programs come in many shapes and sizes and include loans, loan guarantees, forgivable loans, grants, cost-sharing programs (e.g., employee training) and subsidies. As the nature and availability of these programs change from time to time, you should contact your provincial small business department and the Business Development Bank of Canada for further information.

Business Improvement Loan

Business Improvement Loans (BIL) are loans administered by the Small Business Loans Act (SBLA) and are guaranteed by the federal government. BILs are designed to help small businesses obtain intermediate term loans from chartered banks and other designated lenders to help finance specified fixed asset needs. BILs are made directly by approved lenders to small businesses with a loss-sharing arrangement signed between the lenders and the federal government.

Most franchise businesses qualify for funding under the SBLA unless they are involved in certain business sectors such as insurance, finance, real estate, mining, petroleum and natural gas, charitable or religious activities. A small business is defined under the Act as one whose annual gross sales do not exceed $5 million a year.

The loans are designed for financing:

- the purchase of land necessary for the operation of a business enterprise
- the renovation, improvement, modernization and/or extension of premises
- the construction and/or purchase of premises
- the purchase, installation, renovation, improvement and/or modernization of equipment.

The terms and conditions of a BIL may vary from time to time. Check with your lender to get the current policy. Limits are $250,000, and assets can be financed up to 90%. Personal guarantees are capped at 25%. The loan cannot be used for working capital requirements or to repay an existing loan.

The maximum rate of interest approved lenders may charge on BILs cannot exceed 3% over the prime lending rate of the chartered banks. The lender may also charge a one-time front-end fee of 2% of the BIL, which must be paid to the federal government and goes towards an insurance fund to cover defaults. Chartered banks, BDC, credit unions, caisses populaires or other co-operative credit societies, trust companies, loan companies, and insurance companies may provide funds (if approved lenders).

THE CREDIT GRANTING PROCESS

Approximately 87% of small businesses in Canada utilize a chartered bank for financing purposes. This does not mean that a small business uses a bank exclusively, but it usually does for part of its financing requirements. Therefore, it is important that you understand the process involved in the granting of loans. This will assist you in negotiating with the lender.

The financing requirements for a franchise are very similar to those for an independent business. In both instances, it is imperative that the business is not undercapitalized. Sufficient capital should be available until the business is in a break-even position. Provided that you meet the normal loan requirements, it should be easier for a franchise to get a loan than it is for a new independent business because of the lower risk. Some factors involved in selecting a lender and the loan-granting process are:

- your meeting and request for money
- the criteria used by the lender for approving funds
- an agreement between the borrower and the lender regarding terms and amounts of money, security and other factors
- confirmation in writing as to the agreement between the parties
- signing of the necessary security required before the funds are advanced.

Request by Borrower

The franchisor may have established a relationship with a lender who is conversant with the franchise opportunity. Some of the major banks have a bank liaison officer who has the responsibility of collecting information, keeping up to date on the various franchise organizations and making this information available at the branch level. This eliminates the need for the branch loans officer to research the franchise and enables the officer to focus on the borrower's qualifications.

The franchisor may prepare the financial proposal for you, accompany you to your meeting with the lender, or you may be left to make your own arrangements. If you are left to your own devices, it is best to set up an initial appointment to discuss the lender's policies without necessarily going into the details of your proposal.

During the interview you can discuss in general terms such questions as:

- what type of collateral might be required
- limitations that the bank might have on types of business loans that you are considering
- the type of reporting information that you may be required to make
- any other information that the bank needs.

This will prepare you for the type of information needed in your loan proposal. The loans officer may give you a loan application form to complete as shown in Sample 5.2. Many loan applications are rejected because the applicant did not provide all the necessary information.

At the preliminary meeting, the prospective lender may ask questions such as:

- How much money do you need?
- For how long do you need it?
- What do you plan to do with the money?
- How do you intend to repay the loan?
- What are the alternative sources of repayment if you have a problem?
- What types of security are you prepared to provide?

After the meeting, you should finalize your business plan and the financial plan. Set up another meeting with the lender. Present your business plan and financial proposal along with a one-page outline of the essence of your application for funds. (A sample Business Plan Format is provided in Sample 7.1.)

Give the lender a reasonable time to assess your proposal. Depending on the complexity of the proposal, it may need to be referred to another level within the bank.

Lender's Approval Criteria

Prospective lenders want to know as much as possible about you and your business before making a decision to provide you with financing. The lender will be looking at various criteria including character, capital, capacity, conditions and collateral. Risks and bank policy are also considered.

Character

The trustworthiness of a potential borrower will be considered. Your track record and integrity in terms of your business and financial history, such as personal credit history and management ability as demonstrated in your business plan, will weigh heavily in the lender's decision. Your level of commitment to the business, other than financial commitment, is another perception that will be considered.

Capital

This refers to the equity or financial investment that you are going to be putting in the business. Factors are taken into account such as the amount of investment, the quality of the assets that are purchased with your investment, the liquidity of the assets (ability to sell quickly for cash), and the overall liability of the firm. If you have a large financial investment in the business, this demonstrates to the lender a high degree of commitment on your part to ensure that the business succeeds. If you have very little invested, then in the eyes of the lender you could have very little to lose.

Capacity

This refers to the capacity of the business to pay back the loan. The lender, of course, wants to get paid from the cash flow and profits of the business, and not from having to sell the security that you have pledged. The lender is interested in your cash flow projections and the rationale for those projections.

Sample 5.2	**Business Loan Application**

(Format Commonly Requested by Lenders)

Please check:

❑ Proprietorship   ❑ Corporation   ❑ General Partnership
❑ Limited Partnership

Business Name: _____

Nature of Business: _____

Business Address: (Street, City, Postal Code)_____

_____

_____

Business Telephone (___)_____ Year Business established _____

How long under present ownership?____ Number of employees?_____

Amount of loan(s)   1. Please describe below how you plan
$ to use your business loan(s)

_____

_____

2. What will be your primary   3. What are your usual terms
    source repaying the loan(s)?   of sale you offer your
                                          customers?

4. What are the usual terms of   5. Do you wish this loan(s) to be
    sale offered by your major   insured? ❑ YES   ❑ NO
    suppliers?

6. Please describe any seasonality or business cycle requirements related to
    your business.

_____

_____

_____

Principal/Owners

Full Name and Address	% Ownership	Title/ Position
_____	_____	_____
_____	_____	_____
_____	_____	_____

Sample 5.2   Business Loan Application (cont'd)

Historical/Projected Summary

- Existing businesses please provide financial information for the last 3 fiscal years.
- New businesses please provide projected financial information.

Financial Statements Prepared by

❏ Self	❏ Self	❏ Self
❏ Accountant	❏ Accountant	❏ Accountant
❏ Other	❏ Other	❏ Other

Year Ending (Date)   _____   _____   _____

Sales	$_____	$_____	$_____
Gross Profit	$_____	$_____	$_____
Net Profit after Tax	$_____	$_____	$_____
Depreciation/Amortization	$_____	$_____	$_____
Current Assets	$_____	$_____	$_____
Total Assets	$_____	$_____	$_____
Current Liabilities	$_____	$_____	$_____
Total Liabilities	$_____	$_____	$_____
Business Net Worth	$_____	$_____	$_____

Credit Relationships

- Please provide details of your business credit relationships below.

Name of Creditor and Address	Purpose of Loan/ Credit	Original Amount/ Limit	Amount Presently Owing	Repay- ment Terms	Maturity Date If Any
_____	_____	$_____	$_____	_____	_____
_____	_____	$_____	$_____	_____	_____
_____	_____	$_____	$_____	_____	_____
_____	_____	$_____	$_____	_____	_____

Sample 5.2	**Business Loan Application** (cont'd)

Sundry Obligations

- Please provide details below if you answer YES to any of the following questions.

_____

Is the business providing support for obligations not listed on its financial statements? (i.e., co-signer, endorser, guarantor)
❏ YES   ❏ NO

If yes, please indicate total contingency liability $_____

_____

Is the business a party to any claim or lawsuit?   ❏ YES ❏ NO

Has your business ever sought legal protection from its creditors? (i.e., bankruptcy, receiver, receiver-manager)   ❏ YES ❏ NO

_____

Does the business owe any taxes for years prior to the current year? (i.e., sales tax, income tax, property tax, municipal business taxes or provincial corporation taxes) ❏ YES ❏ NO

Amount $_____   Owed to_____

Amount $_____   Owed to_____

Amount $_____   Owed to_____

_____

Details of any of the above

_____

_____

_____

Business References

- Trade creditor, personal, etc., in addition to those noted.

Name	Address	Business Phone

_____

_____

Banker _____

Accountant _____

Other _____

_____

_____

Sample 5.2	**Business Loan Application** (cont'd)

Insurance Coverage

- Existing businesses, please provide details of present coverage.
- New businesses, please state planned coverage.

Type of Coverage	Insurance Company	Amount of Coverage	Annual Premiums
_____	_____	$_____	$_____
_____	_____	$_____	$_____
_____	_____	$_____	$_____

The undersigned declare(s) that the statements made herein are for the purpose of obtaining business financing and are to the best of my/our knowledge true and correct. The applicant(s) consent(s) to the Bank making any inquiries it deems necessary to reach a decision on this application from a credit reporting agency or otherwise, and consent(s) to the disclosure at any time of any credit information about me/us to any credit reporting agency or to anyone with whom I/we have financial relations.

Per:_____   Per: _____

Signature_____   Signature _____

Date_____   Date _____

Title _____   Title _____

Conditions

The lender takes a look at the various economic conditions nationally and locally that are significant to your type of business. In addition, the trends in your industry are important factors. Banks compare your ratios with those of similar industries to see how realistic your projections are. In addition, banks monitor various types of industries that have a high failure or loan default rate.

Collateral

Banks will frequently ask the owners of a corporation to sign personal guarantees or request other forms of collateral.

Risk

The bank will look at the relative degree of risk involved in lending you money, and the return that they are going to get in exchange.

Bank Policy

The lender assesses your application within the overall context of the bank policy. For example, the bank might have a policy against lending any money to someone in a speculative real estate development business at a time when the economy is poor and there are numerous foreclosures. The bank may have a policy that there is a 4:1 security-to-loan ratio required for new start-up businesses. If you are able to provide security which is only three times the value of the loan, then you would not technically comply with the bank policy. The bank may have a policy that all directors of the company have to sign guarantees for the loan. If there are three directors and two of them are not prepared to sign personal guarantees, then the loan can be turned down for that reason alone.

Agreement on Terms and Conditions

During this phase of the loan-granting process, parties agree on the amount, type and structure of the loan, the interest rate that is to be paid for the loan, and the security that is being pledged for it.

There are various factors taken into account in determining the interest rate: the cost of funds (prime rate, money market conditions), administration costs, and the degree of risk involved.

Sufficient lead time must be allowed when making a loan application. Depending on the loan complexity, the length of the process may vary from one day to one month or more from the commence-ment of the preliminary meeting to the finalization of the loan approval.

Confirmation of Loan Agreement and Signing of Security Documents

This is the final phase of the loan-granting process. The lender may provide you with a bank loan confirmation letter setting out the terms and conditions or, if the amount is small, the bank may give you verbal approval. After the bank has accepted the loan applica-tion, the security documents will have to be signed before the funds are advanced to you. Make sure that you have spoken with your lawyer as well as your accountant before you agree to any final loan security documentation. Remember, you are trying to convince the lender of three important factors:

- that your loan application for funds is for a worthwhile purpose and those funds are sufficient to accomplish your business objectives
- that you have the credibility, integrity and commitment to make your business a viable one, and the management skills or access to those skills to make it profitable
- that the loan can be repaid out of the normal operational activities of the business on a realistic cash flow basis, and the bank will not have to realize on its security.

If you are applying for a Small Business Loan, the lender will still evaluate the loan in much the same way as any other loan, although a large percentage is guaranteed by the federal government. The lender will look at the capital, character and capabilities of the appli-cant, and try to assess the probability of success for the type of fran-chise in the proposed location. Its decision will ultimately be based on several factors including one or all of the following:

- ability to repay the loan
- the borrower's collateral
- a secondary source of repayment.

The lender may require collateral, such as a personal residence, in addition to the security of the leasehold improvements or equip-ment.

Types of Security Requested by a Lender

When providing financing to a small business, lenders require security to ensure that they are repaid. Often the value of the security is considerably more than the amount of the loan. If the lender has to "realize" on the security and convert it into money, only a portion of the value of the asset will be obtained after the sale. As well, costs of hiring a lawyer, accountant, receiver or trustee may be involved.

Going Concern Value

This is the most optimistic method, which is an estimate of the business based on its capitalized earnings. This method assumes that the selling price, sufficient to cover the loan, will be obtained if the business is sold as a going concern. This method gives no indication, of course, of the value of the assets if the business is not sold in this manner. Lenders would be interested in a going concern value if they have a debenture on the company.

En Bloc

This is an estimate of a price at which the assets could be sold, without removal or alteration, if the business ceased to operate. The en bloc value is based on the purchase of all the assets, not just some of the assets, and on using the same location for operation.

Current Liquidation Value

This is the most pessimistic method of evaluating the assets of the business. It is based on the estimate of what price the assets might be expected to realize in a forced sale or winding up of the business. Most lenders use this valuation in appraising the security for a loan, because they operate on the conservative premise that in a business problem situation, they cannot be assured of any higher value.

It is critical that you obtain advice from your lawyer and accountant regarding the implications of providing various types of security from legal, accounting and tax viewpoints. Whether you are negotiating with a bank or other lenders, it is important that you agree to a package which is acceptable to you in terms of your risk, personal exposure and leverage.

Comfort Letter from Franchisor

In order to approve the financing, the lender may request that the franchisor provide a comfort letter regarding the financing of the franchised business. Comfort letters take a few different forms depending on the requirements of the lender.

The lender will usually require the franchisor to agree to the following conditions in order to approve the loan:

- provide the lender with a copy of the executed franchise agreement and other documentation such as a lease agreement
- provide the lender with a copy of all financial statements, financial reports and other similar documents relating to the franchisee
- disclose to the lender any financial or credit information which may become known to them about the financial viability of the franchisee's business
- subordinate any security interest in the franchised business in favour of the lender and agree that any security interest that the lender may have in the franchisee's assets has priority
- not demand or commence any actions if any liabilities of the franchisee are guaranteed by the same person until all liabilities to the lender have been paid in full, and any payments received by the franchisor from the franchisee shall be held in trust for the lender
- acknowledge that the lender intends to take security for its loan by way of a security agreement, which may be secured by the franchisee's inventory, leasehold improvements, fixtures, equipment or other assets
- agree that in the event the bank takes possession of the franchisee's inventory, leasehold improvements, fixtures, equipment or other assets, the franchisor will purchase them from the bank within a specified time-frame and according to an agreed formula.

Not all franchisors will agree to providing this type of comfort letter. If the bank insists on such a letter and the franchisor is unwilling to provide it, the franchisee can either change banks or attempt to negotiate some form of compromise as to the terms and conditions of the comfort letter that would be agreeable to the franchisor and the lender.

RECAP

In this chapter we have investigated:

- financial needs when starting-up
- requirements for day-to-day running of the franchise
- plans for expansion
- the sources and methods of financing
- evaluating equity and debt financing
- the credit-granting process
- the security required by lenders

and included were samples of:

- Finance Sources Quick Check
- Loan Proposal Letter
- Loan Application.

....

CHAPTER 6

Which Legal Structure is Best for You?

A verbal contract isn't worth the paper it's written on.

Samuel Goldwyn

One of your first considerations when starting a franchise business is the form of legal structure you should choose. This will be necessary before you set up a company bank account, apply for a business licence, or register your company name. Your main legal choices are sole proprietorship, partnership or corporation. (A description of legal structures follows below, along with the advantages and disadvantages of each.) While a franchisor may provide some guidance, the franchisee is often left to his own devices. The business licence and company name are usually the responsibility of the franchisee.

The higher the potential risk, the greater the necessity for incorporation. About 50% of franchisees are incorporated. Potential risk exposure areas include debt, breach of contract, and liability for negligence. In any case, all shareholders would normally be required by the franchisor to personally guarantee the franchise and lease documents.

If you are involved in a partnership or shareholder situation, it is essential to have a well-constructed agreement in writing, and be sure to get competent legal assistance before signing any agreement.

TYPES OF LEGAL STRUCTURE

The type of legal structure you decide on for your business will depend upon the type of franchise operation, your potential risk and liability, and the amount of money you need to start and expect to earn. If your potential risk and liability are high, the incorporation process will provide protection from possible disasters. On the other hand, a person starting a franchise business with little or no risk should consider the advantages of having a sole proprietorship.

Once you become familiar with the differences between each form of legal structure, you should consult a lawyer and tax accountant. Your decision in this area is an important one.

Sole Proprietorship and Partnership

A sole proprietorship refers to an individual who owns a business in his/her personal name, or operates through a trade name. The business income and the owner's personal income are considered the same for tax purposes. Therefore, business profits are reported on the owner's personal income tax return, based on federal and provincial income tax schedules. Business expenses and losses are deductible. It is advisable, though, to keep personal and business bank accounts separate. For instance, you should pay yourself a salary from your business account and deposit it into your personal account for your personal needs (food, clothing, lodging, personal savings). A proprietor is personally responsible for all debts or liabilities of the business.

A partnership is a proprietorship with two or more owners. The owners may not necessarily be 50:50 partners; they may have whatever percentage properly reflects their investment and contribution to the partnership. Each partner shares profits and losses in proportion to their respective percentage interest. The partnership business itself does not pay any tax. Instead, the individual partners pay tax based on their portion of the net profit or loss, and this is shown on their personal tax return. In a partnership, each partner is personally liable for the full amount of the debts and liabilities of the business. Each individual is authorized to act on behalf of the company, and can bind the partnership legally, except if stated otherwise in a partnership agreement. It is sound business advice not to enter any partnership arrangement without a written agreement between the partners regarding responsibilities for financing the business, sharing the profits and losses, working in the business, specific duties, and other important considerations.

In a proprietorship or partnership, the company continues until the owner ceases to carry on the business or dies. If the business uses a name different from the owner's personal name, the company name (called a "trade style" name and is separate to any federal trade name registration by the franchisor) should be registered with the appropriate provincial registry. The Consumer and Corporate Affairs office of the provincial government will provide the necessary forms to be completed and, if you wish, a copy of the Partnership Act, which governs sole proprietorships and partnerships.

Advantages
- Few government and legal formalities make sole proprietorships and partnerships easy to form. In most provinces, there is a nominal one-time fee for registering the company.
- They are relatively easy to roll over into an incorporated company if necessary or desired at some later point.
- The personal tax rate is lower than the rate for corporations in certain situations. Therefore, during the early phases of the business, it may be more tax advantageous to remain a sole proprietorship or partnership. Once the business is earning substantial sums, the company could be rolled over into a corporation.
- Business losses can be offset against the owner's other income, thereby reducing the owner's overall personal marginal tax rate. There are some exceptions, and you should check with your accountant regarding current tax legislation.

Disadvantages
- The owner is personally liable for all debts and obligations of the business.
- It is frequently difficult to raise capital apart from conventional loans, because of the potential liability and risk.
- Customers and creditors may perceive the proprietorship as having a low level of business sophistication. It may be perceived to be in business for the short term rather than the long term.
- Some government loan, subsidy or guarantee programs are available only to limited companies (corporations).
- Sale of the business could involve having to disclose the

owner's personal tax return.
- If the business fails, the owners are not eligible to collect Unemployment Insurance benefits.

REAL LIFE: The Right Match can Spell Success

Sayeeda Saleswoman had worked in a Best Barter franchise for two years when an opportunity became available to purchase a Best Barter franchise in an adjoining area. Sayeeda did not have all of the required capital so she decided to look for an investor who could contribute the balance of the investment capital.

Sayeeda had discussions with several potential investors and was close to entering into an agreement with a passive investor when Alice Administrator approached Sayeeda and suggested that she would make a good partner. Alice was employed as the office manager in the same Best Barter franchise where Sayeeda worked. Alice explained to Sayeeda that she had received a small inheritance which, added to her personal savings, would provide the balance of the investment, plus their different skill sets would actually complement each other. Sayeeda could do what she did best—go outside of the office and sign up new clients—and Alice could stay in the office and make sure that everything ran smoothly. They discussed how each party would react in various situations that might occur in the running of the business and concluded that they had the potential to form a good working relationship.

After two years Sayeeda and Alice had the number one franchise in the system and were still good friends.

Corporation (Limited Company)

A corporation is a business which is a legal entity separate from the owner or owners of the business. It is a formal business structure which, after being incorporated with the provincial or federal registry, must file annual reports, submit regular tax returns, and pay tax on the profits of the business.

The owners of the business are called shareholders and have no personal liability for the company's debts, unless they have signed a personal guarantee. The liability of the company is limited to the assets of the company. The shareholders elect directors who are responsible for managing the business affairs of the corporation. Directors are usually shareholders. The profits of the corporation may be retained for reinvestment or distributed to the shareholders in the form of dividends at the discretion of the directors.

It is advisable to obtain legal and tax advice to assist with the preparation of the incorporation documents and shareholders' agreements.

Advantages

- The shareholders are not personally responsible for any of the debts or obligations of the corporation, unless a shareholder has signed a personal guarantee.
- A corporation has more financing options available to it, being eligible for government financing incentive programs that may be unavailable to unincorporated businesses. It can attract investors and provide better security to lenders in the form of debentures, common shares, convertible shares and other structures.
- The corporation continues regardless of whether a shareholder dies or retires.
- In general terms, a corporation can imply a higher prestige, more stability, and greater resources in terms of capital and expertise.
- There is increased stability in that shareholders can come and go, but the business continues uninterrupted and all contracts of the corporation remain valid.
- A corporation can convert itself to a public corporation by meeting the requirements of the Securities Commission and other government regulatory departments. It can thereby raise money on the stock exchange by going public.

The following factors can be advantageous in reducing or mini-mizing your personal or corporate tax:

- small business corporate tax rate
- deferring tax on business income
- capital gains exemption
- allowable business investment losses

- bonuses
- estate planning
- income splitting.

You should seek professional tax advice from your accountant that would be customized to your situation.

Disadvantages:

- Costs of incorporating are higher. Legal costs are approximately $300 to $500 plus the lawyer's out-of-pocket disbursements, which are approximately $300. This monetary outlay should be kept in perspective. It is simply another cost of doing business if the reasons for incorporating a business for tax or liability benefits are appropriate.
- The operating losses and tax credits remain within the corporate entity; they are not available to individual shareholders if the corporation is unable to utilize them.

RECAP

In this chapter we have looked at:

- the different types of legal structure
- the advantages and disadvantages of proprietorships
- the advantages and disadvantages of partnerships and limited companies.

CHAPTER 7

Business Planning

Long-range planning does not deal with future decisions,
but with the future of present decisions.

Peter F. Drucker

A business plan is a written summary of what you hope to accomplish by being in business, and how you intend to organize your resources to meet your goals. It is a roadmap of where you want to go in your business, the various routes you will take, stages along the way and, most importantly, where you will be when you have arrived at your destination. It helps eliminate the misunderstandings that can easily arise if you don't put your thoughts and research in writing.

The plan accomplishes a number of things:

- It outlines your organizational and management skills.
- It provides the basis for determining what further information you require.
- It details the availability and use of funds, and management and employee personnel requirements.
- It details the products or services, marketing strategy, production techniques (if a manufacturing company), research and development program, expansion or diversification program, as well as many other goals and objectives.
- It highlights the past, present and future of the business.

The franchisor may prepare a business plan for you, provide you with information for your business plan, or simply require you to complete your own business plan which may require his or her approval. Regardless of the level of assistance and input provided by the franchisor, it is essential that you prepare a business plan. A comprehensive plan is shown in Sample 7.1.

WHY PREPARE A BUSINESS PLAN?

A business plan is one of the most effective management tools available. It can help you focus in a logical and organized manner on the future growth of your company. It helps you anticipate and meet the inevitable changes of the future in a pragmatic fashion. From the business plan you have a device for helping you control the business, allowing you to monitor and assess the progress of your objectives.

A well-prepared business plan provides the following benefits:

- It helps you identify your customers, your market area, your pricing strategy, and the competitive conditions under which you must operate to succeed. This process alone may lead you to discover a competitive advantage or new opportunity as well as deficiencies in your plan.
- It helps to set the guidelines such as the break-even point in profitability and cash flow, and the anticipated return on your investment (ROI).
- It encourages realism instead of over-optimism. When you have to put pen to paper to assess and quantify the various financial and logistic needs of your company, you have a much clearer picture of the next steps to take.
- By committing your plans to paper, your overall ability to manage the business will improve. You will be able to concentrate your efforts on the alterations from the plan before conditions become critical. It helps you look forward to and avoid problems by anticipating them in advance.
- It exposes you to the methods and merits of the planning, budgeting, forecasting and reporting process that is so essential.
- It provides a budget that will help the lender or investor make an early assessment of your business feasibility and viability.
- It establishes the amount of financing for outside investment required, and when it is needed. It helps reduce the time that it takes for a prospective lender or investor to assess and accept or reject your proposal.
- It creates an important first impression to a lender or investor or potential partner in assessing you as a competent business manager.
- It identifies the number of employees needed, when they are

needed, the skills they must have, and the salary or wage they must be paid.

- It helps establish the size and location of plants and facilities for office space. It may show that you could do well with a "packaged office" service, or possibly operate out of your home with a telephone answering service.
- It helps identify the factors critical to the success of your business concept.
- It provides you with the opportunity on a dry-run basis to "operate" your business without financial outlay or risk.

Thoroughly planning your business is essential for your success. Besides the detailed business plan, other factors that have to be taken into account include your personal goals, your business goals, and your financial projections. A potential lender will want to review your business plan before approving financing. Part of planning is also being able to measure the results to ensure that your business plan is on target and accurate. You will, therefore, continue to use your plan to chart the progress and success of your business.

From the point of deciding to go in business, you have started your business plan. You probably already have a fair idea of the overall concept of the operation, the products you will sell, where you will locate the business, and an approximate time-frame for start-up. Your mind will be overflowing with thoughts of how to set your pricing, how much money you will need, and how long it will take to build your customer base. It is at this stage that you need to start mapping these thoughts on paper.

A business plan that is well-researched and documented will largely reduce the risk of going into business. Many people do not venture out on their own because they become overwhelmed with the "what if" syndrome. A comprehensive business plan will enable you to anticipate "what if" problems and develop strategies to overcome them months before you start your business. This enables you to walk through each stage of your business plan on paper, and make many of your crucial decisions before you have invested any money. It will also be required for lenders or investors.

Perhaps after working through your plan, you may come to the realization that there is little profit in the venture, or that it will require a large amount of start-up capital that you may be unable to raise, or that you will be tied to the business with little free time for

Sample 7.1	**Business Plan Format**

Note: Modify as appropriate for your needs. Not all sections will be necessarily applicable to you at this time or at all.

Introductory Page

- Company name: include address and phone number
- Contact person: presenter's name and phone number
- Paragraph about the company describing the nature of the business and market area
- Securities offered to investors (if applicable): preferred shares, common shares, debentures, etc.
- Business loans sought (if applicable): term loan, operating line of credit

Summary

- Highlights of Business Plan: your project, competitive advantage, and "bottom line" in a nutshell—preferably one page maximum in length

Table of Contents

- Section titles and page numbers (for easy reference)

PART I: BUSINESS CONCEPT

Description of the Industry

- Industry outlook and growth potential: industry trends, new products and developments. State your sources of information
- Markets and customers: size of total market, new requirements and market trends
- Competitive companies: market share, strengths and weaknesses, profitability
- National and economic trends: population shifts, consumer trends, relevant economic indicators

Description of Business Venture

- Product(s) or service: pictures, drawings, characteristics, quality

Sample 7.1	**Business Plan Format** (cont'd)

- Product protection/exclusive rights: patents, copyrights, trademarks, industrial design, franchise rights
- Target market: typical customers identified by group; present buying pattern and average purchase in dollars; wants and needs
- Competitive advantage of your business concept: your market niche, uniqueness, estimated market share
- Business location and size: location(s) relative to market, size of premises
- Staff and equipment needed: overall requirement, capacity
- Brief history: principals involved, development work done

Business Goals

- One year: specific goals, such as gross sales, profit margins, share of market; moving out of home and opening a new store, plant or office; introducing new product, etc.
- Over the longer term: return on investment, business net worth, sale of business

Marketing Plan

- Sales strategy: commissioned sales staff, agents, pieceworkers, independent contractors, sales objectives, target customers, sales tools, sales support
- Distribution: direct to public, wholesale, retail, multiple outlets
- Pricing: costings, markups, margins, break-even
- Promotion: media advertising, promotions, publicity—appropriate to reach target market
- Guarantees: product guarantees, service warranties
- Tracking methods: method for confirming who your customers are and how they heard about you

Sales Forecast

- Assumptions: one never has all the necessary information, so state all the assumptions made in developing the forecast
- Monthly forecast for coming year: sales volume in units and dollars

Sample 7.1   Business Plan Format (cont'd)

Note: The sales forecast is the starting point for your project income statement and cash flow forecast in Part II.

- Annual forecast for following two to four years: sales volume in dollars

Production Plan (Manufacturing)

- Brief description of production process (do not be too technical)
- Physical plant requirements: building, utility requirements, expansion capacity, layout
- Machinery and equipment: new or used, lease or purchase, capacity
- Raw materials: how readily available, quality, sources
- Inventory requirements: seasonal levels, turnover rates, methods of control
- Suppliers: volume discounts, multiple sources
- Personnel required: full-time, part-time, skill level, availability, training required
- Cost of facilities, equipment, and materials: estimates and quotations
- Capital estimates: one-time start-up or expansion capital required

Production Plan (Retail or Service)

- Purchasing plans: volume discounts, multiple sources, quality, price
- Inventory system: seasonal variation, turnover rates, method of control
- Space requirements: floor and office space, improvement required, expansion capability
- Staff and equipment required: personnel by skill level, fixtures, office equipment

Corporate Structure

- Legal form: proprietorship, partnership, corporation
- Share distribution: list of principal shareholders

Sample 7.1	**Business Plan Format** (cont'd)

- List of contracts and agreements in force: management contract, shareholder or partnership agreement, franchisor service agreement, service contract
- Directors and officers: names and addresses and role in company
- Background of key management personnel: brief résumés of active owners and key employees
- Professional/consultants under contract: possible outside assistance in specialized or deficient areas
- Duties and responsibilities of key personnel: brief job descriptions—who is responsible for what

Risk Assessment

- Competitor's reaction: will competitors try to squeeze you out
- "What if list" for critical external factors: anticipated effects of strikes, recession, new technology, weather, new competition, supplier problems, shifts in consumer demand
- "What if list" for critical internal factors: effects if sales off by 30%, sales double, key manager quits, workers quit
- Dealing with risks: contingency plans to handle the most significant risks

Action Plan

- Steps to accomplish this year's goals: flow chart by month or by quarter of specific action to be taken and by whom
- Checkpoints for measuring results: identify significant dates, sales levels, production levels as decision points

PART II: FINANCIAL PLAN

Financial Statements

- Previous years' balance sheets and income statements: include past two or three years if applicable

Financial Forecasts

- Opening balance sheet: for a new business only

| Sample 7.1 | Business Plan Format (cont'd) |

- Projected income statements: detailed operating forecast for next year of operation and less detailed forecast for following two years. Use sales forecast as starting point
- Cash flow forecast: budget of cash inflow and outflow on a monthly basis for next year of operation

Financing and Capitalization

- Applying for a term loan: amount, terms, when required
- Purpose of term loan: attach detailed description of assets to be financed with cost quotations
- Owner's equity: your level of commitment to the financing needed
- Summary of term loan requirements for a particular project or for a business as a whole

Example

If the purpose of the Business Plan is to attract a new investor, further details would be given here concerning share participation, role in company, etc.

Operating Loan

- Line of credit applied for: new or increase, security offered
- Maximum operating cash requirement: amount, timing. (Refer to cash flow forecast)

Present Financing (if applicable)

- Term loans outstanding: balance owing, repayment terms, purpose, security held
- Current operating line of credit: amount, security held

References

- Name of present lending institution: branch, type of accounts
- Lawyer's name: include address and telephone and fax numbers
- Accountant's name: include address and telephone and fax numbers

Appendix

The following documents *may* be requested by your banker or potential investor:

Sample 7.1	**Business Plan Format** (cont'd)

- Personal net worth statement: include personal property values, investments, cash, bank loans, charge accounts, mortgages and other liabilities. This will substantiate the value of your personal guarantee if required for security
- Letters of intent: potential orders, customer commitments, letters of support
- List of inventory: type, age, value
- List of household improvements: description, when made
- List of fixed assets: description, age, serial numbers
- Price lists to support cost estimates
- Description of insurance coverage: insurance policies, amount of coverage
- Accounts receivable summary: include aging schedule
- Accounts payable summary: include schedule of payments
- Copies of legal agreements: contracts, lease, franchise agreement, mortgage, debenture
- Appraisals: property, equipment
- Financial statements for associated companies: where appropriate

FINALLY...

Preparing a business plan requires much thought and will generate a lot of paper! Keep in mind, however, that the final document is a summary of your planning process. You can always refer to your working papers later on to substantiate a particular point.

Have your key employees and two or three impartial outsiders review the furnished plan in detail. There may be something you have overlooked or underemphasized. Also, a critical review will be good preparation for your presentation to potential investors and lenders.

Approaching Lenders

When approaching any financial institution, you are effectively selling the merits of your business proposal. As in all sales, consider the needs of the other party:

Sample 7.1	Business Plan Format (cont'd)

- Ability to serve the debt with sufficient surplus to cover contigencies (i.e., carry interest charges, eventually repay in full). Cash flow forecast and projected income statement will show this
- Track record/integrity (i.e., personal credit history, management ability as demonstrated in your business plan, company results)
- Your level of commitment (i.e., your equity in business or cash investment in the particular asset being purchased)
- Secondary source of repayment (includes security in the event of default and other sources of income). Discuss this subject with your lawyer before submitting your proposal
- Lead time. Lender needs a reasonable time to assess your proposal; also, the loan may have to be referred to another level within the financial institution
- Don't overdo it. Be sensible with the amount of documentation you provide initially; for example, the Introductory Page, Summary, and Financial Plan sections alone provide a good basic loan submission if the amount requested is small

Attracting Investors

Start first by approaching people you know (i.e., friends; bank, credit union, or trust company manager; lawyer; accountant; doctor). They, in turn, may know of possible investors. If your business concept exhibits high growth potential, a second alternative is to approach a venture capital company. Either way, take a moment to consider the investor's needs, which may differ from a lender's needs:

- Your level of commitment: to be sure that you are sharing the risk
- Share participation: investors may demand more equity than you are willing to give
- Rate of return: investors are willing to take a high risk, but they also expect a high rate of return (e.g., to double their money in two or three years)
- Involvement in key decisions: possibly as a director or even an officer of the company
- Regular financial reporting: investors usually want to see tight financial controls in place and prompt financial reporting

yourself and your family. If this is the case, you may decide either to modify your business concept to build in these missing factors, operate the business on a part-time basis (if the franchise agreement provides that you do not have to be a full-time operator) or cancel your plan altogether. If the risk is too great, then your best business decision may be not to start the business.

Your goals, if not clear in your mind before you start your plan, will become more obvious as you go through the planning stages. Your personal as well as business goals will need to be considered thoroughly and discussed with your support network. Your network may include your spouse, children, parents, business associates, lawyer, accountant, friends or relatives—those people who may be directly affected by your decision to go into business and whom you trust to give you honest, candid feedback and assist you in realizing your goals.

DETERMINING YOUR GOALS

In *Alice's Adventures in Wonderland*, Alice has several roads to choose from and is having a difficult time deciding which way to go when she meets the Cheshire Cat.

"Would you tell me, please, which way I ought to walk from here?" she asks.

"That depends a good deal on where you want to get to," says the Cat.

"I don't care where—" responds Alice.

"Then, it doesn't matter which way you walk," grins the Cheshire Cat.

A common denominator among successful people is that they have learned to set goals for themselves and they are focused on and committed to reaching their goals. The reason that most people fail is not that they don't work hard—it's just that they are usually working hard at the wrong things. If you don't know where you're going, you might end up somewhere else and you won't know when you get there.

Before working on a plan for your business, it is important to establish your personal goals. These will largely dictate the type of business that you go into, whether it is a part-time or full-time business, whether you work out of your home or an office, or whether you travel a lot or stay in one location.

When you are considering your personal goals, it is important to know your present financial net worth. For an example of a personal net worth statement, see the Franchise Application Report at Sample 3.1. The Personal Cost-of-Living Budget form will be useful in determining your existing as well as future financial needs. Do you have sufficient financial resources to support yourself and your family during the initial stage of your business? (Sample 7.2 provides a format for calculating your needs.) Do you have available funds to inject into your business during the start-up phase? The solo family wage-earner may be faced with the additional stress of unmet family expectations, in terms of time spent away from home. Such factors should be discussed openly beforehand.

Other goals you may consider include minimizing taxes, having a home, and providing security for your dependants. Quality-of-life goals include your recreational activities, trips and vacations, challenge and fulfillment, and time spent with your family. Your personal goals may change from time to time throughout your life, and your business goals will have to be modified accordingly, based on changing circumstances.

An honest personal assessment of your skills, qualities, personality style, strengths and weaknesses, and likes and dislikes will help you further refine the type of business suited to your needs. For example, a person who enjoys meeting people and has natural sales ability can become easily frustrated and discouraged if most of his or her time is spent behind the scenes and processing paperwork. You may recognize certain weaknesses that you have and make a conscious decision on how to deal with them. For instance, if careful record-keeping is an area you tend to neglect, the decision to hire a bookkeeper can alleviate possible frustrations, problems and stress.

Reviewing your personal goals and reasons for going into business will help you clarify specific goals for your business that parallel your personal needs. For example, if one of your reasons for choosing the entrepreneurial route was to make more money, then this will have a bearing on the type of franchised business you go into. You may decide to start the franchise and build it to its optimum level of activity and then sell it for a profit while it's at its peak. On the other hand, if you are motivated by the idea of being your own boss, then this short-term goal of selling the franchise business would not necessarily meet that personal need.

Sample 7.2	Personal Cost-Of-Living Budget

A. Income (average monthly income, actual or estimated)

Salary, bonuses, commissions, dividends $_____ $_____

Interest income $_____ $_____

Other:_____ $_____

Total Monthly Income   (A) $_____

B. Expenses (average monthly, actual or estimated)

1. Regular Monthly Payments

Rent or mortgage payments $_____

Automobile loan $_____

Personal loan $_____

Credit card payments $_____

Insurance premiums (medical, life,
    house, auto) $_____

Investment plan deductions (RRSP, etc.) $_____

Other:_____ $_____

Total Regular Monthly Payments $_____

2. Household Operating Expenses

Telephone $_____

Heat, gas and electricity $_____

Water and garbage $_____

Repairs and maintenance $_____

Other:_____ $_____

Total Household Operating Expenses $_____

3. Personal Expenses

Clothing, cleaning, laundry $_____

Food (at home, away from home) $_____

Medical/dental $_____

Day care $_____

Sample 7.2	Personal Cost-Of-Living Budget (cont'd)

Education $_____

Gifts, donations and dues $_____

Recreation and travel $_____

Newspapers, magazines, books $_____

Automobile maintenance, gas and parking $_____

Spending money, allowances $_____

Other:_____ $_____

Total Personal Expenses $_____

4. Tax Expenses

Federal and provincial income taxes $_____

Home property taxes $_____

Other:_____ $_____

Total Tax Expenses $_____

Total Monthly Expenses   (B) $_____

TOTAL MONTHLY DISPOSABLE INCOME
 AVAILABLE $_____

(Subtract total monthly expenses from   (A–B)
total monthly income)

Sample 7.3	Projected Financial Needs for the First Three Months

This worksheet will help you to estimate the amount of money you will need for the first three months of business operation. Note: This worksheet relates to your business expenses only. You will have to also calculate your personal cost-of-living expenses on a separate sheet, making certain not to duplicate income or expense items.

Cash Available

Owner's cash on hand $_____

Loan from relative or friend   _____

Other:_____   _____

Total Cash on Hand $_____

Start-up Costs

Repairs, renovations and decorating $_____

Equipment (including installation costs)   _____

Furniture   _____

Insurance (homeowners' rider, personal
   and product liability)   _____

Inventory   _____

Product materials and office supplies   _____

Advertising and promotion (Yellow Pages,   _____
   business cards, stationery, flyers,
   newspaper ads, etc.)   _____

Other:_____   _____

Total Start-up Costs $_____

Operating Costs

Wages of owner $3 \times \$_____ = $ $_____

Utilities $3 \times \$_____ = $ _____

Supplies and inventory $3 \times \$_____ = $ _____

Advertising $3 \times \$_____ = $ _____

Auto and travel $3 \times \$_____ = $ _____

Contingency $3 \times \$_____ = $ _____

Total Operating Costs $_____

Total Start-up and Three-Month
  Operating Costs   _____

TOTAL MONEY NEEDED FOR FIRST THREE
  MONTHS OF BUSINESS (APPROXIMATION) $_____

When identifying your goals, you should be specific regarding the outcome, so that your degree of success can be measured. For instance, "making more money" should be rewritten to read "making at least $30,000 by the second year of operation, and $60,000 by the fourth year." It is important to do extensive research so that you can realistically project your goals, taking into account factors such as competition, suppliers, financing, personal resources and personal commitment. Your goals should include short-term (first year) and long-term (years two to five) objectives.

In reviewing your personal and business goals along with your personal profile of skills and attributes, you should be able to objectively assess if you are suited to the franchise business you have chosen, and if it will meet your needs.

REAL LIFE: Plan and Leave Your Options Open

Mario Manystores wanted to go into business for himself and felt that buying a franchise offered him the greatest chance of success. However, he still had two areas of concern: the type of franchised business he was able to afford could not provide the level of income he desired, and having been employed as an area manager the thought of being restricted to working in one store did not appeal to him. Mario decided that he should seek a franchise that allowed him to add additional franchises as his business developed. Conversely, if he discovered that he did not like the specific line of business he could sell his single unit franchise and try something different.

He entered into a multi-unit franchise agreement with EyeCanSeeYou optical stores to open one franchise in a local mall and have the option to open up to five more units within a specific time-frame. Mario was very successful in running his first franchise and over a period of five years was able to open four more stores. This provided him with job satisfaction and ultimately provided the level of income he desired.

HOW TO PREPARE AN EFFECTIVE BUSINESS PLAN

Not all business plans are alike, although they have many features in common. The content of your plan will vary depending on whether you have a service, retail, manufacturing, wholesale, high tech, or research and development firm. A typical business plan outline is provided at Sample 7.1.

Other business plans covering various industry sectors are available from provincial small business ministries, banks and major accounting firms. You may wish to obtain free copies of the material available and decide which format is appropriate for your needs.

The business plan should be word-processed, well-spaced and well-organized with a table of contents. As you can see from the sample plan, it should have a summary that outlines your goals concisely so that a potential investor, partner or lender may have a capsule overview. This overview tends to be one to three pages in length, and hopefully convinces the reader to continue reviewing your plan. Although the brief summary occurs first, it should be the last part you write. The rest of the business plan covers such subjects as:

- market analysis and strategy
- products or services
- fixed assets—land, building, equipment
- staff and product operations management
- financial data
- risks and opportunities.

Government Regulations

There are certain government regulations and licences you will have to apply for, depending on the type of business you have chosen. Part of your planning process should include checking with the various municipal, provincial and federal governments to become aware of the regulations that may affect your business. Some may be identified by the franchisor, but knowing the regulations is the responsibility of the franchisee as many are local or regional in nature.

Preparing Financial Projections

An integral part of your business plan is the preparation of financial projections. This is a critical component for a realistic assessment of the viability of your business. If you have received financial projections from the franchisor you may wish to rely on those, modify them or start from scratch so that nothing is left to chance. The projections, of course, will be based on various uncertain factors. You must identify your assumptions about the financial and operating characteristics of your business start-up. You must develop sales and budget projections. Then you must assemble these into an income projection (profit-and-loss statement projection). This information must then be translated into a cash flow projection. A cash flow projection is an analysis of when you expect the money to flow in and out of the business on a monthly basis. You need to know when you will be receiving money, how and when you will be able to make necessary payments to the landlord, suppliers and staff. For instance, if you bill regular customers on the last day of the month and 80% of your customers pay within 15 days of receiving their invoices, then you can expect to have a good cash flow around the 20th day of the following month. If, however, your bank-loan payment comes due on the 15th of every month, then you may decide to close off sales a week before the actual month-end to accelerate the process by one week in order to meet your major financial commitment. In many cases lenders rely very heavily on the capacity of your cash flow to service the debt rather than on the equity base that you might have or collateral security that you may be prepared to give. See the cash flow projection in Sample 7.4 with an explanation of the component parts. You should work out your cash flow for the first 12 months of the business.

After completing your cash flow projections, you must check your results by projecting your balance sheet. And finally, you have to do a thorough ratio analysis to compare your company's projected performance with that of similar companies.

As you go through the preceding steps, you will begin to see how decisions on such factors as advertising, marketing, production, distribution and financing will have an effect on the viability, profitability and liquidity of your company. You can readily see how important it is that you do a dry run on paper of all aspects of your business operation before committing yourself to the time, expense and risk of a business venture.

Sample 7.4   Cash Flow Projection

Month #	1	2	3	4
Cash Receipts (Cash In)				
1. Cash sales	$_____	$_____	$_____	$_____
2. Collection from accounts receivable (credit sales payments)	$_____	$_____	$_____	$_____
3. Term loan proceeds	$_____	$_____	$_____	$_____
4. Sale of fixed assets	$_____	$_____	$_____	$_____
5. Other cash received	$_____	$_____	$_____	$_____
6. **Total Cash In**	$_____	$_____	$_____	$_____
Cash Disbursements (Cash Out)				
7. Rent (for premises, equipment, etc.)	$_____	$_____	$_____	$_____
8. Management salaries	$_____	$_____	$_____	$_____
9. Other salaries and wages	$_____	$_____	$_____	$_____
10. Legal and accounting fees	$_____	$_____	$_____	$_____
11. Utilities (heat, light and water)	$_____	$_____	$_____	$_____
12. Telephone	$_____	$_____	$_____	$_____
13. Repairs and maintenance	$_____	$_____	$_____	$_____
14. Licences and municipal taxes	$_____	$_____	$_____	$_____
15. Insurance	$_____	$_____	$_____	$_____
16. Other operating expenses	$_____	$_____	$_____	$_____
17. Payments on purchase of fixed assets	$_____	$_____	$_____	$_____
18. Interest paid on loans (short-term loans, lines of credit, overdrafts)	$_____	$_____	$_____	$_____

Sample 7.4	Cash Flow Projection (cont'd)

19. Payments on mortgages/term loans	$_____	$_____	$_____	$_____
20. Income tax payments	$_____	$_____	$_____	$_____
21. Cash dividends paid	$_____	$_____	$_____	$_____
22. Payments on accounts payable/inventories	$_____	$_____	$_____	$_____
23. Other cash expenses	$_____	$_____	$_____	$_____
24. **Total Cash Out**	$_____	$_____	$_____	$_____

Reconciliation of Cash Flow

25. Opening cash balance	$_____	$_____	$_____	$_____
26. Add: Cash In (line 6)	$_____	$_____	$_____	$_____
27. Deduct: Cash Out (line 24)	$_____	$_____	$_____	$_____
28. Surplus or (deficit)	$_____	$_____	$_____	$_____
29. **Closing cash balance**	$_____	$_____	$_____	$_____

EXPLANATION

Lines 1, 2, and 22 of the cash flow can be completed after doing the exercises shown in examples 24A and 24B that follow (Projected Cash Sales and Accounts Receivable plus Projected Accounts Payable), and their total should be inserted on the worksheet.

Line 3   **Loans** If you take possession of borrowed money during the month, list this cash receipt.

Line 4   **Sale of fixed assets** If you sell a fixed asset such as a piece of office furniture or a vehicle, list the cash income in the monthly column when payment is received.

Line 5   **Other cash** List all other cash income such as interest, rent, shareholders' loans, etc.

Line 6   Total of lines 1-5.

Lines 7-16 **Operating expenses** Enter the amount of cheques that you write for your monthly expenses. This is actual cash outlay for the month; for example, if you write a cheque in January for the full year's insurance, the amount of the cheque would be put in the January column and nothing would be entered for the rest of the year.

        Other operating expenses The expense items listed in the format may not be applicable to your business. The headings should be changed so that they are applicable to your situation.

Sample 7.4	**Cash Flow Projection** (cont'd)

Line 17 **Payments on purchase of a fixed asset** If money is spent for the purchase of fixed assets such as a vehicle or a filing cabinet, list the amount for the month when the cheque is written.

Line 18 **Interest paid on loans** This is the interest paid monthly on short-term loans such as bank overdrafts or lines of credit. Since you are in the process of working out the amount of money you will need to borrow, this interest figure may be very difficult to estimate. Consequently, you may decide to leave the line blank for now. If it is likely to be a small amount, you may decide to omit it altogether.

Line 19 **Payments on mortgage/loans** Indicate the monthly payment for the principal and interest on long-term loans. For example, if you borrow $20,000 to purchase a half-ton truck and monthly payments are $550 with the first payment due in March, then $550 will be entered in line 19 for each month beginning in March.

Lines 20-21 Income tax payments and cash dividends paid The amounts you expect to pay, if any.

Line 23 **Other cash expenses** The expense items listed in the format may not be applicable to your business. The headings should be changed so that they are appropriate for your situation.

Line 24 **Total cash out** Total all possible cash payments for the month.

Line 25 **Opening cash balance** The amount of money with which you started the month.

Line 28 **Surplus or deficit for the month—cash in minus cash out** If line 28 is a deficit, the operating bank loan should be increased to cover the deficit. Sometimes a bank will require a minimum balance to remain in the account at all times. If line 28 is a surplus, excess funds should be applied on the operating loan.

Line 29 **Closing cash balance** The amount of money you started out with plus (or minus) the amount of cash surplus at month's end. The closing cash balance becomes next month's operating cash balance.

Example 24A

PROJECTED CASH SALES AND ACCOUNTS RECEIVABLE

Month #	1	2	3	4
Projected sales	$_____	$_____	$_____	$_____
Cash sales (line 1)	$_____	$_____	$_____	$_____
Collection of previous month's sales	$_____	$_____	$_____	$_____

Sample 7.4	Cash Flow Projection (cont'd)

Collection of sales from
   two months previous $_____ $_____ $_____ $_____

Collection of sales from
   more than two months
   previous $_____ $_____ $_____ $_____

Collection from accounts
   receivable (line 2) $_____ $_____ $_____ $_____

Example 24B
PROJECTED ACCOUNTS PAYABLE

Month#	1	2	3	4
Planned purchases	$_____	$_____	$_____	$_____
Payments on current month's purchases	$_____	$_____	$_____	$_____
Payments on purchases from two months previous	$_____	$_____	$_____	$_____
Payments on purchases from more than two months previous	$_____	$_____	$_____	$_____
Payments on accounts payable (line 22)	$_____	$_____	$_____	$_____

RECAP

In this chapter we have looked at:

- the reasons for a business plan
- the care and thought needed to prepare a plan
- your financial requirements during the start-up period
- the elements of a well-prepared plan

and included were samples of:

- the Business Plan
- a Personal Budget
- Financial Needs for the First Three Months
- Cash Flow Projection.

Buying an Existing Franchise

If there were dreams to sell...what would you buy?

George Herbert

As an alternative to buying a brand-new franchise, you may consider purchasing one that is fully operational. Existing franchisees need to sell their businesses for a variety of reasons, which creates opportunities for buyers to take over established and profitable franchises.

In buying an existing franchised business you are actually doing two things simultaneously: (1) buying an operating business from the vendor, and (2) buying a franchise from the franchisor. Much of the due diligence process will remain the same as when buying a new franchise, but there should be much more information regarding the track record of the franchisee. Assuming that the franchise business is operating successfully, some of the risks associated with a start-up franchise will be eliminated, as a customer base and cash flow will already be established. You will be required to meet the selection criteria of the franchisor in the same way as if you were buying a new franchise.

The vendor may be the actual operator of the franchise, or alternatively it may be the franchisor who is selling either a company-owned location (branchising), or a previously franchised unit that has been repurchased or terminated. The first thing to determine is why the vendors are selling, if they are permitted to sell or assign the franchise, and what are the franchisor's terms and conditions regarding an assignment of the franchise. The franchisor may require that you assume the remaining term of the franchise agreement or execute a new franchise agreement which may reflect different terms and conditions to the original agreement. It is important to find out if you will be required to make any upgrades or alterations to the premises, uniforms, signage, vehicles, etc. to conform with the franchisor's current image or colour schemes, as these could prove to be very substantial expenses.

There may be an opportunity for you to acquire a resale unit that has not been operating to its full potential, and with a few changes and some effort, turn it into a profitable business. If it has been operating below standard, then you must ascertain how much, if any, damage has been done in the marketplace and whether or not it is irreparable. If the unit has a good track record, you should expect to pay something for goodwill over and above the cost of the initial franchise fee originally paid by the vendor. Conversely, if the unit has been performing unprofitably, the value may be discounted.

Buying any small business is a complicated and potentially risky transaction, and buying a franchised business is no different in this respect. You have to assess carefully the advantages and disadvantages of buying an existing franchise by determining the type and size of franchised business you prefer, searching for available opportunities, evaluating the business, negotiating the purchase price, and then signing all of the necessary legal documents. It is essential that you have the counsel and advice of a lawyer and an accountant to protect your interests, especially before you sign an offer.

ADVANTAGES AND DISADVANTAGES OF BUYING AN EXISTING FRANCHISE

Whether the advantages of buying an existing franchise outweigh the disadvantages depends in part on your financial situation, your business knowledge and experience. Following are some of the advantages and disadvantages of buying an existing franchise.

Advantages

- It is a faster way of getting into business without the cost, energy, time and risk involved in starting up a new franchise.
- You can examine the track record of the business and analyze the financial statements showing its revenue, expenses and cash flow. In this way you can determine whether the profits are increasing or decreasing, and whether it's a viable business opportunity.

- It is easier to project the potential of the business in terms of revenue and profit, thereby minimizing the uncertainty and risk that would be involved in starting from scratch.

- After you have negotiated a purchase price, you know the fixed amount you are dealing with. You also know the state of the business in terms of its income and cash flow and its potential for growth based on its history and other factors. (When starting a business from scratch, you would have no idea of how much money you might have to expend to bring the business up to the same financial state and potential as the one that you are buying.)

- You may obtain a return on your investment much sooner than if you start from scratch.

- A franchise that is performing below established levels of the franchise system may be purchased at a low price and then turned around under good management to result in attractive profits. The reason for the weak performance may vary from a partnership split, poor health or marital problems, to burnout or unskilled management. If you have the skill to be able to take over such a situation, this could be a viable option.

- You may be able to obtain financing more easily because the lender can assess the history of the franchise in terms of its financial statements and proven sales rather than optimistic projections.

- It could be easier to obtain supplier financing because suppliers who have dealt with the franchise in the past are familiar with its potential and viability. A trade creditor would therefore be more likely to extend a larger amount of credit and more favourable terms than if you started from scratch without any track record.

- A buyer might be able to purchase leasehold improvements which are already in place, at a considerable savings compared to what it would have cost to have put them in the business in the first place.

- Trained personnel who were directly responsible for the success of the franchise may stay with the new owner.

- An existing franchise might have an excellent location with high-traffic volume, public familiarity and acceptance. It could take a considerable time for somebody starting from scratch either to find a similar location or reach the same point in terms of sales volume, reputation and customer loyalty.

Disadvantages

- The existing location of the business may not be as attractive as it was originally. This may be due to changing traffic flow, nearby competition, declining population base, and other factors.
- You could be locked into the present physical layout and location of the franchise because the lease comes as part of the purchase price. This could present problems if you want to expand at some future point but still have a long-term lease, or if you want to make alterations to the premises but it is not financially feasible.
- The franchise location that you are buying, or a lease that you are assuming, could be an older building that could cost you more money in heating, maintenance or improvements than you are prepared or able to pay.
- You may be required to pay for a goodwill factor which you otherwise would not have to pay if you started your own franchise from scratch. The present owner's goodwill (the value that is placed on the present established customer base, business reputation, the initial franchise fee and net profit) may be difficult to assess in a manner which is acceptable to both sides.
- The seller may have had a poor credit and collection system, of which the customers took advantage. It could take some considerable adjustment to retrain the customers into a more responsible approach. Customers may be lost in the process.
- Some of the equipment might be obsolete or defective and therefore require early repair or replacement.
- The previous owner's employees may not be suitable for the type of business operation you intend to run. They may be accustomed to sloppy procedures or lack of systems, and could resent your desire to operate a "tight ship." Employees might quit quickly if they do not like your style as a new owner, and this could create difficulties or delay in getting replacement employees and training them promptly.
- If the business you are considering has customer ill-will for any reason, you will inherit that problem, which could impair your business growth and investment.
- You could buy a franchise which has inherently serious problems that you might not be aware of prior to the purchase. (Again, due diligence is very important.)
- Some agreements, such as the franchise agreement or the lease of

the premises, may be assigned to a purchaser which means that the purchaser only has the benefit of any remaining term under that agreement. In the case of a lease, this could translate into an increase in rent in the near future.

REAL LIFE: Check Out the Reasons for Poor Performance

Debby Dobetter was interested in buying a franchise to operate a small restaurant when she saw an advertisement in her local newspaper to purchase an existing Ms. Monicka's Restaurant. The asking price for the business was about 60% of the cost of purchasing a Ms. Monicka's franchise and setting up a new restaurant.

Debby met with the franchisee, William Wantamove, who explained that because of his recent divorce he was unable to focus on the business and wanted to move to another city. William Wantamove's operating financial statements for the business showed that the restaurant was performing at about 50% of the average of other Ms. Monicka's Restaurants. Debby asked if she could spend a day working in the restaurant to see what it would take to improve the performance.

Her conclusion was that it was a combination of items, such as: poor customer service, low staff morale, high staff turnover, inconsistent food quality, and excessive food wastage. These were mainly attitudinal things that required time and effort rather than large investments of capital, although Debby thought it would be worth spending some money on interior painting and a new exterior sign.

Debby purchased the business and after just three months she was able to achieve her initial target of the average sales of the other restaurants in the chain. She went on to surpass her goal by 25% at the end of the first year.

Many of the disadvantages of buying an existing franchise can be avoided through careful research and investigation. The following sections will assist you in this process.

SEARCHING FOR AVAILABLE OPPORTUNITIES

Once you have decided that you want to buy an existing franchise, identified the type of business that you want to buy, established your objectives clearly, determined your financial resources and the location that you want, among other factors, you now have to seek out the sources of available opportunities. Some of the sources to consider are listed below.

Newspaper Ads

Ads frequently appear in the business section and the business opportunities section of the classifieds. Check the classified sections of all the newspapers in your locale and national newspapers such as *The Globe and Mail*, and The *Financial Post*. You may decide to place an ad in the paper, either in the business opportunity section or a classified ad under the business wanted section.

Magazine Ads

Local, provincial and national business magazines (e.g., *Profit, Canadian Business, Canadian Business Franchise, Opportunities Canada*) have a classified section which lists businesses for sale.

Trade Sources

Trade publications may advertise businesses for sale. Contact the trade association and ask if there are any businesses for sale, or place an ad in the monthly trade publication stating business wanted and a description. Other trade sources include manufacturers, distributors, suppliers, wholesalers and salespeople.

Franchise Consultants

Franchise consultants often re-sell franchises on behalf of the franchisor or the franchisee. Some franchise companies prefer franchise consultants to handle re-sales rather than real estate salespeople as they understand the unique characteristics of franchised business and can screen applicants for suitability as franchisees.

Franchise Companies

Franchise companies may have a company-owned location or be aware of a franchised unit that is, or is going to be, for sale. Some companies handle the sale of the franchised business on behalf of their franchisees.

Business Brokers

Business brokers specialize in the buying and selling of all types of businesses, including franchises. Ask to be included on their mailing list to receive updated lists of businesses for sale. The broker can act as an intermediary in terms of the preliminary negotiating process on factors such as financing, terms, price, takeover date and other matters. Investigate the broker's reputation, services and contacts.

Realtors

Frequently, small franchise businesses are listed for sale through realtors on the multiple listing service (MLS). Search out realtors who specialize in commercial real estate and are sophisticated in negotiating leases, buildings and businesses. You should be able to find several realtors who either will have listings or will attempt to source out potential opportunities.

Professional Advisors

Your lawyer and accountant may know of franchise businesses for sale that may be of interest to you.

Chambers of Commerce

Become a member of the local Chamber of Commerce to gain a better knowledge of the business in the geographic area in which you are interested. You might consider putting an ad in the chamber newsletter stating "franchise business wanted," along with details.

Cold Call Prospecting

You could contact the owners of a franchise and ask them if they are currently interested, or might be at some point in the future, in selling their business. They may not be interested immediately, but you could encourage them to consider the idea that they otherwise may not have thought about.

Business Matchmaking

The Business Development Bank of Canada administers a match-2making service for people with businesses to sell and for those who are looking for businesses to buy. In addition, most provincial governments have a similar type of arrangement.

RISKY BUSINESSES

When searching for existing franchise businesses, there are a number of classic warning signs that should alert you to potential problems. Buying the wrong type of franchise business could result in a financial disaster for you. Use Quick Check 8.1 to help you in your evaluation. The following is a list of common warning signs that you should watch for. Additional cautions are presented in the next section on evaluating a business.

High Pressure to Buy Business

If you are experiencing a situation in which the seller or an agent of the seller is putting a lot of pressure on you to buy the franchise business, resist and be wary. Possibly the seller is close to going under or is desperate to sell for some other negative reason. Possibly the agent is eager to make a commission or feels that the listing is going to run out. Never put yourself in a situation where you have to make a quick decision on something as critical as buying a business.

Price is Below Market Value of Existing Franchises

From time to time franchises are advertised below the total investment cost of a new franchise being offered by the franchisor. This is definitely a red flag, particularly if the franchise is being marketed directly by the franchise company.

Partner Wanted Business

Some business partnerships that are based on sound economic data can work out well and may be worthy of your consideration. On the other hand, many business partnerships do not survive in the long run. This could be because of conflicts of personality, philosophy, policy and priorities, or unequal contribution of money, time or skill to the business. Some unstable and undesirable business operations attempt to defraud the unwary investor by obtaining an injection of funds into the business and then using those funds in an inappropriate fashion without any controls. For example, investment funds could be used for paying past creditors' debts rather than be available as working capital for future needs and growth. Be cautious of any business partnerships that promise a disproportionate return based on the investment of money or time.

Quick Check 8.1 Buying an Existing Business

Check when
answered to
your satisfaction

Preliminary

1. What are your reasons for considering buying a business rather than starting from scratch or buying into a franchise? _____

2. Have you made a list of what you like and don't like about buying a business someone else has started? _____

3. Have you compared the cost of buying a business with the cost of starting a new business? _____

4. Have you talked with other business owners in the area to see what they think of the firm? _____

5. Have you fully explored the alternative types of businesses you might be interested in? _____

6. Have you selected the type of industry that would most interest you? _____

7. Have you expertise and experience in the type of business you are considering? Is it compatible with your personal goals, personality and financial resources? _____

8. Have you established the criteria that you require in an existing business for your needs? _____

9. Are you comparing identical types of businesses for sale so that you can make a comparative value judgment? _____

10. Do you know the real reasons as to why the business is for sale? How do you know they are accurate? _____

11. Have you checked out the firm's reputation with the Better Business Bureau, credit bureaus, Dun & Bradstreet, suppliers, creditors, competitors? _____

Quick Check 8.1 **Buying an Existing Business** (cont'd)

12. Have you made sure that you have escape clause conditions in any offer to purchase contract (e.g., subject to satisfactory review by purchaser's lawyer and accountant, financing, inspection of records, receiving licences, rights, and other transfers)? _____

Costs

13. Is inventory accurately shown at true current value for calculating actual cost of goods sold? _____

14. Did the seller prepay some expenses? Must you reimburse him for your share? _____

15. Are expenses all-inclusive? Will new ownership change them? _____

16. Is another business involved in the accumulation or payment of expenses? _____

17. Will some annual expenses be due soon? _____

18. Have some expenses been delayed (e.g., equipment maintenance)? _____

19. What new or increased expenses should you anticipate? _____

20. Was interest paid for money lent to the business? _____

21. Are wages as well as an attractive profit margin provided for working owners? _____

22. Must staff salaries be adjusted soon? _____

23. Does equipment value reflect reasonable annual depreciation? _____

24. Has your lawyer checked out the lease? _____

25. What expenses do similar businesses have? _____

26. How will sales fluctuations affect cost? _____

27. What costs are allocated to which product? How would a change in product mix affect costs? _____

Quick Check 8.1 Buying an Existing Business (cont'd)

Sales

28. What's the future of your product or service? Is it expanding? Becoming oversold? Obsolete? _____

29. Can sales increase with current resources? _____

30. Have you checked with the suppliers in terms of the history of the business for sale? _____

31. Is the location good, or is poor location the reason for the sale? _____

32. Are bad debts deducted from records or are they still shown as receivables? _____

33. Have all sales been reliably recorded? Are the total sales broken down by product line, if applicable? _____

34. Are some goods on consignment and able to be returned for full credit? _____

35. Are some goods on warranty? If so, will financial allowance be made for possible warranty commitments? _____

36. What is the monthly and annual sales pattern? Is it consistent? Seasonal? Related to other cycles? _____

37. Are sales fluctuations due to one-shot promotions? _____

38. Is the seller's personal role critical to success? _____

39. Is there a salesperson who contributes significantly to success? Can you keep him/her? _____

40. Will existing suppliers be available to you? _____

41. Is reported stock turnover in line with industry practice ratios? Does existing stock include items from another business? _____

42. Are sales figures solely from this business? _____

Quick Check 8.1 Buying an Existing Business (cont'd)

43. Are prices competitive? Who are the competitors and are their price strategies gaining them a larger market share? _____

Profits

44. Do you know minimum and maximum levels of sales? _____

45. How will sales fluctuations affect profits? _____

46. What are the book values, market values and replacement values of the fixed assets? _____

47. If inventory and/or work in progress are included, has a value been agreed upon at time of offer? Have you agreed on how it will be adjusted at time of closing, and within what limits? _____

48. Is there inventory sold but not shipped? _____

49. How will inflation affect sales and costs? _____

50. Are profits enough to take the risk? _____

51. Based on the history, have you projected future cash flow and profitability? Have you determined your break-even point? _____

52. Have records been well kept? _____

53. Have you and a qualified accountant analyzed the records thoroughly? Balance sheets? Profit-and-loss statements? Tax returns? Purchases and sales records? Bank statements? How far back have you gone? _____

54. Must you build up your own accounts receivable? How will this affect cash flow? _____

55. Is some equipment leased? At what cost? _____

56. Is equipment in good repair? Efficient? Up-to-date? Easy to service? Saleable? _____

Quick Check 8.1 Buying an Existing Business (cont'd)

57. Have you checked with comparable industry profit
    ratios and are they consistent with the business you
    are examining?   _____

Liabilities

58. Is the seller co-operative in supplying financial
    information?   _____

59. Are there any contingencies such as warranties or
    guaranteed debts or accounts?   _____

60. Are your assets free and clear of debts and liens?
    Do you have in writing the terms of debts you are
    assuming?   _____

61. Will cash flow cover debts?   _____

62. Are you assuming any risk of liability for the seller's
    actions (e.g., if you are buying shares of a limited
    company)? Will customers expect you to make
    refunds or honour warranties or risk losing good-will,
    even though you are not legally obliged to do so?   _____

63. How is the business' credit rating with suppliers?   _____

64. Are there advances or prepayments that should be
    turned over to you?   _____

65. Are there goods that have been prepaid to the
    business but not delivered by the business? Should
    these advance payments be given to you?

66. If buying part of a company or entering a partnership,
    what limitations are there, and what authority will
    you have in the management of the firm? Have you
    read the chapter that covers shareholders' agreements
    and partnership agreements?   _____

The Purchase Agreement

67. Is the business a limited company? Are you buying
    assets or shares? Have you consulted with your lawyer
    and accountant on the pros and cons of this issue?   _____

Quick Check 8.1 **Buying an Existing Business** (cont'd)

68. Does the contract of sale cover assets to be purchased, liabilities to be assumed, when business is to be taken over? _____

69. Are you prepared to negotiate, remembering a business is only worth what someone will pay and what a seller will accept? Do you have the skills to negotiate directly yourself? _____

70. Did you include escape clauses in the proposed offer to purchase contract covering obtaining finance, inspection of records, receiving licences, rights and other transfers, and satisfactory review by your lawyer and accountant? _____

71. Have you discussed the proposed business with someone who understands this type of business? _____

72. Will the seller agree not to set up in competition with you for an specified time and within a specified geographic area? _____

73. Will the seller train and assist you after the purchase?

74. Have you selected a lawyer who is skilled in business law, including buying a business? Are you going to discuss the purchase terms with your lawyer before removing the escape clauses or better still, before formally submitting an offer? _____

75. Have you selected an accountant who is skilled in the financial evaluation and assessment aspects of buying a business? Are you going to discuss the purchase terms with your accountant before removing the escape clauses or, better still, before formally submitting an offer? _____

Franchisor Is Offering Exceptional Financing Terms

If the franchisor offers to carry all, or a large part, of the financing for the purchaser, or provide exceptional terms, there is probably good reason. Some franchise companies have resold locations three or four times, continually reducing the price until the capital investment is at a low enough level to stand a chance of being profitable for a franchisee. Of course, along the way a number of franchisees have lost their investments to allow this devaluation of the franchised business. Check any such offer out very carefully. If it looks too good to be true, it probably is.

Buy-back Business

A seller may attempt to induce a prospective purchaser by promising to buy back the franchise if the buyer is not satisfied. Once the money has changed hands, the seller could renege on the commitment or perhaps use up all of the funds and disappear. Although you would have recourse to sue, in practical terms you could be wasting further money. The franchise agreement should be examined to ascertain if a buy-back is permitted by the franchisor, or if it would approve the previous franchisee reacquiring the franchise.

Owner Claims Skimming

A business owner may try to induce a sale by claiming that the financial statements do not accurately record the amount of cash that has come into the franchise. For example, if the franchise is essentially a cash-only business such as a delicatessen, the seller could state that in fact 50% more revenue was made than the records show. In other words, the seller would be stating (discreetly and obviously not in writing) that half of the cash was pocketed without recording it or paying royalties or tax on it.

Don't purchase such a business. The situation would mean that you cannot rely at all on the financial records, which places you at high risk. In addition, you cannot base your purchase price on the assurance of the seller that he or she evaded taxes. Obviously the seller is not credible, and consequently the business is not credible enough to consider any longer. Sales figures can often be validated by comparing them with the franchisee's sales reports submitted to the franchisor. It is unlikely that a franchisee will overstate revenues that are subject to royalty payments.

Purchases Which Use Up All Investment Capital

If you are considering a franchise which would require all of your financial resources to pay the purchase price, you could be in a situation that you are starting off undercapitalized, without working capital or reserve for future needs. For example, if you take over a franchise, and there is a decline in sales and profit during the transition phase, you would not have any resources to be able to buffer the financial crunch. Never buy a business without taking into account your working capital and contingency fund.

Personal Service Business

There are special concerns you should be aware of if you are considering buying a personal service business (e.g., an architectural, engineering, law, dental or legal practice). The main concern relates to the bonding and goodwill which has occurred on a one-to-one relationship between clients and the professional. Once the franchise is purchased, a substantial portion or possibly most of the clientele could leave and go to other professionals because of a difference in style and operation. For example, you may require retainers in advance and send bills promptly every two weeks for services that you render. The previous owner of the personal service business may have been very sloppy in credit and collection procedures, never asked for retainers, and frequently left accounts unbilled for months on end. If you do buy a personal service business, you should build in protections because of the high risk that the goodwill may not necessarily stay when the other party leaves, despite the brand-name recognition normally associated with a franchise.

Declining or Changing Neighbourhood

If you are considering a franchise in an area which is geographically changing rapidly in terms of the population base, reconsider. For example, perhaps the location is becoming more commercialized and older residential buildings are being torn down for office buildings. If your target market is the homeowner and the population is declining in that area, this could cause sufficient loss of income to the point where your franchise would not survive.

Emotionally Based Interest

If you are considering a franchise for which you have a very positive emotional feeling, and that feeling rather than objective business criteria tends to dominate the decisions you are making, then don't proceed any further. Emotional over-enthusiasm, unrealistic expectations, inflated projections, and blind optimism can very quickly turn into financial disaster. A business that you buy has to make objective good business sense first by being a viable idea at a price that you can afford.

Failing or Distressed Business

Don't proceed any further if you are considering a franchise which is going through serious financial problems. The exception would be if you are an expert in that type of business, have clearly identified the reasons for the financial difficulties, and know that you have the expertise and management resources to turn it around. There are people who buy businesses with a turnaround strategy in mind, and skilfully negotiate a purchase package which is very attractive. This can be done effectively, of course, only if the buyer knows what he or she is doing and is sophisticated in this type of distress purchase.

EVALUATING AN OPERATING FRANCHISE

After you have completed all the preliminary steps and have decided on the specific franchise business that you are interested in, the next step is to calculate the worth of the enterprise. The buyer, of course, is hoping to buy the franchise with as little financial outlay as possible. The seller is frequently looking emotionally at the many years of time, energy and stress that went into the franchise, and the small returns in the first years of growth. In addition, most business owners have an inflated assessment of the value of goodwill, which may have little or no bearing on the value of the business. There could be a considerable difference between the proposed selling price and the eventual purchase price after a thorough evaluation is done and negotiations completed.

After taking into account all the factors and input in evaluating the franchise, rely on your accountant's advice plus your own judgement. As in any business, ultimately the price of the franchise is really determined by the buyer, not the seller.

Why Is the Franchise Being Sold?

One of the first steps in the evaluation process is to determine why the franchise is being sold. Some of the reasons may not have any impact, while other reasons could have a serious impact and could cause you to lose your investment completely. Here are some of the common reasons why franchised businesses are sold:

- Facilities are obsolete and it would be too expensive to upgrade or move to a new location.
- The lease is about to expire and the landlord does not want to renew the lease or wants to renew it at a much higher price.
- The franchise agreement is about to expire or be terminated.
- Sales are declining, possibly due to changing economic or market factors, poor location, or unmarketable services or products.
- Competition has just come into the area or will be coming soon and the owner wants to sell before that factor makes the franchise unattractive.
- The owner is having partnership problems.
- The owner is having marital or health problems, or wants to retire.
- The owner has lost his commitment to the franchise after many years of frustration and hard work, and wants to do something different in life.
- The owner wants to sell so that the money can be used to buy another, more attractive business opportunity.
- Government regulations (federal, provincial or municipal) have just come in or will be coming in which would require the owner to expend monies to comply with regulations, and the enterprise cannot afford to make the changes and remain competitive.
- The location of the business is no longer attractive because of changing zoning by-laws, traffic patterns or transportation services.
- The owner is concerned about potential law suits and wants to sell quickly before they commence.
- Due to a poor credit and collection policy, the franchise is unable

to collect receivables, is suffering serious cash flow problems, and cannot obtain further financing.

- The franchise has lost one or more key employees, which will have a negative impact on the operation.
- The franchise has lost one or more major contracts, without which it is no longer financially viable.
- The reputation, support or financial stability of the franchise company is deteriorating or the franchisee is experiencing a personality problem with the franchisor.

Factors that Affect a Business Evaluation

There are many factors which determine the ultimate evaluation and pricing of a franchise. In fact, an appraisal is largely an estimate or opinion of value which can vary considerably. Value is in the eyes of the beholder. For example, the value placed on the business by the seller, which will determine his or her asking price, is in many cases unrealistic. This is because the seller frequently sees value in emotional terms, and does not necessarily heed current market realities. The franchise that may have cost the owner $40,000 to equip four years ago may be worth anywhere from $10,000 to $100,000 today, depending on factors which bear on the business market value.

At the onset of your inquiry, obtain from the seller financial records including:

- income statements (profit-and-loss statements) and balance sheets for the past three years
- tax returns for the past three years
- lists of accounts payable and accounts receivable
- all other liabilities of the company
- the books of the business.

In addition, you should have a copy of:

- the franchise agreement
- current lease
- any contracts the company has with employees, suppliers or others
- other documentation that your lawyer and accountant may request.

You should also obtain copies of the franchisor's projections of income and expense for this particular business or similar locations. Most franchisees are on their own in terms of selling the business, but require franchisor approval to do so.

Here are the most common factors considered in establishing a selling price for a franchise:

Accounts Receivable

If these are to be included in the purchase price, they should be examined closely. Accounts under 30 days have a higher incidence of reliability, while those between 30 and 60 days are a higher risk. Any receivables over 60 days may be uncollectable. Before purchasing any accounts receivable, contact the customers to make sure that they agree with the outstanding balances. You may want to arrange with the seller that you will defer payment or partial payment to the seller until you have received the accounts receivable.

Fixed Assets

These include such things as the building, fixtures and leasehold improvements. Although the original owner may have put a considerable amount of money into leasehold improvements, he or she may not have maintained their market value. Perhaps the improvements stay with the landlord at the end of the lease.

Movable Assets

These would include such items as equipment, furniture and furnishings. The value of the equipment may be based on its original value, its replacement value, its auction-sale value as used equipment, or its depreciated value.

Inventory

You may want to use the franchisor or an independent, qualified appraiser to determine the dollar value of the inventory. A manufacturer may have several different types of inventory, such as finished goods, work in process, and raw materials. The inventory should be examined for style, condition, saleability, quality, age, freshness and balance. Personally inspect the inventory to know what you are buying. Some of the inventory might be outdated and would be difficult to sell. If possible, purchase inventory at a discounted price. Normally inventory is paid for separately from the purchase price of the business and after it has been accounted for as of the day that the business is taken over. Other considerations that you have to take into account when dealing with inventory include:

- Is the inventory in character with your target market?
- Is the inventory in accord with what the buyer would like to sell and the franchisor approves?
- How much of the inventory would have to be cleared out at a loss and what would that loss amount to?
- Does the inventory list contain items that have already been sold and paid for and not yet shipped?
- How does the average industry ratio of inventory to sales compare with the business for sale?
- Has the seller kept adequate records of inventory, in what form, and for how long?
- Are all the items in inventory owned by the business or are some of those on consignment?
- Does a lender have any security documentation covering inventory, such as to a bank?

Customer List, Business and Creditor Records, Mailing Lists

These items could be valuable assets for you. Make sure that they are included in the sales agreement and that the seller is not entitled to use these lists for the seller's own purpose in competition with you, or to give the lists and records to any other party without your written consent.

Licences

Are those licences necessary for the operation of the franchise (e.g., a liquor licence) included in the sale price and are they transferable to you? Make sure that the completion of the purchase is conditional upon the licence being transferred. Have you checked all the licensing requirements and municipal by-laws (e.g., health, fire and safety regulations, zoning by-laws, and other matters)?

Leases

A lease is an essential part of the purchase price of the franchise, unless of course you are buying the whole building. The length and terms of the lease are important considerations in establishing the value of a business. You will want to have answers to such questions as:

- Is the lease held directly with the landlord or is it a sub-lease from the franchisor?
- Is the lease transferable to the buyer with or without the consent of the landlord?
- Is the present lease negotiable with the landlord?
- Should you negotiate a brand-new lease?
- Are there restrictions in the lease?
- Are there options for renewal in the lease?
- What rent-escalation clauses are built into the lease?

Apart from leases with the landlord, there could be leases for equipment, signs, furniture, telephone systems and many other items. In some cases, these leases are assignable. Obtain the actual lease documents for your lawyer's review. Possibly you will not want to keep some of the items leased.

Franchise Agreement

Is the transfer or assignment of the franchise permitted by the franchisor? Are there any special terms and conditions regarding such a transfer? Is there an assignment fee and, if so, how much is it? Who pays the assignment fee? Will you be signing a new franchise agreement with different terms and conditions than the existing agreement, or will the existing agreement be assigned to you? What training will you receive from the franchisor? Is there a cost for this training? What is the exclusive territory?

Non-Competition Clause

When buying a franchise, it is important that you protect yourself from having the owner open up a competing business across the street and putting your investment at severe risk. To avoid this situation, you should have a clause in the sales agreement prohibiting the seller from establishing a business in competition with you. Built into that restriction should be a time-limit and a specified geographic area. There will probably be a non-competition clause in the franchise agreement, but that is between the owner and the franchisor, and not the owner and the purchaser, so the purchaser is unable to rely on it. In addition, courts have been reluctant at times to enforce restrictive covenants that are part of franchise agreements, so it is prudent for the purchaser to incorporate any restrictive covenants into an agreement that is separate and distinct to the franchise agreement.

Accounts Payable

This factor is relevant in terms of potential litigation and credit history. For example, are all the accounts current or are some of them past due, and how long past due? Do any of the creditors have liens or encumbrances against the assets of the franchise, or have they made claims for monies owing?

Prepaid Expenses

Sometimes a franchise will have prepaid expenses such as insurance or last month's rent, or if the building is owned then property taxes for the year have possibly been paid in advance. Check to make sure that the items which have been prepaid can be assigned to you without penalty.

Patents, Copyrights, Trademarks, Industrial Designs and Business Names

These intangible rights can have very real monetary benefit to your business. If you want them as part of your agreement, they should be specifically included in the sales agreement.

Employees

Ideally, you would try to keep the key employees who are experienced in the franchise and know the customers, the product or service, and the suppliers. Try to find out how many of the key employees would be prepared to remain with the franchise after you buy it.

Income/Earnings

The net income after expenses and before taxes is an important factor that has to be taken in context. For example, the net income is relative to

- how the franchise operator keeps his or her books
- how efficient he or she is in buying and controlling labour costs

- how competent in managing the franchise
- how well the business is marketed and promoted
- how careful he or she is about overhead and expenses
- how committed he or she is to making the franchise financially successful.

Some buyers or sellers put a high reliance on the gross sales figure and feel this is the true value of the business because it reflects the volume of activity and cash flow.

Type of Business

Some franchises are more popular than others and therefore have a greater buyer appeal. The higher the appeal, the higher the demand, and therefore generally the higher the price.

Competition

The amount of competition in the trading area plays an important part in the potential profitability and gross volume of the franchise. Do your research thoroughly and look for the following warning signs:

- nearby major shopping centres which offer more attractive one-stop facilities for shoppers
- heavy competition by discounters
- the presence of many competing businesses engaged in the same type of business that you are considering
- competitors who offer special features such as cheque cashing, delivery service, credit, delayed payments and other inducements to attract customers.

If these factors are present, you could be forced to try to meet the competition by offering the same features.

Customers

A significant factor for many buyers is the type of existing customer base that the franchise currently enjoys. Does the franchise cater to a few customers that make up the majority of the purchase volume? If this is the case, what would be the effect on the business if a few, or several, of these customers ceased doing business with you?

Warranties

If the franchise that you are buying offers products which are covered by warranty, you would need to know what warranties have been extended and the lifetime of each warranty. Possibly they are renewal contracts in terms of extended coverage which could generate a cash flow for the business. To maintain customer goodwill, you might be obligated to honour the warranties.

Accounting Practices

Make sure that the financial statements are current and prepared by a professional, qualified accountant such as a chartered accountant (CA) or certified general accountant (CGA). The strength of the financial statements in terms of the accounting opinion must be a credible one. Obtain your professional accountant's advice in interpreting the financial information. Auditing can be an expensive procedure, but depending on the nature of the franchise that you are buying and the amount of purchase price, that might be a condition that you require before you finalize the purchase. Other factors that you should be aware of include:

• unusually high depreciation which can artificially alter the profit figures by increasing them
• financial statements that are unrealistically overstated or understated
• statements that reflect a lower-than-normal product cost or net profit percentage.

Management

Assess the quality and nature of the current management of the company. This factor will make a difference in terms of continuity of the franchise when a new owner takes over. For example, if the management has shown disinterest or incompetence, you should be able to purchase a franchise at a reduced rate and hopefully turn it around in terms of improving the operation and therefore building up a customer base. However, if the reputation of the franchise is bad and has been for a long time, it may not be possible to substantially increase the customer base.

Financing

Determine if the seller is prepared to take a sizeable downpayment and carry the balance of the purchase price over time with security. The security could be a debenture or a chattel mortgage on equipment and vehicles, or assignment of accounts receivable. The lower the downpayment, the more potential buyers there will be, and the seller can therefore ask a higher price for the franchise. The converse holds true in cases where the seller demands the transaction be done in cash. Check the franchise agreement to determine if there are any restrictions on using the assets of the franchised business as security in this kind of situation.

Geographic Area

A franchise situated in an affluent area where the population has a higher disposable income may be more attractive than one situated in a low-income or less-travelled area.

Industry Ratio Comparison

A factor in influencing the evaluation of a franchise and the eventual purchase price is the comparison with published industry standards. If the comparison shows that the business for sale is more efficiently and profitably run in comparison to key ratios, that could increase the purchase price. This is assuming, of course, that the financial records and the backup documentation supporting them are shown to be accurate and not artificially contrived.

A sophisticated buyer will be able to review all the factors discussed and, after analyzing all the data, make an evaluation of the worth of the enterprise. This would at least provide a basis on whether to consider buying the franchise, assuming that the asking price is realistic enough to commence negotiations. It is critical that the buyer obtain competent legal and accounting advice—and possibly consulting advice—before making the decision to present an offer.

Evaluating Goodwill

The area of greatest divergence of opinion in the evaluation of any small business is the value of goodwill. There is no firm rule for computing goodwill. The initial franchise fee originally paid by the owner of the business will not be paid again by the purchaser; however, it will probably be shown as an asset although it is now really part of the goodwill. The term "goodwill" is interpreted differently by different people. Some people define goodwill as simply the expectation of continued patronage. Others define it more precisely as the value of a business in excess of its suggested book value. Still others construe goodwill to be that amount which is the difference between the tangible net worth of the company and its fair market value. The price the buyer should be willing to pay for goodwill depends on the earning power and potential of the franchise. If the earning power is low, the buyer will probably resist paying any amount for goodwill.

Goodwill must result in profits or it cannot have value. Profit in this context is a residue after operating costs, salaries and a return on the investment. The buyer looks at the franchise for its ability to earn a fair return on investment, and looks at the present and future earning power of the business as of prime importance. The seller adopts a position that goodwill relates to the franchise agreement, lease benefits, location, customer base, sales and inventory records, exclusive lines, connections with suppliers, licences, patents, trademarks and copyrights. In the opinion of the seller, all these factors contribute to the earning power of the business and therefore deserve compensation. Goodwill is an intangible because it is an opinion of the person evaluating it.

There are various factors to take into account when attempting to establish a value for goodwill, such as:

- reputation of the franchised business and franchisee
- desirability and exclusiveness of the franchise
- reputation of the franchisor and any associated trademarks
- location
- stability of company and industry trends
- age of the business
- profitability
- transition period in ownership changeover for training purposes
- key personnel staying with the company under the new ownership
- a broad customer base.

The buyer should be careful in apportioning the value to goodwill because of the tax implications. The seller is able to use the amount paid for goodwill as a capital gain. For this reason, the seller may want to apportion as high a factor as possible for goodwill. The buyer on the other hand, for tax reasons, should try to have the value for goodwill as low as possible because the buyer cannot get the same tax advantages for the goodwill component. The other aspects of the purchase—for example, chattels, leasehold improvements and inventory—also have values apportioned to them. Make sure that you receive tax advice before committing yourself in any way to the apportioning of the purchase price.

METHODS OF EVALUATING A FRANCHISED BUSINESS

There are numerous methods and techniques used for determining the value of a business. In most cases, a small business is priced by the seller based on a set of values. The methods used by the seller do not necessarily reflect a realistic or actual value of the business, but for the purpose of selling it some value has to be determined. As mentioned earlier, the suggested sale price could differ considerably based on what a professional accountant would advise, what the banker would suggest, and what a business broker would recommend.

Many of the evaluation methods require a thorough understanding and analysis of the financial information from the franchise, including income statement (profit-and-loss statement) and balance sheet. In many businesses, the price may not necessarily include accounts receivable, cash and inventory. These items are frequently negotiated separately and are not included in the overall purchase price.

The market value of a business means the highest estimated price which the buyer would be warranted in paying, and the seller would be justified in accepting, without any undue or outside influence involved. Undue or outside influence would include factors such as foreclosure, bankruptcy, receivership, competition, marital or partnership disputes, or health problems. If any of these factors is present, as a consequence the price should be lowered. As a buyer, you should look for these factors in order to apply leverage in your negotiations.

Some of the methods used to evaluate a franchise include book value, liquidation value, replacement value, and gross multiplier value. The capitalization of income value (CIV) is one of the more reliable methods. It also involves a determination of the rate of return on investment. A brief description of the CIV method follows, plus an outline of a typical selling price formula.

Capitalization of Income Value

This method is concerned with the present worth of future benefits from investment in the franchise. In other words, the value is determined by capitalizing the franchise's earnings at a rate that reflects the risk associated with that business. A high capitalization rate would be chosen if the buyer perceives a high degree of risk. The rate could vary from as little as 15% to as high as 100% or more, depending on the perceived risk of the franchise. A capitalization rate of 20% is frequently the minimum amount for the purchase of a small business that shows reasonable prospects for continued success and growth, and has relatively no risk. As you can see, the higher the capitalization rate used, the lower the valuation arrived at for the franchise.

The capitalization of income value is used frequently because the business value is based on income or profit before depreciation, interest and income taxes, and by using an appropriate capitalization rate which is acceptable to the buyer, considering all the circumstances as illustrated in this situation.

1. Determine the level of future earnings of the franchise based on average net earnings over the past several years, together with an estimate of the increase in earnings expected. Average net earnings include owner's salary.
2. Select an appropriate capitalization rate based on the return on investment which buyers would be expected to demand. This is based on a fair return on investment: for example, 10% to 25%. The risk factor plays an important role at this stage.
3. Capitalize the income by dividing the income by the selected capitalization rate. The outcome would constitute the selling price.

REAL LIFE: View Your Investment Fairly and Set a Price

Sam Slim wanted to sell his DropWeight franchise and needed to place a valuation on the business. During the three years that Sam had operated the business it had averaged net earnings of $60,000 (including Sam's salary). As sales had increased by 5% each year it was reasonable that they would continue to increase by the same amount, so Sam projected net earnings of $63,000 (i.e., $60,000 × 5% = $3,000) for the following year.

He assumed that a potential purchaser would require a return on their investment of 40% (the capitalization rate) so he capitalized the income of $63,000 by dividing it by the selected capitalization rate of 40%, which constituted a selling price of $157,500.

Based on a 40% return on investment, it would take a purchaser two-and-a-half years to recover their initial investment.

Selling Price Formula

The formula given on the following worksheet is based on an evaluation of the franchise's existing earning power and profit potential. The selling price approach is given from the perspective of the buyer. Keep in mind that because each business and sales transaction is unique, the formula that is shown should be used only as a guideline to indicate some of the major considerations in the pricing of a franchise.

Pricing Formula Worksheet

1. Tangible net worth $_____
2. Current earning power $_____
3. Reasonable annual salary $_____
4. Total earning capacity $_____
5. Average annual net profit $_____
6. Extra earning power (line 5 minus line 4) $_____
7. Value of intangibles (line 6 x multiplier figure) $_____
8. Final price (a total of lines 1 and 7) $_____

Here is an explanation of each step in the worksheet:

1. Determine the tangible net worth of the franchise. This consists of the total market value of the tangible assets (excluding goodwill), including all current and long-term assets less total current and long-term liabilities.

2. Estimate the current earning power of the tangible net worth of the franchise; in other words, if the buyer is going to invest this amount elsewhere, such as in stocks, bonds, term deposits, and other investments, what would the return be on an annual basis. Naturally this is calculated based on current interest rates, and the earning power would fluctuate based on economic trends and other factors. When determining the interest rate, try to make the comparison realistic by using a comparable risk investment or business.

3. Determine a reasonable annual salary that the buyer would anticipate earning if employed elsewhere. For the purpose of this calculation, this would be the same salary that an owner/operator would take out of the franchised business. When making a salary calculation, take into account that if employed elsewhere, the salary would also include fringe benefits which may be equivalent to 15% to 20% over the base salary. Take into consideration that if a buyer is employed in his or her own business, he or she could also receive benefits such as Canada Pension Plan, medical and dental coverage, and the use of an automobile.

4. Calculate a total earning capacity of the buyer by adding steps **2** and **3**; in other words, if the buyer was going to invest the equivalent of tangible net worth outside the business plus an income from employment outside the business, what would the total earning capacity be? For the purpose of comparisons, don't take taxes into account.

5. Determine the average annual net profit of the business over a minimum of the past three years. Ideally, five years would provide a more accurate result. This average will be the total of all profit as obtained from the financial statements, and before any management salaries are taken off for the owners, or taxes are paid. The average is determined by dividing the total profit over the time period used by the number of years used in the analysis. The reason that income taxes are not taken off is to make the calculations comparable with earnings from other sources or by individuals in different tax brackets. Admittedly, when comparing alternative investments, there could be tax benefits that are not available from employment in a small business. When calculating the earnings, take a look at the trends. The earnings may have been increasing or decreasing steadily, or fluctuating widely or remaining constant. Take these factors and trends into account when adjusting the earnings figure as might be required.

6. Calculate the extra earning power of the franchise by subtracting the figure in step **4** from the figure in step **5**. This figure represents the additional benefit in terms of extra earning income if you buy the business rather than if·you obtained outside employment and invested the equivalent of the tangible net worth. In other words, this figure might make the difference by providing the incentive to buy the business and justify the risk.

7. Calculate the value of intangibles by multiplying the extra earning power outlined in step **6** times the factor that is referred to as the years-of-profit figure. This multiplier figure is based on various factors. The questions to which you would have to obtain answers to determine the multiplier factor include:

- What expenses and risks would be involved in setting up a similar type of business?
- How long would it take to set up a similar type of business and bring it to a similar stage of development?
- What would be the price of goodwill in similar firms?
- Are the intangibles offered by the firm unique (franchise, trade name, trademarks, patents, location)?
- Will the seller sign a covenant agreeing not to compete?

After evaluating the above factors, if you determine that the franchise is successful and well-established, you may use a multiplier factor of five or more. You may use a multiplier of three for a moderately seasoned firm in terms of growth and length of time in business. A profitable but younger business may only rate a factor of one. To a certain extent the multiplier factor is related to the number of years in business, but that is just one of the factors when trying to determine the correct multiplier factor for your needs.

8. Calculate the final price, which is obtained by adding the tangible net worth of the business (outlined in step **1**) to the value of intangibles (outlined in step **7**). This final price figure gives an estimated guideline only when determining a potential price for a business. As discussed in other parts of this chapter, there are many other variables which have to be taken into account.

METHODS OF BUYING A BUSINESS

There are two common methods of buying a business. One way is to buy the assets, which includes a goodwill component, and the other way is to buy the shares, assuming it is a corporation. If you have the alternative of buying either assets or shares, there are various considerations that have to be taken into account and discussed with your accountant and lawyer before committing yourself. Here are some points to consider:

- company financing
- potential liability
- company credit rating
- franchise agreement
- leases and contracts held by the company
- tax implications (i.e., depreciation of fixed assets, sales tax payable).

Purchase of Assets

If the business is a sole proprietorship or a partnership, the sale must be conducted as a transfer of assets, as there is no corporation in which shares can be purchased. When purchasing assets of a corporation, the buyer typically sets up his or her own corporation and transfers all the assets and the lease into the new corporate name.

If a buyer is buying the assets of the company and therefore has a new corporation without any track record, the lack of a credit history could impair the amount of credit that would be extended to the company in the initial stages of operation. You will want to allocate as low a price as possible for goodwill because the tax write-off benefits are not as attractive to you as they are for the seller. Conversely, you want to allocate as much of the purchase price as possible to equipment, fixtures and other depreciable capital assets so that you have as high a depreciation deduction as possible.

If the assets of the franchise are secured by a creditor's lien, mortgage or other form of encumbrance, the transfer of assets cannot occur without the approval of the creditor. The creditor may not release the seller from the security, and may insist on having personal covenants of the buyer as well. Or, the creditor may consent to an asset transfer conditional to a renegotiation of the terms of the security. Protections can be built in to make sure that the assets are free and clear of any liabilities. Your lawyer should check the appropriate registries to see if there are any encumbrances or liens against the assets. Find out if there are any assignment or training fees payable to the franchisor that are not listed in the information provided. If there are, who is responsible for paying them?

Purchase of Shares

The buyer may purchase the shares of the incorporated company from the shareholders. At the time of the sale, the shareholders resign as directors and officers. The buyer elects his or her own directors and officers. A modification to this approach is for the existing shareholders to sell their shares back to the corporation. The corporation then sells new shares to the buyer. A buyer may be able to purchase the shares of the business if the company has a high amount of debt by paying the owners the difference between the debt and the purchase price. For example, if the business assets were worth $200,000 and the debt was $175,000, the buyer could pay $25,000 to the owner and assume the shares of the business.

In many instances, it may be difficult to have leases, contracts or licences assigned to a new company. If this is the case, then a purchase of shares in the corporation would permit the business to continue without others necessarily knowing that there has been a change in ownership. Another reason for buying the shares of a company is that a tax loss could be available that could benefit the buyer.

If you buy the shares of a business that enjoys a very good credit rating, you would be obtaining the ongoing benefit of the excellent credit rating. On the other hand, if the credit rating is poor, that could have an adverse effect on obtaining future credit and overall goodwill.

If a buyer is making a share purchase, then any and all liabilities that the business might have from the past remain with the business. For example, there could be contingent liabilities in claims by Revenue Canada for back taxes or reassessment of taxes, creditors may sue for past debts, customers may sue for an injury that was sustained in the past on the premises of the business, customers may make a claim on an express or implied warranty on products that have been purchased, and product liability claims may be commenced due to injury from the product.

PURCHASE DOCUMENTATION

After you have decided on the structure of the purchase transaction, you will want to make sure that you are properly protected with legal documentation. The legal documents include the offer to purchase and the formal purchase-and-sale agreement. The purchase and sale agreement would be for either an asset or share transfer.

Offer to Purchase

This is a common first step in buying a business. Whether you are making the offer directly yourself or through a franchise consultant, realtor, business broker or lawyer, the offer-to-purchase agreement must be in writing and specific. Never make an offer-to-purchase agreement without obtaining legal and accounting advice in advance. The terms of the offer-to-purchase agreement normally include such matters as:

- the apportioning of purchase price if you are buying the assets
- employees
- transition phase clause (owner staying on to assist in training)
- non-competition clause
- franchisor's approval of assignment of the franchise
- financing considerations
- timing of completion and possession date
- a provision that all the financial records of the company such as financial statements, balance sheet, income statement (profit-and-loss statement), sales records, franchise documentation, contracts, lease and all other necessary documentation have been or will be supplied to the prospective buyer for review before any offer is firm.

You want to make sure that you can back out of the contract and avoid liability if for any reason you change your mind. For example, you may discover hidden problems with the franchise or the franchise organization. There could be many other factors not covered in the offer-to-purchase that you will want to include once you become aware of the situation.

It is necessary in most situations to have a clause stating that a formal purchase-and-sale agreement will be negotiated and drawn up by the parties after all the subject conditions in the offer-to-purchase have been removed.

There are several tips that will help minimize your risk when making an offer-to-purchase, as follows:

Keep the Purchase Deposit to a Minimum

As a general rule of thumb, a deposit of 5% to 10% of the purchase price is requested as a gesture of good faith and sincerity. In practical terms, a minimum deposit is usually required. In fact, the broker or realtor involved generally wants to have the amount of their commission (approximately 10%) as the amount of the deposit. As the amount of the deposit is negotiable, attempt to pay as little as possible. An alternative is to pay a small deposit such as $1,000 and then have a clause that states that the deposit will be increased to a larger amount—for example, 10% of the purchase price—once all of the conditional (escape) clauses have been removed.

Use Escape Clauses

Escape clauses are conditions that have to be met before the offer to purchase becomes a binding contract. Some of the most common escape clause conditions which benefit the buyer of a franchise include:

- review and approval of offer to purchase by the buyer's lawyer and accountant
- verification of all records by the buyer's accountant to the satisfaction of the accountant and buyer
- appraisal of the business by an independent appraiser of the buyer's choosing
- inspection of the business by a third party (potential partners or associates of the buyer)
- franchisor's approval of the assignment
- approval by the buyer's bank for financing.

These clauses are often referred to as unilateral conditions because it is totally up to the buyer as to whether or not the escape clauses are removed.

Buy the Business Through a Corporation

You will probably want to incorporate a company to purchase the assets of the franchise, so you should make sure that the offer-to-purchase is in a corporate name. This would also help you when the formal purchase-and-sale documentation is complete, because if you default on the final agreement, your company may be sued, but not you personally. It will be necessary to execute the correct franchise documentation such as an Assignment to a Controlled Corporation to be able to operate the franchise through a company.

The franchise agreement may include restrictions on the issue of shares. (See Chapter 4, "Understanding the Franchise Agreement" for more information on assignment and transfer of the franchise agreement.)

Avoid Signing Personal Guarantees

If you have incorporated a company and signed the offer-to-purchase in the corporate name, avoid signing a personal guarantee. Have all the risk assumed by your corporation; however, the franchisor will require a personal guarantee of the franchisee's performance of the franchise agreement if it is to be operated through a corporation.

Insert a Liquidated Damage Clause

The buyer should ensure that in the event the contract is breached, the deposit shall be deemed to be liquidated (total) damages.

Purchase-and-Sale Agreements

If the escape clauses in the offer to purchase have been removed, then a purchase-and-sale agreement and the franchise documentation is normally prepared on behalf of and at the expense of the buyer by the buyer's lawyer. The document is sent to the seller's lawyer for review and approval. The contract is signed by all parties, followed by the transfer of payment and possession. These contracts are formal and can be lengthy, sometimes 25 to 100 pages, depending on the type of the franchise business being purchased, and other factors. Frequently there can be collateral agreements, in addition to the main agreement, that have to be signed by the parties, or one of the parties. In addition, key documents are attached to the contract as exhibits. This would include such items as financial statements, lists of assets, lists of inventory and supplies, copies of leases and other major contracts, lists of creditors, lists of customers, and other documentation.

You can see now why there is generally a two-step documentation process before the franchise actually changes hands, the first step being the offer-to-purchase which is relatively simple and short and shows an agreement in principle, and the second step which has just been described and which sets out the binding agreement between the parties.

There are key terms that should be included in any contract involving a purchase of shares or assets. Each contract should cover these basic questions:

- What is the amount of the purchase price?
- How will the purchase price be paid?
- How will the purchase price be apportioned?
- What assets are to be sold?
- What assets will be retained by the seller?
- How will inventory adjustments be made?
- How will accounts receivable be handled?
- How will other adjustments be determined?
- What about the seller's liabilities?
- What protection does the seller have if the buyer does not pay the assumed liabilities?
- What other warranties should the seller make to the buyer?
- What are the rights of the seller to compete?
- What restrictions should be imposed on the seller in operating the business prior to transfer?
- What performance conditions has the seller included as part of the agreement?
- What happens to the records and books for the business at the time of closing?
- How are any disputes under the agreement resolved?
- What training will be provided to the purchaser and who is responsible for the delivery of the training?

Like any other legal document, the contract to buy a business must be designed to meet the specific needs of the transaction. No two documents are or should be identical. The agreement therefore may contain most but not necessarily all of the points mentioned here, as well as other provisions to fully protect yourself.

PROFESSIONAL ASSISTANCE IN PURCHASING A BUSINESS

Throughout this chapter, as well as the rest of the book, we frequently advise obtaining qualified legal and accounting assistance at all stages of a business operation. This is particularly important when dealing with buying an existing franchise business.

Buying a franchise is serious business, involving serious money. It is false economy and very unwise to attempt to save on legal fees by doing all the work yourself. If problems occur in the purchase transaction, which is likely to happen if you do it yourself, then you will certainly be retaining a lawyer at that time to initiate a law suit or protect you from one. Discuss your concerns and needs with your lawyer in the preliminary interest stage, and always before signing an offer-to-purchase or a formal agreement.

RECAP

In this chapter we have evaluated:

- the advantages and disadvantages of buying an existing franchise
- where to find franchise opportunities
- risks of some businesses
- evaluating an existing franchise, from the financial, legal and day-to-day viewpoints
- how to evaluate, using a worksheet
- the value of "goodwill"
- methods of purchasing an existing franchise

and included was a sample of:

- Existing Business Quick Check.

CHAPTER 9

The Ten Golden Rules

A prudent person profits from personal experience,
a wise one from the experience of others.
Joseph Collins

At this point you have probably decided whether or not franchising is for you; what type of franchise business suits you best; if a new or an existing franchised business best serves your purposes; and what type of franchise business you can afford.

You may have already researched certain franchises or entered into discussions with some franchisors. Before you reach the point of no return in your decision-making, you should take some time to reflect on some of the key points made throughout the book and make sure that you have covered all the bases before you proceed. Remember to give equal consideration to your emotional, logical and financial needs.

To assist in your deliberations we have included our Ten Golden Rules of Franchising. Follow these rules and you should enjoy the benefits of profitable franchising.

THE TEN GOLDEN RULES

1. Read and understand the contents of the Franchise Agreement and other documentation.
2. Understand what self-employment is all about.
3. Capitalize the business properly.
4. Talk to other franchisees.
5. Confirm oral representations made by the franchisor.
6. Get professional advice.
7. Meet the franchisor's operational staff.
8. Visit the corporate office.
9. Get the most out of the initial training.
10. Follow the system.

APPENDIX

FRANCHISE REGULATORY AUTHORITIES

CANADA

Alberta is the only province in Canada that has legislation specifically pertaining to franchising. For information, contact:

Alberta Municipal Affairs, Housing and Consumer Affairs Division
Director of Industry Standards
16th Floor, Commerce Place,
10155-102nd Street,
Edmonton, Alberta T5J 4L4
Phone (403) 422-1588
Fax (403) 427-3033
E-mail palovr@censsw.gov.ab.ca

UNITED STATES

Division of Marketing Practices
Bureau of Consumer Protection
Federal Trade Commission
6th and Pennsylvania Ave., N.W.
Washington, D.C. 20580
Phone: (202) 326-3128
Fax: (202) 326-2012
E-mail: consumerline@ftc.gov

FRANCHISE ASSOCIATIONS

Canadian Franchise Association
5045 Orbitor Drive
Building 9, Suite 401
Mississauga, ON L4W 4Y4
Phone: (905) 625-2896
Toll Free: 1-800-665-4232
Fax: (905) 625-9076
E-mail: info@cfa.ca
Website: www.cfa.ca

International Franchise Association
1350 New York Avenue, N.W.,
Suite 900
Washington, DC 20005
Phone: (202) 628-8000
Fax: (202) 628-0812
E-mail: ifa. franchise.org
Website: www.franchise.org

The Top 500 Franchises in Canada (by Number of Units)

The list below simply relates to the factor of size, from the franchise company with the most units or locations, to the company with the least units. There are over 1,000 franchise companies in Canada, so we have selected the top 500 in size.

As you know from reading this book, size is only one factor. There are many variables to consider when selecting a franchise, however it is one comparative reference point.

The information was obtained from the December 1997 listing compiled by the National Franchise Database Systems Inc. of Toronto, Ontario. It is updated every year.

To find out more about the franchises below and other franchise operations, contact the Canadian Franchise Association in Toronto to obtain information about their members. In addition, refer to page 64 for publications listing details about Canadian franchise operations. Some of the publications also detail U.S. franchise operations.

Rank	Units	Company	Rank	Units	Company
1	8500	Scharecorp	54	269	Pizza Pizza
2	2200	Canada Post Corporation	55	266	Horne & Pitfield Inc.
3	1500	Tim Horton's	56	260	Amerispec Home Inspections
4	1207	Yves Rocher Canada Ltd.	57	256	First Choice Haircutters
5	1198	Subway	58	255	Burger King
6	1140	Uniglobe Travel International	59	254	Provi-Soir
7	1049	McDonald's Restaurants	60	243	Midas Muffler Shops
8	1000	Student Works Painting	61	241	Pet Valu
9	900	H & R Block	62	240	Robins Donuts & Deli
10	883	Radio Shack	63	235	Coldwell Banker
11	838	Kentucky Fried Chicken	64	229	Kumon Educational Institute
12	823	Shoppers Drug Mart	65	226	M & M Meat Shops
13	700	IGA Canada Limited	66	225	Choice Hotels
14	670	Mr. Crispy's Hot Fries	67	220	Rust Check Center
15	628	Metro Richelieu	68	216	Mail Boxes Etc.
16	600	Rodier, Rodier Hommes	69	215	Thomas Cook/Marlin Travel
17	590	A & W Restaurants	70	210	Dunkin' Donuts
18	589	Becker Milk Company	71	208	Wendy's
19	551	Mr. Sub	72	206	Country Style Donuts
20	525	True Value Hardware Stores	73	200	Private Postal Centre
21	525	UAP Auto Parts	74	200	Realty World Canada
22	525	V & S Department Stores	75	194	Color Your World
23	504	Travel Professionals Int'l.	76	192	Custom Auto Restoration Systems
24	477	Dairy Queen	77	191	Pharmasave Drugs Ltd.
25	476	Re/Max International	78	190	Domino's Pizza
26	450	Ro-Na L'Entrepot	79	187	A Buck Or Two!
27	450	Save-Easy	80	187	O.K. Tire Stores
28	425	Canadian Tire	81	183	Sketchley Cleaners
29	418	Petro Canada	82	180	Valu-Mart/Freshmart/Mr. Grocer
30	400	National Tilden	83	176	Avis Car And Truck Rental
31	396	Mr. Tube Steak	84	171	Great Canadian Bagel
32	385	National Real Estate Service	85	170	Goodyear Certified Auto Centres
33	380	Pizza Hut	86	170	Hertz Canada Ltd.
34	375	Budget Rent-A-Car	87	165	Molly Maid
35	375	Snap-On Tools	88	164	Discount Car & Truck Rentals
36	350	Harvey's Restaurant	89	160	Fabricland
37	350	Pro Hardware	90	160	Uni Pro
38	349	Agnew, Aggies	91	159	Alimentation Couche Tard
39	347	Second Cup	92	159	Thrifty Car Rental
40	338	Mohawk Oil Co. Ltd.	93	158	Little Caesar's Pizza
41	331	General Business Services	94	155	Speedy Muffler King
42	317	Clover Farm	95	152	Rooster's B.B.Q.
43	313	Sooter Studios	96	151	Swiss Chalet
44	310	Coffee Time Donuts	97	150	Service Master
45	305	Yogen Fruz	98	149	Treats
46	275	Century 21	99	149	Work World
47	287	Uniclean Systems	100	147	Academy of Learning
48	285	Homelife	101	147	Certigard Car Repair
49	279	Jani-King	102	147	St. Clair Paint and Wallpaper
50	275	Gateway Newstands	103	146	Jean Coutu Group
51	272	Sheraton Hotels	104	145	Beaver Lumber Company Ltd.
52	271	Wildwood Travel	105	145	Mark's Work Wearhouse
53	270	Baskin Robbins	106	144	Faces

Rank	Units	Company
107	144	Grower Direct Fresh Cut Flowers
108	144	National Money Mart
109	144	Video Update
110	142	Pizza Delight
111	139	Japan Camera 1 Hour Photo
112	136	Valentine
113	135	Novus Glass Repair & Replacement
114	135	Roto-Static International
115	132	Weed Man
116	131	Chem-Dry Carpet Cleaning
117	127	Best Western International
118	126	Minute Muffler and Brake
119	126	Sports Experts
120	125	Apple Auto Glass Limited
121	125	Ferplus Decorating
122	125	Rona Dismat
123	125	Saint Cinnamon Bake Shoppe
124	122	Dixie Lee Fried Chicken
125	122	Mikes Restaurants
126	120	Smitty's
127	120	Taco Time
128	119	U & R Tax Depot
129	117	Baker's Dozen Donuts
130	116	Padgett Business Services
131	114	Arby's
132	114	The Body Shop
133	112	Pilon Pal Depot
134	111	Main Street Financial Services
135	110	mmmarvellous mmmuffins
136	109	Decorating Den
137	108	Boston Pizza
138	108	Camera Expert
139	107	A.L. Van Houtte
140	107	New York Fries
141	106	Panagopoulos Pizza
142	104	Buns Master Bakery
143	103	Mountain Boy Chicken 'N Taters
144	103	Orange Julius
145	102	Gold Pro Canada
146	102	Super Gard Canada Ltd.
147	101	Coverall Cleaning Concepts
148	101	Jazzercise
149	100	Herbrand Tools & Equipment
150	97	Bobby Lawn Care/Pest Control
151	97	Just New Reeleases
152	96	Algonquin Travel
153	93	LGC Smithers & Assoc.
154	93	Money Concepts
155	92	Canway Carpet Cleaning
156	92	St. Hubert Bar-B-Q
157	90	International Master Care
158	90	Thruway Muffler Centre

Rank	Units	Company
159	89	Moneysworth & Best Shoe Repair
160	88	Mr. Lube
161	87	Grandma Lee's Restaurant/Bakery
162	86	Alibi's Cafe Bakery
163	86	Chatel Votre Nettoyeur
164	86	Master Care Janitorial
165	86	Mister Transmission
166	85	Joe Loue Tout Rent All Inc.
167	84	Ontario Paralegal
168	82	The Keg Steakhouse
169	81	Monsieur Muffler
170	81	Mrs. Vanelli's Italian Foods
171	80	Groupe Tecnic Driving School
172	80	Microplay Video Game Stores
173	80	Student Paint Works
174	56	Videomatic 24 Hr. Movie Rentals
175	79	Kwik Kerb
176	79	Kwik Kopy Printing
177	78	Sunitron Inc.
178	77	Manchu Wok
179	77	Rent-A-Wreck
180	76	Lebeau Vitres D'Autos
181	76	Timothy's World Coffee
182	76	Travelodge/Thriftlodge
183	75	Excellence Sports
184	74	Giant Tiger Stores Ltd.
185	74	Our Baby Impressions
186	74	Stretch-N-Grow
187	75	241 Pizza
188	73	Le Naturist Jean-Marc Brunet
189	73	Surface Doctor
190	72	Young Drivers of Canada
191	71	Bun King Bakeries
192	71	Cantor's
193	71	Play It Again Sports
194	70	Grand & Toy
195	70	Pillar To Post Home Inspection
196	70	R.X. Soleil
197	70	Sakkio Japan
198	70	Sandwich Tree
199	70	Sure Stop Brake Centers
200	68	Knechtel Associate Stores
201	67	Kernels Extraordinary Popcorn
202	67	Le Club International Video Film
203	67	Steamatic
204	65	Double Double Pizza & Chicken
205	65	Goliger's Travel Ltd.
206	65	Oil Gard Anti-Rust
207	65	Pizza Nova
208	64	Fabutan Sun Tan Studios
209	60	Canadian 2 For 1 Pizza
210	63	Joey's Only Seafood Restaurant
211	63	Jumbo Video

Rank	Units	Company	Rank	Units	Company
212	63	We Care Home Health Services	265	50	Panda
213	62	Beverly Hills Weight Loss Clinic	266	50	Paulmac's Pet Food
214	62	Framing Experience	267	50	Personal Edge
215	62	La Bonbonniere 'Sweet Factory'	268	50	Please Mum
216	62	Stereo Plus	269	50	Rafters
217	61	Culligan Of Canada Ltd.	270	50	White Spot Restaurants
218	61	Mary Brown's Fried Chicken	271	49	Alliance Security Systems
219	61	Panda Shoes	272	49	Humpty's Family Restaurants
220	61	Shefield & Sons Tobacconists	273	49	Maple Leaf Maintenance
221	60	Bagel Builders	274	49	Priority Management Systems
222	60	Bonanza Restaurants	275	48	ADL
223	60	Foodland	276	48	Cruiseship Centers
224	60	Golden Griddle Restaurants	277	48	Gourmet Cup
225	60	Kelsey's Restaurants	278	48	OCTO Brakes Mufflers
226	60	Lormit Process Services	279	48	Original Panzerotto & Pizza
227	60	Minuteman Press	280	47	Perma-Shine
228	60	Reddi Mart Convenience Stores	281	46	Compucollege School of Business
229	60	Rug Doctor	282	46	Druxy's Famous Deli Sandwiches
230	52	Super 8 Motels	283	46	Husky House Restaurants·
231	59	East Side Mario's	284	46	International Business Schools
232	59	Grabbajabba	285	46	Kit Atout
233	58	The #1 Store Plus	286	46	Nettoyeur Michel Forget
234	59	U Frame It/ Flair Custom Framing	287	46	Tiki-Ming
235	59	Windsor Plywood	288	45	Cultures Restaurants
236	58	American Speedy Printing Centres	289	45	Days Inn
237	58	Cruise Holidays	290	45	Dollar Rent A Car
238	58	Speedpro Signs Plus	291	45	Framing & Art Centre
239	58	Sweet Factory	292	45	Hale Contact Lens Service
240	57	Ziebart Tidy Car	293	45	Howard Johnson Hotels
241	57	Zippy Print Enterprises	294	45	Identification Services of Canada
242	56	Compucentre	295	45	Nevada Bob's
243	56	Motophoto & Portrait Studio	296	45	Pizzaville - Pizza & Panzerotto
244	56	Schwab's Meats	297	45	Trident Key Mart
245	55	Bulk Barn	298	45	Vag Coiffer
246	55	Greco Pizza Donair	299	45	Video Cube
247	55	Trans-Action Real Estate Services	300	45	Wee Watch Home Day Care
248	54	Call N' Cut	301	44	Fibrenew Industries Ltd.
249	54	Drake Office Overload/Personnel	302	44	Kampground of America KOA
250	54	Nectar Bath & Beauty Shop	303	44	Magicuts
251	54	The Cyclepath	304	43	Colorworks
252	53	Guaranteed Muffler Shops	305	43	Made In Japan
253	53	Medpro Billing Systems	306	43	Ricky's Family Restaurants
254	53	Productivity Point International	307	42	Custom Home-Watch Int'l.
255	52	Athena	308	42	House Of Knives, The Edge
256	52	Bizou	309	42	Lawn Care The Professional Way
257	52	Dufferin Game Room Store	310	42	Minit-Tune & Brake Auto Centers
258	51	Action-Student Window Cleaning	311	42	Nutrite
259	51	Al-Vin Aluminum Siding Cleaners	312	42	Ramada Inns
260	51	Centre Du Rasoir	313	42	Val-Pak
261	51	Mini-Golf	314	42	Wine Kitz
262	50	Edo Japan	315	41	Academy For Mathematics
263	50	Holiday Inn Worldwide	316	41	Bevinco Bar Systems
264	50	It Store	317	41	Cash Converters

Rank	Units	Company
318	41	Mini-Putt
319	41	Sanibrite
320	41	Soapberry Shop
321	41	University First Class Painters
322	40	Actual Reality
323	40	Bestsellers
324	40	Certa Propainters of Canada
325	40	Comprehensive Business Services
326	40	Maaco Auto Painting & Bodyworks
327	40	1 Hour Martinizing Dry Cleaning
328	40	Sylvan Learning Centers
329	40	Toronto School of Business
330	40	Videoflicks
331	39	Cafe Supreme
332	39	Chicken Delight
333	39	Measure Masters
334	39	Nutri-lawn
335	39	Ryan's Quality Pet Food
336	39	Sangster's Health Centres
337	38	Croissant + Plus
338	38	Jug City
339	38	Sure Copy Centres
340	37	Bathtub Doctor
341	37	International Business Opps.
342	37	Screen Printing North America
343	36	Cleaning By Page
344	36	Hoj Car & Truck Rentals/Leasing
345	36	Pretzel Twister
346	36	Select Sandwich
347	35	Gestion Montemurro
348	35	Global Pet Foods
349	35	Gone Hollywood Video
350	35	Monsieur Felix/Mr. Norton Cookies
351	35	Sports Traders
352	35	Square Boy Pizza And Subs
353	34	Alarmforce Industries Inc.
354	34	Caryl Baker Visage
355	34	Chicken Chef
356	33	Aloette Cosmetics
357	33	Beavertails Pastry
358	33	Bee-Clean
359	33	Garry Robertson Music Services
360	33	Le Muffin Plus
361	33	Legs Beautiful
362	33	Merle Norman Cosmetics
363	33	Mighty Dollar
364	33	Pizza Donini
365	33	Renew Works - Wood Renewers
366	32	Casey's Grillhouse
367	32	Cityscapes Internet
368	32	Envoy Business Services
369	32	Kiddie Kobbler
370	32	Mini Donal Ltd.
371	32	Pacini
372	32	Realty Executives
373	32	Zellers Portrait Studio
374	31	Cookies by George
375	31	Fabri-Zone Cleaning Systems
376	31	Futurekids
377	31	Glacier Clearwater Enterprise
378	31	Hickory Farms Of Canada
379	31	Housesitters
380	31	Janstar Cleaning Systems
381	31	MEDIchair
382	31	Pointts
383	31	Schooley, Mitchell, Telecom
384	31	The Bagel Stop
385	30	C.S.T. Consultants
386	30	Flair Custom Framing Centre
387	30	Giorgio Restaurants
388	30	Great Canadian Dollar Store
389	30	In'Flector Control Systems
390	30	Jersey City
391	30	Le Print Express
392	30	Nutter's Bulk & Natural Foods
393	30	Paul Davis Systems Canada Ltd.
394	30	Roto-Rooter Sewer-Drain Service
395	29	Active Tire and Auto Centre
396	29	C.K.M. Window Fashions
397	29	EKW Systems
398	29	Enviro Masters Lawn Care
399	29	Hygenicomp Computer Cleaning
400	29	The Panhandler
401	27	#1 Nautilus/Good Life Club
402	28	Automax
403	28	Cash on the Spot
404	28	Furniture Medic of Canada
405	28	Gold Coast Dog's
406	28	Q Lube
407	28	Row Entertainment
408	28	Shine Factory
409	28	Wackyputt
410	27	Carstar Automotive
411	27	Coast To Coast Collision Centres
412	27	Living Lighting Limited
413	27	Master Mechanic
414	27	Permacrete Systems
415	27	Records on Wheels
416	27	Ribbon Xchange
417	27	Winks
418	26	Betonel Ltee.
419	26	Budget Brake & Muffler
420	26	Dollar Bill's
421	26	Merry Maids
422	26	Mystery Pizza & Chicken

Rank	Units	Company	Rank	Units	Company
423	26	Pet Paradise Inc.	462	22	Sandwich Board
424	26	Restaurant Normandin	463	22	Soap Exchange
425	26	Signs Now	464	21	Albert's Family Restaurant
426	25	Ceiling Doctor	465	21	Company's Coming Cafe
427	25	Interface Financial Group	466	21	Fat Albert's/Ralph's Sports Bar
428	25	JDI Cleaning Systems	467	21	Great Wilderness Company
429	25	Les Pres Restaurant	468	21	Heavenly Muffins
430	25	Mini Maid Services	469	21	Koya Japan
431	25	Mister C's Donuts & More	470	21	Mr. Rooter Plumbing
432	25	Mr. Mugs	471	21	Pingouin
433	25	Ross Dixon Financial Services	472	21	Professional Carpet Systems
434	25	Shake Shoppe	473	21	Rainbow Int'l. Carpet Cleaning
435	25	Sutton Group	474	21	Super Seamless Steel Siding
436	25	Yogurt Shoppe	475	21	The Paper Factory
437	24	Chips Away	476	21	Wandlyn Inns
438	24	Chocolaterie Bernard Collebaut	477	20	Chemwise
439	24	Great Clips	478	20	Coffee Way
440	24	Pantry Family Restaurants	479	20	Edelweiss Deli Express
441	24	Sizzling Wok	480	20	Fontaine Sante
442	23	AAMCO Transmissions	481	20	Fragrance
443	23	ABC Family Restaurants	482	20	Hillary's
444	23	Bargain Tire Auto Centres	483	20	Langenwalter Carpet Dyeing
445	23	Ho-Lee Chow	484	20	Music City
446	23	La Cache	485	20	Patio Vidal Restaurant
447	23	Magi Seal Services	486	20	Phase One Restaurants
448	23	Money Mailer Canada	487	20	Pictures
449	23	Muffin Break	488	20	Proshred Security
450	23	Open Window Bakery	489	20	Tele-Tech Communications
451	22	Acadamy Florists	490	20	Tint King Auto World
452	22	Comcheq Services Ltd.	491	20	Two Small Men With Big Hearts
453	22	Don Cherry's Grapevine	492	20	Vin-Bon
454	22	Donut Delite Cafe	493	20	Wynn's X-Tend Auto-Link
455	22	Duraclean International	494	19	Badge Maker
456	22	Fax-9	495	19	Cen-Ta Group
457	22	Haircrafters	496	19	Color-Glo International
458	22	London Cleaners	497	19	Fruits & Passion
459	22	Mr. Wizard Glass Tinting	498	19	Just Desserts
460	22	New Orleans Pizza	499	19	Kenny Rogers Roasters
461	22	Resort Publications	500	19	Mr. Mike's Grill

Index

About the Authors

Douglas A. Gray, B.A., LL.B., formerly a practising lawyer, is an internationally recognized authority on entrepreneurial development and small business management. He is frequently consulted by government, business, financial and educational institutions, and professional associations. In his capacity as a business and real estate lawyer, he has represented numerous clients wanting to buy a franchise (become a franchisee) or start a franchise (become a franchisor). Mr. Gray has founded 12 successful small businesses, and is the president of the Canadian Enterprise Institute Inc. He is the author of 16 bestselling books.

As a public speaker and educator, Mr. Gray has conducted seminars and presentations to more than 250,000 people throughout Canada, the U.S. and internationally. Many of these presentations included how to buy or start a franchise business. Mr. Gray is a member of the National Speakers' Association and Canadian Association of Professional Speakers. He is frequently interviewed by the media as an authority on small business entrepreneurship and writes various national small business columns in *Opportunities Canada*, *Profit*, *Computer Paper* and *Canadian Computer Wholesaler*. Mr. Gray has given over 2,000 media interviews (newspaper, magazine, television, radio.

Mr. Gray lives in Vancouver, B.C.

Norman P. Friend is president of The Franchise Group. This company provides assistance on a national basis to start-up franchisors, consultancy services to established franchise organizations, and markets franchise opportunities for selected franchisors. Mr. Friend has been involved in franchising since 1980 and is recognized as an expert in recruitment. His experience as both franchisor and franchisee provides him with a valuable perspective on the unique franchising business relationship and contributes to his success in the recruitment of quality franchisees. He is a Founding Member of the Pacific Franchise Association.

Mr. Friend was managing partner of a group of companies which included real estate, insurance, construction and a mortgage investment corporation, and in partnership with his son owned a restaurant franchise. The real estate company was a Century 21 franchise, and Mr. Friend earned their "Achievement in Management" designation.

Mr. Friend is an accomplished professional public speaker and member of the National Speakers' Association. He has also contributed articles on franchising, sales and marketing to national publications.

Mr. Friend resides in Vancouver, B.C.

Reader Feedback and Educational Resources

Your candid feedback and constructive suggestions for improvements for future editions of the book are welcomed. Please write with your comments to the address below. In addition, if you would like information about educational seminars, books, and other educational products and material relating to small business and franchising in Canada, please contact:

CANADIAN ENTERPRISE INSTITUTE INC.
#300 – 3665 Kingsway
Vancouver, B.C. V5R 5W2
Phone: (604) 436-3337
Fax: (604) 436-9155
Website: http://www.small.biz.ca

THE SMALL BUSINESS REFERENCE SERIES

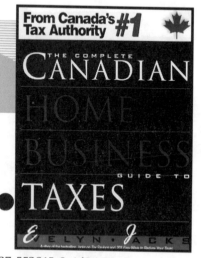
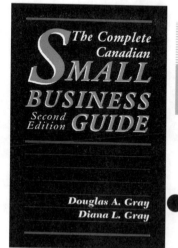